Merging the Instructional Design Proc Learner-Centered Theory

Merging the Instructional Design Process with Learner-Centered Theory brings together the innovations of two previously divided processes – learning design strategies/theories and instructional systems development – into a new introductory textbook. Using a holistic rather than fragmented approach that includes top-level, mid-level, and lower-level design, this book provides guidance for major topics such as non-instructional interventions, just-in-time analysis, rapid-prototype approaches, and learner-centered, project-based, anytime-anywhere instruction. Informed by the authors' considerable experience and leadership throughout dramatic shifts in today's learning landscape, this book offers the next generation of instructional designers a fresh perspective that synthesizes and pushes beyond the basics of design and development.

Charles M. Reigeluth is Professor Emeritus in the Instructional Systems Technology Department at Indiana University, USA.

Yunjo An is Associate Professor in the Department of Learning Technologies at the University of North Texas, USA.

Merging the Instructional Design Process with Learner-Centered Theory

Theory

The Holistic 4D Model

Charles M. Reigeluth and Yunjo An

Routledge
Taylor & Francis Group

NEW YORK AND LONDON

First published 2021
by Routledge
52 Vanderbilt Avenue, New York, NY 10017

and by Routledge
2 Park Square, Milton Park, Abingdon, Oxon, OX14 4RN

Routledge is an imprint of the Taylor & Francis Group, an informa business

Library of Congress Cataloging-in-Publication Data
A catalog record for this title has been requested

ISBN: 978-0-8153-6078-0 (hbk)
ISBN: 978-0-8153-6079-7 (pbk)
ISBN: 978-1-351-11754-8 (ebk)

Typeset in Garamond
by Deanta Global Publishing Services, Chennai, India

Contents

Preface

Since the beginning of this millennium, knowledge about learning, instructional strategies, technological tools, and instructional design (ID) processes has advanced considerably, but most ID process models have not kept pace. This prompted the US Air Force to hire one of us for a year to update their ID process model. The result was a model with many novel features to greatly improve the effectiveness and efficiency of the ID process and the resulting instruction. Building on the Air Force model, we have created a new model, called the Holistic 4D Model, that takes a holistic approach to the ID process and is organized into four major activities: Define, Design, Develop, and Deploy. Its most notable features include:

1. A holistic design process
2. Analysis-design-evaluation (ADE) cycles and design document templates
3. Integration with instructional theory
4. Teaching topic and task expertise
5. Holistic instructional sequences
6. Learner-centered instruction
7. Non-instructional interventions
8. Rapid prototyping
9. Designer objectives and demonstration objectives
10. Product and process evaluations

Each of these is described next.

1. Holistic design process. To address the problem of fragmented and "cookie cutter" instruction, the Holistic 4D Model uses a holistic design process. Rather than beginning the design process by analyzing the content into small pieces and designing instruction for each of those pieces, it begins with a top-level ADE that creates a fuzzy vision of both the content and methods, followed by a mid-level ADE that works out more details on the fuzzy vision, and finally a lower-level ADE is conducted that fills in all the details for both content and methods. This allows for more creativity in the design process and more coherence in the resulting instruction.

2. ADE cycles and design document templates. When an ID project tries to complete all the analysis before doing any design, some things get analyzed that are not needed, and some things that are needed are not analyzed. Also, memories fade when a lot of time passes between the analysis and the use of its results in design. Therefore, the Holistic 4D

Model offers guidance for just-in-time (JIT) analysis. Similarly, it helps to do some formative evaluation of each design decision as soon as possible, so any improvements can be incorporated into future design decisions. Thus, we offer guidance for cycles of ADE that uses JIT analysis and immediate evaluation for your design decisions. We also offer templates for ADE on the top, mid, and lower levels of design. These templates greatly facilitate the process of documenting the results of the design process, including important analysis and formative evaluation results.

3. Integration with instructional theory. The biggest influence on the quality of the instruction you design is the instructional methods you choose. Therefore, instructional theory is integrated into the Holistic 4D Model. That integration improves the efficiency of the ID process and the effectiveness of the resulting instruction.

4. Teaching topic and task expertise. Due to its behaviorist roots, most ID models look at all that is to be learned as tasks, so the primary analysis is task analysis. That works well in most training contexts, but not so well in many educational contexts where topics reign supreme. Analysis and design activities need to be quite different when the learning is focused on topic expertise. The Holistic 4D Model provides guidance for developing both task and topic expertise.

5. Holistic instructional sequences. Schema theory has helped us understand that learning is improved when it occurs within a meaningful context of broader and more inclusive knowledge. Hierarchical sequences that begin with small, component skills and proceed to combine them into ever-larger skills violate this important principle of learning. The Holistic 4D Model provides guidance for designing holistic instructional sequences that don't ignore the existence of learning prerequisites – for both task and topic expertise.

6. Learner-centered instruction. There is growing recognition of the power of learning by doing (project-based, problem-based, inquiry-based, maker-based, task-based learning), as well as competency-based, personalized, collaborative, self-directed, and anytime-anywhere instruction, yet the guidance for designing such learner-centered instruction is sketchy. Therefore, the Holistic 4D Model includes guidance for designing such instruction, thereby helping designers to make their instruction more motivational and effective.

7. Non-instructional interventions. The Holistic 4D Model includes guidance about how to identify non-instructional interventions to improve performance, thereby enhancing performance and avoiding the development of instruction when other interventions are more effective – or the development of instruction alone when it should be accompanied by other interventions.

8. Rapid prototyping. The model also includes guidance for using either of two kinds of rapid prototyping – qualitative reduction or quantitative reduction – thereby increasing the efficiency of the ID process.

9. Designer objectives and demonstration objectives. Designers use objectives to help guide the design of their instruction, and learners sometimes benefit from objectives to help guide their learning. The problem is that different kinds of information are needed for these two different purposes. The Holistic 4D Model provides guidance for the design of these two very different types of objectives. Furthermore, objectives are typically abstract to learners and thereby not very helpful. Therefore, we provide guidance for designing a more concrete and useful kind of objective that we call a demonstration objective.

10. Product and process evaluations. It is important to conduct formative evaluations of the instruction you are designing, but it is also important to conduct formative evaluations of the ID process you are using. The Holistic 4D Model provides guidance for both kinds of evaluation and when to do them throughout the ID process, not just at the end. Of course, it also provides guidance for summative evaluation after the instructional system is implemented.

This book is intended for three audiences: (1) practicing instructional designers, to guide their design efforts, (2) students of instructional design, to help them learn how to be good instructional designers, and (3) teachers, instructors, and trainers, to help them design and develop leaner-centered instruction. Supporting resources are available at www.reigeluth.net/holistic-4d.

Chapter 1 addresses what instructional design is, its origins, why it is important, and what kinds of skills are needed to be a good instructional designer. Next, it provides a brief introduction to some of the most well-known ID models. Finally, it provides an overview of our updated ID model, the Holistic 4D Model – Define, Design, Develop, Deploy.

Define

Chapter 2 describes activities that are important to conduct before you begin the ID process. They include performance analysis (to identify any organizational performance problems and decide what kinds of interventions will best address them, including both instructional and non-instructional interventions), instructional needs assessment (to identify what needs to be taught – major instructional goals), project planning (to develop a project management plan for the ID process), and instructional system planning (to develop a plan to carry out all the instructional system functions after the instruction has been developed).

Design

Chapter 3 introduces readers to categories of learning and explains their importance in determining which instructional methods are likely to be most effective for any given instructional situation. It then provides a brief description of learning theories (behavioral, cognitive, and constructivist), followed by a few of the best-known instructional theories.

Chapter 4 describes nine major considerations for one to keep in mind during the ID process: (1) the distinction between task expertise and topic expertise, (2) the diverse kinds of analysis that one must conduct, (3) the concept of just-in-time analysis, (4) the role of subject-matter experts, (5) the two kinds of rapid prototyping, (6) the nature of a design document, (7) the variety of learner-centered and teacher-centered approaches to instruction, (8) motivational strategies, and (9) media selection.

Chapter 5 offers detailed guidance for three major ADE activities on the "top level" of our Holistic 4D Model – the level on which you create a "fuzzy vision" of the instruction, including a top-level view of the content, sequence, and instructional methods, along with indication of when to do formative evaluation and revision during those activities.

Chapter 6 provides detailed guidance for eight major ADE activities on the "mid level" of our model – the level on which you provide the next level of clarity about the vision, including the mid-level content, sequence, objectives, assessments, instructional methods, and media for both task expertise and topic expertise, each of which requires somewhat different guidance. It also indicates when to do formative evaluation and revision during those activities.

Chapters 7 and 8 provide detailed guidance for eight major ADE activities on the "lower level" of our model – the level on which you provide the final level of clarity about the vision, including content, sequence, and instructional methods, based on resources and existing instruction, for both task expertise and topic expertise. Specifically, Chapter 8 provides guidance for designing just-in-time tutorials. They also indicate when to do formative evaluation and revision during those activities. And they conclude with guidance for developing the implementation plan and updating the project management plan.

Develop

Chapter 9 provides major considerations and detailed guidance for the third D, Developing the instruction. Some development occurs periodically during the design process. The development process varies depending on many factors, which are discussed, along with guidance for producing instructional media, scriptwriting and storyboarding, graphic design, developing technology-enhanced instruction, and developing a learner guide and an instructor guide. The chapter also emphasizes the importance of frequent evaluation and revisions during the development process.

Chapter 10 provides major considerations and detailed guidance for conducting ongoing formative evaluation of both the instructional design and the ID process throughout the ID process. References to these formative evaluation activities appear throughout the guidance in Chapters 5–9, showing the iterative and recursive nature of the ID process.

Deploy

Chapter 11 provides detailed guidance for the fourth D (Deploy) in our Holistic 4D Model. It includes guidance for ensuring that the delivery, management, and support functions of an instructional system are operating well.

Chapter 12 provides detailed guidance for conducting summative evaluation of the instructional system.

An **Afterword** provides some concluding remarks.

An **Appendix** provides all the templates or forms offered in this book, as a convenience for you to photocopy. Also, Word documents for those templates and forms are available at www.reigeluth.net/holistic-4d.

The authors welcome suggestions for improving the next edition of this book. Please contact them at reigelut@indiana.edu or yunjo.an@unt.edu.

Acknowledgments

This book – a combination of textbook and job aid – has been extensively formatively evaluated by 11 professionals, who are either full-time instructional developers, professors of instructional design, or a combination of the two. We would like to thank them (listed below) for their expert review of an earlier manuscript of the book.

We would like to thank Katherine Burk and Wendy Johnson of the U.S. Air Force Air Education and Training Command for their contributions to early ideas for this book.

We would also like to thank Alexander Romiszowski for his review and comments on early drafts of the book and for his contribution of some personal experiences and case examples which we have included in the first four chapters.

Janet Annelli
Sinem Aslan
Brian Beatty
Pratima Dutta
Jake Enfield
Herb Fiester
Melissa Goodrum
John Keller
Minkyoung Kim
Seolim Kwon
Kurt Richter

1 Instructional Design

Overview

What Is Instructional Design?

Instructional design (ID) is a deliberate and orderly, but flexible, process for planning, analyzing, designing, developing, implementing, and evaluating instruction in education or training settings, formal and informal.

Design and development are confusing terms because they have both a macro and a micro sense. As we just stated, the ID process involves activities that are called design and development, among others. But the ID process also needs a name, and unfortunately it is called the instructional development process by some people and the instructional design process by others. So, "design" and "development" are terms that can refer to the whole process (a macro meaning) or to one kind of activity within the process (a micro meaning). The context will (or should) indicate the correct meaning.

To further complicate matters, the whole process is referred to by some people as instructional design and by others as instructional development or, alternatively, instructional systems design or instructional systems development (ISD). Since the activity of design is what largely determines the nature of the instruction, we view it as the "key" activity of the ID process and therefore prefer to call the overall process the instructional design process, but from now on we just refer to it as the ID process.

In practice, design should always lead to development (unless the design process is just an intellectual exercise). Similarly, development of a product should always be preceded by design. And development (with subsequent evaluation) may often lead back to (re)design of some aspects of the original design. We must therefore expect design and development activities to interact, each influencing the other. But as you read through the later chapters, you will study the nature of these two activities separately: design in Chapters 5–8 and development in Chapter 9. Please keep in mind that in practice they are done interactively and recursively.

The "Why and How" of ID

A lot of knowledge has been developed about how people learn (learning science) and how best to help people learn (instructional science), as we discuss in Chapter 3. A lot has also been learned about the process for using that knowledge to create high-quality instruction – to help people learn more effectively, efficiently, and motivationally, as we discuss in Chapter 4. ID utilizes both these kinds of knowledge, and ID models and design theories offer them in the form of practical guidance for instructional designers.

Instructors often approach the design of instruction from a content perspective – that is, *what to teach*. In contrast, instructional designers approach the task from a problem-solving perspective that includes what to teach but pays considerable attention to *how to teach it* in a way that is effective, efficient, and motivational. Instruction – the process of helping others to learn something new – can sometimes be straightforward, such as demonstrating the steps of a simple procedure followed by supervised practice. But other times, when the topic is complex and the learners may be ill-prepared to understand it, deciding how best to teach it may be a complex, ill-structured problem that doesn't have a single correct solution – there are usually many possibilities.

How can the designer find a good design from all the many possibilities? In general, there is no well-defined, or "algorithmic," procedure that is guaranteed to lead to a good solution. Designers have to apply "heuristics" for solving their problems. A *heuristic* is a rule or general principle which, if applied, works most of the time, but it may sometimes fail and is often incomplete or imprecise (see Table 1.1 for examples). Therefore, heuristic problem-solving is an iterative process – it involves analysis, design, evaluation, and then (if necessary) further loops of analysis, design, and evaluation. ID is a method for solving such problems – a method for deciding how best to teach given content to given target learners under given sets of practical and contextual conditions.

Instructional designers first define the problem; second determine what knowledge, skills, and attitudes need to be taught, focusing on what the learner needs to know and be able to do; and third determine the methods that will best help the learner to master that content. In training contexts, organizations often waste lots of resources by developing instruction that requires employees to spend extra hours away from the job to learn content that ends up having little or no impact on performance. Well-designed instruction makes learning more effective, efficient, and motivating, saves time and money, improves performance, and increases employee satisfaction. In education contexts, ID helps teachers better meet learners' needs, motivate them, and accelerate their learning.

Design problems, in most contexts, usually have many possible solutions – and ID is no exception. This is what makes design exciting, challenging, and rewarding.

The "When and Where" of ID

ID can be applied in any context in which people engage in purposeful learning, formal or informal. Table 1.2 provides some general examples of ID projects in different contexts.

Quality Issues in Design and the Activity of Designing

To understand quality in the context of ID, let us look at common features and recurring themes found in many different design contexts. A good design is one that appropriately answers a requirement or meets a stated need. Good design also anticipates and satisfies the "needs and wants" of the *clients* (those who request the project) and the *consumers* of

Table 1.1 Examples of Heuristics

One heuristic used in solving problems with many possible solutions is to **reduce the options** by asking questions that may identify and eliminate inadequate or inappropriate solutions before beginning to investigate the remaining possibilities.
Another heuristic often used by designers is to see if there is already a **solution to a similar problem** that can be adopted or adapted to the problem under analysis (with permission, as appropriate).

Table 1.2 Examples of ID Projects in Diverse Contexts

Context	Examples of ID Projects
P-12 Education	Help teachers design technology-enhanced lessons Design and develop multimedia learning resources Design online projects for high school students
Higher Education	Design and develop training materials for faculty and staff Help faculty improve courses Help faculty adapt their face-to-face courses to online project-based courses
Business	Design online training for employees or external clients Design on-the-job training Develop job aids Design classroom training or workshops
Healthcare	Design training for healthcare professionals (e.g., doctors, nurses, nurse practitioners, pharmacists) Create patient education resources
Military	Design and develop training courses for soldiers Design and develop military games and simulations
Informal Learning	Design and develop game-based projects for tasks of general interest Design and develop instruction and assessments for popular digital badges

the final product (the target learners). This has been jokingly described as the "dog food syndrome": the issue of designing a solution that satisfies both whoever uses/consumes it and also whoever chooses and pays for it. Sometimes, these are one and the same, but very frequently they are not.

To be a good designer in any field means using skills (researching, creating, testing), knowledge (about things, people, principles), abilities (e.g., time planning and management), and sensitivities (to values, contexts, markets, aesthetics, elegance, beauty, etc.). Good ID also involves knowledge about human learning, perception and acquisition of skills, attitudes and values, and information about the content to be learned.

Terminology

Instruction, education, and training. While the meanings of education and training are fairly universally understood, the term "instruction" is understood differently in different parts of the world. In the USA, it is typically defined in terms of "activities that promote learning" and is used in both education and training contexts. In the United Kingdom, however, it tends to be understood only as training – what happens in military, industrial, and animal contexts – rather than what happens in schools or colleges. Other countries and cultures have yet different terms. France translates "instructional design" as "conception pédagogique" (pedagogical design). In the 1970s, Brazil used the term "planejamento pedagógico" (pedagogical planning), but the currently accepted technical term is "design instructional" (Romiszowski & Romiszowski, 2005).

Technology. Technology has become one of the most frequently used – and most often misused or misunderstood – terms, not only in education or training but in just about any context. In general, technology is applied knowledge, but it takes two forms: hard and soft technology. Hard technology refers to equipment, such as computers, mobile devices, and such. Soft technology refers to knowledge, such as methods, processes, and principles.

We offer two pieces of advice about terminology:

1. Make sure you really understand the meaning of terms as used by others
2. Reflect on how you would ensure that others with whom you work share the same understanding of the terms you use

Origins of ID

USA Contributions to the Origins of ID

During the Second World War, the USA military needed to train a large number of untrained draftees in a very short period of time. In the words of Robert Gagné, they had to "transform farm boys into airplane mechanics in thirty days instead of two years" (Munzenmaier, 2014, p. 6). Several psychologists and educators, including Robert Gagné, Leslie Briggs, and John Flanagan, were called on to conduct research and develop training materials for the military services. Most tasks to be trained were physical ones (e.g., operating military equipment), and the behavioral approach (e.g., breaking a task into small steps, providing practice and reinforcement) was ideal for the situation.

The success of the behavioral approach led to ongoing research into behavioral objectives and programmed instruction during the 1950s and 1960s. Many of the psychologists who were responsible for the military training and research during the war continued to do pioneering work in the ID field (Reiser, 2001, 2018). But ID has morphed considerably since then, due to advances in cognitive science, constructivism, learning sciences, and digital technologies. We shall address these topics when relevant in later chapters. However, a general review of some of this early work provides a broader context for understanding the rise of ID as a discipline and profession.

One important contributor to both the theory and the practice of ID in those early days was Professor B.F. Skinner. Although much of his research both before and immediately after the Second World War was laboratory-based experimentation on the principles of "operant conditioning" using a variety of animals (and sometimes also humans) as experimental subjects, from the 1950s onward he also devoted effort to defining and applying research-based principles and procedures for effective instruction in classroom settings and for the systematic design and development of self-instructional materials to be used in educational and training contexts (programmed instruction). In a paper entitled *The Science of Learning and the Art of Teaching*, Skinner (1954) summarized the potential impact of the results of his research and development activities as follows:

> From this exciting prospect of an advancing science of learning, it is a great shock to turn to that branch of technology which is most directly concerned with the learning process – education. … [T]he advances which have recently been made in our control of the learning process suggest a thorough revision of classroom practices and, fortunately, they tell us how the revision can be brought about. This is not, of course, the first time that the results of an experimental science have been brought to bear upon the practical problems of education. The modern classroom does not, however, offer much evidence that research in the field of learning has been respected or used.
>
> (pp. 90–91)

Ten years later, in a paper entitled *The Technology of Teaching*, Skinner (1968) presents his views and proposals for the improvement of instruction – and much more. He opens as follows:

> More than sixty years ago, William James (1899) in *Talks to Teachers on Psychology*, said: "You make a great mistake, if you think that psychology, being the science of the mind's laws, is something from which you can deduce definite programs, schemes and methods of instruction for schoolroom use. Psychology is a science, and teaching is an art; and sciences never generate arts directly out of themselves. An intermediary inventive mind must make the application, by using its originality."
>
> (p. 59)

Skinner then argues that the "intermediary inventive mind" which James called for is an educational or instructional "technologist."

Skinner (1968) included this paper as chapter 4 in an 11-chapter book with the same title, in which he outlines how the behavioral sciences are the basis for procedures that may not only transform teaching (aka instruction), but also develop in the learner such competencies as productive thinking, creativity, motivation to learn, discipline, ethical behavior, and self-control – and, in addition, principles and procedures for the organization and management of the "establishment" (i.e., schools, colleges, etc.).

European Contributions to the Origins of ID

Considerations about "what to teach" and "how to teach it" have, of course, existed ever since the birth of formal education. The ancient Greeks – Plato and Aristotle among others – wrote books devoted to these issues, and the birth of a scientific approach to the study of teaching and learning dates from the 17th century. John Amos Comenius (1592–1670) was a philosopher, pedagogue, and theologian considered by some as the "father of modern education" (see Figure 1.1). He was born in Central Europe but travelled and worked in many other countries across Europe. His native language was German, but being a scholar and theologian, he was obliged by the norms of the time to use Latin as an academic working language. However, he introduced school textbooks profusely illustrated with pictures and diagrams and written in native languages instead of Latin. He introduced many other innovations, including teaching procedures based on gradual development from simpler to more complex concepts, curriculum focused on logical thinking and problem-solving, educational opportunities for women and the economically disadvantaged, and lifelong learning.

Comenius was also one of the first champions of universal education, a concept he described in his book, *Didactica Magna*, published in 1638.[1] This book introduced *didactics* as the theory of teaching and defined it in a less formal and wider sense as the practical application of the science of teaching. Comenius also contrasted "didactica" with "mathetica," a term he derived from the classical Greek word for learning and defined as "the science of learning." Soon, many Central European schools of education founded departments of didactics. In time, most European nations and many in other parts of the world (e.g., Latin America) followed suit – but not the Anglo-Saxon world. Universities in the UK and USA founded similar departments in terms of their academic focus, but with different names (e.g., teaching theory and practice in the UK; curriculum and

---

1   For an English translation, see Comenius (1907).

Figure 1.1 John Amos Comenius.

instruction in the USA). In the past, these academic communities did not interact much with European didactics, but times have changed. The current situation is well illustrated by a recent conference.

The International Commission on Mathematical Instruction (ICMI) is a part of the International Mathematical Union, an internationally acting organization founded in 1908 at an International Congress in Rome. It was a relatively small, Europe-based organization until the 1950s, when it expanded worldwide to over 90 member countries, including the USA and most of the Americas. Since the 1960s, the ICMI has organized an International Congress on Mathematics Education every four years.

ID Competencies and Skills

In this section of the chapter, we examine several research-based lists of the competencies and skills that have been identified as required to effectively and efficiently perform ID – and also manage the development and implementation phases of ID projects. Because of the broad range of skills, ID projects typically involve a team of people. We also "look into the future" of how these competency profiles may change.

ID Competencies According to ibstpi

In 1986, the International Board of Standards for Training, Performance, and Instruction (ibstpi), a not-for-profit corporation with up to 15 board members, published the first set of ID competencies. The latest ibstpi (2012) ID competencies are composed of 22 competencies clustered into five domains (see Table 1.3):

- Professional foundations
- Planning and analysis
- Design and development
- Evaluation and implementation
- Management

The competencies are also categorized as essential (for all instructional designers), advanced (for experienced instructional designers), and managerial (for managers of ID teams).

The ATD / IACET / R&A Study of ID Competencies

Through a partnership between the Association for Talent Development (ATD), the International Association for Continuing Education and Training (IACET), and Rothwell & Associates (R&A), a research team conducted a study to examine the ID competencies

Table 1.3 2012 ibstpi ID Competencies

Domain	Competencies	Level of Expertise
Professional Foundations	1. Communicate effectively in visual, oral, and written form	Essential
	2. Apply research and theory to the discipline of ID	Advanced
	3. Update and improve knowledge, skills, and attitudes pertaining to the ID process and related fields	Essential
	4. Apply data collection and analysis skills in ID projects	Advanced
	5. Identify and respond to ethical, legal, and political implications of design in the workplace	Essential
Planning and Analysis	6. Conduct a needs assessment in order to recommend appropriate design solutions and strategies	Advanced
	7. Identify and describe target population and environmental characteristics	Essential
	8. Select and use analysis techniques for determining instructional content	Essential
	9. Analyze the characteristics of existing and emerging technologies and their potential use	Essential
Design and Development	10. Use an ID process appropriate for a given project	Essential
	11. Organize instructional programs and/or products to be designed, developed, and evaluated	Essential
	12. Design instructional interventions	Essential
	13. Plan non-instructional interventions	Advanced
	14. Select or modify existing instructional materials	Essential
	15. Develop instructional materials	Essential
	16. Design learning assessment	Advanced
Evaluation and Implementation	17. Evaluate instructional and non-instructional interventions	Advanced
	18. Revise instructional and non-instructional solutions based on data	Essential
	19. Implement, disseminate, and diffuse instructional and non-instructional interventions	Advanced
Management	20. Apply business skills to managing the ID function	Managerial
	21. Manage partnerships and collaborative relationships	Managerial
	22. Plan and manage ID projects	Advanced

most valued by instructional designers themselves (ATD Research, 2015). When asked which skills are most important to the role of instructional designer, participants selected soft skills, such as critical thinking and interpersonal skills. Technology skills (e.g., coding, programming, graphic design) were deemed less important, perhaps because designers often work with technology experts when such special skills are needed. The top ten skills identified were:

1. Skill to not only listen but also synthesize what's being said
2. Analytical skills
3. Knowledge of ID principles, practices, and adult learning theory
4. Organization, prioritization, time management skill
5. Writing skills
6. Interpersonal skills
7. Attention to detail
8. Project management
9. Lifelong learner, the hunger to learn new things
10. Customer service skills

The eLearning Guild Study

The eLearning Guild identified the skills most desired by managers advertising for instructional designers through the content analysis of 60 job advertisements for instructional designers placed on Indeed.com during June 2014 (Munzenmaier, 2014). The results of the content analysis showed that the most desired skills were:

- Evaluate courses
- Manage projects
- Collaborate with subject-matter experts (SMEs)
- Conduct needs analysis
- Develop content
- Write objectives
- Manage courses
- Document/administer courses

A Look into the Future

The roles of instructional designers are continually evolving to meet the needs of changing knowledge, tools, and environments for learning. Keep in mind that the roles and responsibilities of instructional designers may vary depending on where they are (e.g., different countries, different settings, different organizations) and the nature of the ID project. For example, some instructional designers design and develop a wide variety of instructional materials – from simple job aids to classroom training to e-learning courses to game-based learning – while others focus on a very specific type of instruction (e.g., e-learning or games). Further, some instructional designers are required to play multiple roles in the ID process (e.g., project manager, instructional designer, graphics designer, developer), while others focus on design and work in one role, with many other specialized professionals in a large team.

More recently, several authors, in commenting on the accelerating rate of technological change, have proposed and described the emerging role of *learning engineer*

(Saxberg & Hess, 2013; Saxberg, 2015; Educause, 2018; Lieberman, 2018; Wagner, 2019), offered by Simon in 1967. The main reason for proposing this role is that nowadays instructional designers are dealing with an ever-growing and increasingly complex list of tasks due to the appearance and use of new digital tools and technologies. These authors suggest that learning engineers, by using knowledge and skills from scientific disciplines such as data science, computer science, and learning science, would support and complement the work of instructional designers and ID project managers and may also help learners and instructors to obtain more benefits from new learning technologies. But if we have learning engineers, then why not also learning architects? We believe that these terms reflect the evolution of skills in roles that are already defined by ibstpi and others.

ID Models

A number of ID models have been developed to guide instructional designers and trainers in the ID process. Here, we only briefly describe a few of the best-known models. A comprehensive list and descriptions can be found elsewhere (see e.g., Dills & Romiszowski, 1997; Gustafson & Branch, 2002).

ADDIE Model

One of the most commonly used terms in the ID field is "the ADDIE model." ADDIE is an acronym for Analysis, Design, Development, Implementation, and Evaluation. Although the origin of the label is unknown, ADDIE has been widely used by ID practitioners as a model for ID. It is generally agreed that ADDIE is an illustration of the generic, essential steps of the ID process (Molenda, 2003; Reiser & Dempsey, 2002). A number of adaptations of ADDIE have been developed. Figure 1.2 shows one.

The Dick and Carey Systems Approach Model

The Dick, Carey, and Carey (2014) model is a well-known ID model that uses a systems approach to the design of instruction (see Figure 1.3). In this model, the ID process is viewed as a system, and the components of the system, including the learners, the instructor, the instructional materials, and the learning environment, interact with one another

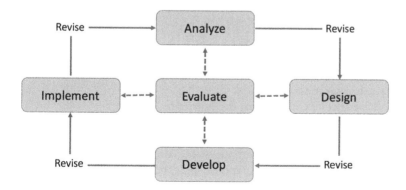

Figure 1.2 The ADDIE Model.

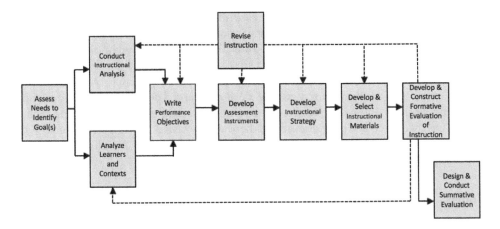

Figure 1.3 The Dick and Carey Model.

and work together to achieve the goal of learning. The systems approach model consists of the following interconnected components:

- Identify instructional goal(s)
- Conduct instructional analysis
- Analyze learners and contexts
- Write performance objectives
- Develop assessment instruments
- Develop instructional strategy
- Develop and select instructional materials
- Design and conduct formative evaluation of instruction
- Revise instruction
- Design and conduct summative evaluation

The Morrison, Ross, and Kemp Model

The Morrison, Ross, Kalman, and Kemp (2010) ID model is composed of the following nine elements (see Figure 1.4):

- Instructional Problems: identify the need of the client or the performance problem the client wishes to solve
- Learner Characteristics: define the characteristics of the target audience
- Task Analysis: determine what knowledge and procedures you need to include in the instruction to help the learner master the objectives
- Instructional Objectives: specify exactly what the learner must master
- Content Sequencing: sequence content in a logical order
- Instructional Strategies: design creative ways of presenting the information that help the learner integrate the new information with ideas they already understand
- Designing the Message: select appropriate graphics, text, and typographical design to enhance the readability and the learner's understanding of the instruction

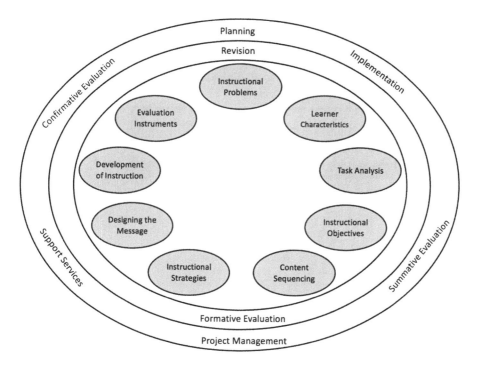

Figure 1.4 The Morrison, Ross, and Kemp Model.

- Development of Instruction: put all the parts together to produce instructional materials
- Evaluation Instruments: assess the learner's mastery of the objectives

In addition to these nine elements, the Morrison, Ross, and Kemp model includes eight processes that are ongoing throughout the life of an ID project: planning, project management, support services, formative evaluation, revision, implementation, summative evaluation, and confirmative evaluation.

Rapid Prototyping

Critics argue that traditional approaches to ID are too linear, too slow, overly analytical, and inflexible (e.g., Zemke & Rossett, 2002). In response to these criticisms, rapid prototyping (see Figure 1.5) was proposed to reduce the time and cost of an ID project, while increasing effectiveness and flexibility. Rapid prototyping is a non-linear, iterative approach that is characterized by the "parallel processes of design and research, or construction and utilization" (Tripp & Bichelmeyer, 1990, p. 37). Basically, it produces the prototype of a part of the whole instruction and allows the client to see early in the process what the completed instruction will look like and how it will work (Piskurich, 2015), whereas in the traditional ID process the client does not see the product until the whole instruction is almost completed. Since the prototype is developed and presented early in the process, the client is able to provide more detailed feedback and formative recommendations early and frequently in the ID process, which can result in customized design

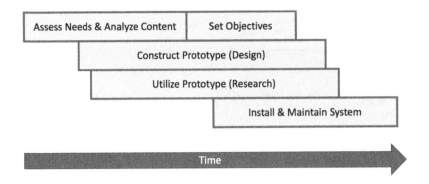

Figure 1.5 Rapid Prototyping.

and lower development costs. Rapid prototyping is particularly effective for large-scale, technology-based projects.

Design Layering

Brand (1994) describes the design of a building in terms of multiple coordinated and integrated sub-designs, which he calls layers. According to Brand, virtually all modern buildings are composed of six layers (the six Ss: site, structure, skin, services, space plan, and stuff). Based on the philosophy that designed artifacts can be characterized in terms of decomposable functional "layers," Gibbons and Rogers (2009) proposed a layered approach to ID. Specifically, they identified and described the following seven design layers of an instructional design:

- Content layer: a design must specify the structures of the content to be taught
- Strategy layer: a design must specify the physical organization of the learning space, social organizations of participants, their roles and responsibilities, instructional goals, allocation of goals to timed event structures, and strategic patterns of interaction between the learner and the instructional experience
- Message layer: a design must specify the tactical language of message structures through which the instructional experience can communicate content-derived information to the learner in conversational form
- Control layer: a design must specify the language of control structures through which the instructional experience can communicate content-derived information to the learner in conversational form
- Representation layer: a design must specify the representations that make message elements visible, hearable, and otherwise sense-able
- Media-logic layer: a design must specify the mechanism by which representations are caused to occur in their designed or computed sequence
- Data management layer: a design must specify data to be captured, archived, analyzed, interpreted, and reported

These layers represent major functions of an instructional artifact. Gibbons and Rogers (2009) explain that there might be more or fewer layers, depending on the insight of the instructional designer.

The Pebble-in-the-Pond Model

The pebble-in-the-pond model, developed by David Merrill (2002), consists of a series of expanding activities initiated by casting a pebble in the design pond (see Figure 1.6):

- Specify a problem (the first ripple): specify a typical problem that represents the whole task that learners will be able to do following the instruction
- Progression of problems (the second ripple): identify a progression of problems that gradually increase in complexity and difficulty
- Component analysis (the third ripple): identify all the knowledge components required to complete each of the tasks in the progression
- Instructional strategy (the fourth ripple): determine the instructional strategy that will be used to engage the learner with the content that has been specified through problem identification, problem progression, and task analysis
- Interface design (the fifth ripple): adapt the knowledge components and instructional strategy to the delivery system and instructional architecture of the learning situation
- Production (the sixth ripple): produce the instructional materials or situation

The pebble-in-the-pond model addresses some of the major objections to traditional ID models raised by Gordon and Zemke (2000) by developing the content first. The model is effective for designing problem-centered instruction.

Our Holistic 4D Model

Holistic

This book offers a holistic approach to ID, which stands in contrast to the prevailing fragmented approach that begins with an exhaustive hierarchical analysis process that breaks "what should be taught" down into tiny pieces and proceeds to design instruction for each of those pieces. The holistic approach begins the design process by creating a "fuzzy vision" of the instructional system (top-level design) and proceeds to work out progressively more details for each part of it in two more cycles (mid-level and lower-level design) so that each part is designed with the other parts in mind.

Our holistic approach also entails doing analysis within each part of this process rather than all at once at the beginning of the process, so that (a) designers do not get mired in details during the initial envisioning process, (b) information gleaned from an analysis activity is used immediately for designing while it is still fresh, and (c) only useful

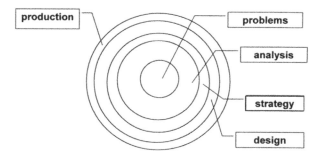

Figure 1.6 The Pebble-in-the-Pond Model.

information – and all necessary information – is analyzed. We offer this approach because there is strong evidence that it makes the resulting instructional system more effective and less fragmented. It also makes the ID *process* more creative and more efficient (less expensive and time-consuming) and makes rapid prototyping more effective and efficient.

We propose three stages for holistic ID – an adaptation of Romiszowski's (1981) division of "the analysis and the instructional development procedures … into [two] levels of detail" (pp. 81–93) and later (Romiszowski, 1986, pp. 11–12), to four levels, the fourth being concerned with development of instructional materials rather than design. The three levels of design that we propose are:

1. **Top-level** (strategic) design to create a "fuzzy vision" of the instruction, including top-level content, sequence, and preliminary instructional methods
2. **Mid-level** (operational) design to provide the next level of clarity about the vision including the mid-level sequence, objectives, assessments, and instructional methods
3. **Lower-level** (tactical) design to create a detailed blueprint of the instruction including the lower-level objectives, assessments, and instruction for both a task focus and a topic focus

While it is possible to configure the design process in any number of levels (realistically, one to perhaps six), using three levels seems to be a "happy medium" that keeps the number of design cycles manageably small while allowing for a more creative, coherent, and efficient process.

Each stage of design requires its own analysis:

1. **Top-level analysis** identifies just enough about the course content to create the top-level design. The purpose of analysis during the top-level design is to begin to determine what to teach (given the instructional goals identified in the needs assessment) and how to teach it. It identifies the general content that is later examined during mid-level analysis and allows you to create a fuzzy vision of what the instruction should be like for each task and/or topic. A top-level analysis is not required if all major parts of the content have already been identified. In such a case, you should go directly to mid-level analysis.
2. **Mid-level analysis** identifies just enough more about the content to elaborate it to a mid-level design. Having identified general information about what to teach and the general instructional methods in the top-level analysis, you will have a meaningful context within which to gather more detailed information about what to teach and how to teach it for each task and/or each topic listed.
3. **Lower-level analysis** identifies details about the kinds of learning involved in order to elaborate the design to a detailed blueprint of the instruction. Different kinds of learning require different kinds of mental processing for learning to occur, which in turn require different methods of instruction to foster those cognitive processes. Therefore, it is important to analyze each version[2] of a task and each subtopic of a topic in order to identify the different kinds of learning and consequently the different methods of instruction that will be most helpful for mastering the content.

---

2   A version of a task is one of several classes of ways that a complex task is performed in the real world. A simple task typically has a single version. The more complex the task, the more versions it is likely to have. This is explained more in Activity 1A.2 in Chapter 6.

4D

These three levels of design may be visualized within the overall instructional system design, development, and evaluation process as shown in Figure 1.7. This "systems diagram" is an attempt to visualize the overall instructional system design, development, and evaluation process as it is described and explained in this book. The large box occupying "center stage" in the diagram represents the ID functions with just-in-time analysis and ongoing evaluation – perhaps a real-world ID department of an educational or training organization, or perhaps just a theoretical visualization of the functions performed by instructional designers and developers working on some project.

Define. On the left of the diagram is a box representing the activities that precede the ID process. These are explained in Chapter 2. They include analysis of the need for instruction, carried out in a holistic and integrated manner that considers other forms of intervention that may be necessary in addition to, or in place of, instruction. These activities, therefore, evaluate whether there is a need for instruction and clearly define that need in the form of ID project goals and objectives.

Design. In the left-hand part of this box, are the three levels of design. They are organized vertically, indicating that top-level design is followed by mid-level and lower-level design, involving ever deeper just-in-time analysis at each of the levels. Also, at each of these three levels, we see a cyclical, or iterative process of analysis, design, evaluation and, if proved to be necessary, further analysis, design, and so on. Analyses of learners, resources, and context are also conducted to inform the design decisions about both what to teach and how to teach it.

It is not always necessary to do all these kinds of analysis. The nature and scope of each ID project determine which of the various kinds to conduct. For example, revising

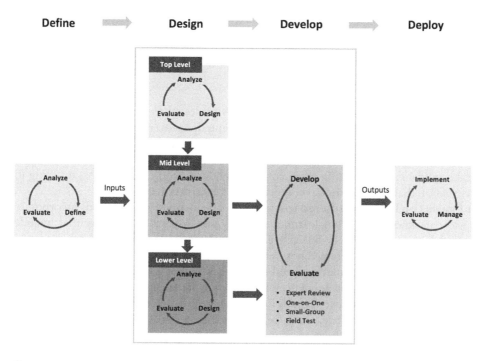

Figure 1.7 Our Holistic 4D Model of ID.

an existing course to cover a new piece of equipment would not require another top-level, mid-level, or learner analysis, but only a lower-level (tactical) focus. The three levels of design and guidelines on when and how to perform design at each of the levels will be presented and explained in Chapters 5–8.

Develop. In the right-hand part of the box, we see the instructional development process, intimately linked to the design activities as shown by the arrows interlinking the subsystem boxes. Development may be performed at several levels of detail, as required by a given project. Development also involves careful evaluation at each stage. However, in contrast to the design stages, where evaluation entails expert review by instructional designers and subject-matter experts to improve the decisions taken at each design level, evaluation during the development process involves trying out the instruction with real learners to improve it. The stages and activities of the development process are discussed in Chapter 9, and those for formative evaluation are discussed in Chapter 10.

To complete our picture of the process, on both sides of the diagram are inputs and outputs of the core instructional analysis-design-development-evaluation process: define and deliver.

Deploy. Finally, on the right of the diagram, there is a box representing the activities that follow design and development. These entail implementing the instructional system for regular, full-scale use in the school, training department, workplace, or informal learning environment (as appropriate), where the regular instructors and/or other ancillary staff will deliver the instructional system by implementing, managing, and evaluating it. This will include the process we call summative evaluation, as well as further formative evaluation. These activities are discussed in Chapters 10 and 13.

Thus, the ID process may be summarized as *Define – Design – Develop – Deploy*, with three levels of holistic design and iterative cycles of analysis, design, and evaluation. Hence it is called the Holistic 4D Model of ID.

Why Should You Use the Holistic 4D Model?

In our preface, we outlined ten innovations that appear in our Holistic 4D Model. Here we elaborate some more on them.

1. **It uses a holistic design process**. The cycles of design from top-level to mid-level to lower-level make the instruction less fragmented, more creative, and consequently more effective. They also make the ID process more efficient.
2. **It includes guidance about instructional theory**. Unlike most ID models, it integrates guidance for selecting instructional methods into the ID process, resulting in instruction that is more effective, efficient, and motivational.
3. **It focuses on learner-centered instruction**. The instructional methods incorporate up-to-date knowledge from learning sciences and instructional theory that include project-based, competency-based, self-directed, and anytime anywhere learning, thereby improving the effectiveness, efficiency, and appeal of the instruction.
4. **It focuses on holistic instructional sequences**. Based on schema theory, it offers guidance for instructional sequences that are holistic and thereby place all learning within a meaningful context, thereby increasing the effectiveness (especially for retention and transfer), efficiency, and appeal of the instruction.
5. **It addresses "topic" expertise as well as "task" expertise**. Based on the distinction between education and training, it offers guidance for designing instruction that is primarily focused on mental models (understandings) as well as instruction that

is primarily focused on tasks (how to). This greatly improves the effectiveness, efficiency, and appeal of both kinds of instruction, but especially for understanding topics – an area largely overlooked in ID.

6. **It addresses non-instructional interventions**. In contexts for which training is important, many performance problems cannot be solved by instruction. The Holistic 4D Model includes guidance about how to identify non-instructional interventions to improve performance, thereby producing more effective solutions and avoiding the expense of developing instruction that is not needed.

7. **It uses just-in-time analysis**. It provides guidance for conducting analysis activities immediately before the information is needed to create a part of the design, rather than trying to do all the analysis before any designing is done. This avoids doing unnecessary analysis, avoids overlooking information that later turns out to be important, and makes the information fresh in the designer's mind just when it is needed, considerably increasing the efficiency of the ID process.

8. **It uses rapid prototyping**. It includes guidance for using either (or both) of two kinds of rapid prototyping: quantitative reduction whereby a small amount of the entire instructional system is developed rapidly, and qualitative reduction whereby it is developed more rapidly by making it a simpler facsimile of the final instructional system. Rapid prototyping increases the efficiency and, to a lesser extent, the effectiveness of the ID process.

9. **It addresses the objectives controversy**. Research on behavioral objectives yields mixed results, which has created protagonists and antagonists. The Holistic 4D Model distinguishes between what may be helpful for designers and what may be helpful for learners. It offers guidance to create designer objectives, which contain certain specific kinds of information to guide the design process, and guidance to create learner objectives, which can be either abstract or concrete (what we call "demonstration objectives"). This results in more effective instruction.

10. **It utilizes more frequent evaluations**. Guidance is offered for doing smaller, more frequent formative evaluations of both the instructional designs and the ID process, thereby increasing the efficiency of the ID process and the effectiveness of the instruction.

Where Are We?

In this chapter, we have discussed the origins and the evolution of ID and have briefly described a selection of some of the ID models which have been proposed over the years. We introduced a new model, which includes the strong points of many other models and also places design in a broader, multi-level context of ID which may be summarized as *Define – Design – Develop – Deploy*. Hence it is called the Holistic 4D Model of ID.

The following chapters further describe this model and its use:

- **Unit 1, Define** describes how to determine what instruction (if any) is required and how to plan an appropriate ID project (Chapter 2)
- **Unit 2, Design** describes theories and other considerations that underlie the model (Chapters 3 and 4), followed by detailed guidance for designing the instruction (Chapters 5–8)
- **Unit 3, Develop** describes some considerations for creating the instruction from the design, followed by detailed guidance for developing the instruction (Chapter 9) and formatively evaluating it (Chapter 10)

- **Unit 4, Deploy** describes some considerations for implementing the instructional system, followed by detailed guidance for implementing it (Chapter 11) and summatively evaluating it (Chapter 12)
- The **Epilogue** provides some concluding remarks

Exercises

Here we offer suggestions for a teacher using this book as a textbook in a course, to help the students understand more deeply the contents of this chapter. We suggest these exercises be conducted in discussion groups of, say, three to five students each, so that those students who are shy will have more opportunity to talk. Of course, these exercises can be done individually by any reader who wants to deepen their understanding.

1. Discuss the ways that ID projects might vary from each other. Then discuss the major ways that ID needs to differ for those variations. Finally, report your conclusions to the whole class.
2. Discuss the major criticisms of ID models that you have or have heard.
3. Discuss why ID models can be useful.
4. Discuss the importance and merits of each of the ten innovations of the Holistic 4D Model.

References

ATD Research. (2015). Skills, challenges, and trends in instructional design. Retrieved from https://www.iacet.org/default/assets/File/pdfs/2015%20ATD_Research_Skills_Challenges_and_Trends_in_Instructional_Design.pdf.

Brand, S. (1994). *How buildings learn: What happens after they're built.* New York, NY: Penguin Books.

Comenius, J.A. (1907). *The great didactic: Setting forth the whole art of teaching all things to all men.* London: Adam and Charles Black.

Dick, W., Carey, L., & Carey, J.O. (2014). *The systematic design of instruction* (8th ed.). Boston, MA: Pearson.

Dills, C.R., & Romiszowski, A.J. (Eds.). (1997). *Instructional development paradigms.* Englewood Cliffs, NJ: Educational Technology Publications.

Educause Learning Institute. (2018). 7 Things you should know about learning engineering. Retrieved from https://library.educause.edu/-/media/files/library/2018/9/eli7160.pdf.

Gibbons, A.S., & Rogers, P.C. (2009). The architecture of instructional theory. In C. Reigeluth & A. Carr-Chellman (Eds.), *Instructional-design theories and models* (Vol. III, pp. 305–326). New York, NY: Routledge.

Gordon, J., & Zemke, R. (2000). The attack on ISD. *Training, 37,* 43–53.

Gustafson, K.L., & Branch, R.M. (2002). *Survey of instructional development models* (4th ed.). Syracuse, NY: ERIC Clearinghouse on Information & Technology.

International Board of Standards for Training, Performance and Instruction (Ibstpi). (2012). Instructional design competencies. Retrieved from http://ibstpi.org/.

Lieberman, M. (2018). Learning Engineers Inch toward the Spotlight. What is a learning engineer, and how is it different from other roles? Retrieved from https://www.insidehighered.com/digital-learning/article/2018/09/26/learning-engineers-pose-challenges-and-opportunities-improving.

Merrill, M.D. (2002). A pebble-in-the-pond model for instructional design. *Performance Improvement, 41*(7), 39–44.

Molenda, M. (2003). In search of the elusive ADDIE model. *Performance Improvement, 42*(5), 34–36.

Morrison, G.R., Ross, S.M., Kalman, H., & Kemp, J.E. (2010). *Designing effective instruction* (6th ed.). Hoboken, NJ: Wiley.

Munzenmaier, C. (2014). *Today's instructional designer. Competencies and careers.* Santa Rosa, CA: The eLearning Guild. Retrieved from https://momentum.gevc.ca/wp-content/uploads/2014/12/Todays-Instructional-Designer-2014.pdf.

Piskurich, G.M. (2015). *Rapid instructional design: Learning ID fast and right* (3rd ed.). Hoboken, NJ: John Wiley & Sons, Inc.

Reiser, R.A. (2001). A history of instructional design and technology: Part II: A history of instructional design. *Educational Technology Research and Development*, *49*(2), 57–67.

Reiser, R.A. (2018). A history of instructional design and technology. In R. A. Reiser & J. V. Dempsey (Eds.), *Trends and issues in instructional design and technology* (4th ed.). New York, NY: Pearson Education.

Reiser, R.A., & Dempsey, J.A. (Eds.). (2002). *Trends and issues in instructional design and technology*. Upper Saddle River, NJ: Merrill/Prentice Hall.

Romiszowski, A.J. (1981). *Designing instructional systems: Decision making in course planning and curriculum design*. London: Kogan Page. Reprinted 1990, 1996.

Romiszowski, A.J. (1986). *Developing auto-instructional materials: From programmed texts to CAL and interactive video*. London: Kogan Page. Reprinted1990, 1996.

Romiszowski, A.J., & Romiszowski, H.P. (2005). Retrospectiva e perspectivas do design instrucional e educação a distância: Análise da literatura [History of and perspectives for instructional design in distance education: A literature review]. *Revista Brasileira de Aprendizagem Aberta e a Distancia*, *4*. Originally published in the online journal of the Brazilian Association for Distance Education (abed.org.br). (http://seer.abed.net.br/index .php/RBAAD). Retrieved from https://www.researchgate.net/publication/242090526_Retrospectiva_e _Perspectivas_do_Design_Instrucional_e_Educacao_a_Distancia_Analise_da_Literatura.

Saxberg, B. (2015). Why we need learning engineers. *Chronicle of Higher Education*. Retrieved from https://ww w.chronicle.com/article/Why-We-Need-Learning-Engineers/229391.

Saxberg, B., & Hess, F.M. (2013). *Breakthrough leadership in the digital age: Using learning science to reboot schooling*. Thousand Oaks, CA: Corwin Press.

Simon, H. (1967). The job of a college president. *Educational Record*, *48*. Retrieved from http://digitalcollec tions.library.cmu.edu/awweb/awarchive?type=file&item=33692.

Skinner, B.F. (1954). The science of learning and the art of teaching. *Harvard Educational Review*, *24*(2), 86–97.

Skinner, B.F. (1968). The technology of teaching. In B.F. Skinner (Ed.), *The technology of teaching* (pp. 59–91). New York, NY: Appleton-Century-Crofts.

Tripp, S., & Bichelmeyer, B. (1990). Rapid prototyping: An alternative instructional design strategy. *Educational Technology Research and Development*, *38*(1), 31–44.

Wagner, E. (2019). Learning Engineering: A primer. Elearning Guild. Retrieved from https://www.elearnin gguild.com/insights/238/learning-engineering-a-primer/.

Zemke, R., & Rossett, A. (2002). A hard look at ISD. *Training*, *39*(2), 26–34.

Unit 1

Define

This unit contains one chapter. It describes how to determine what instruction (if any) is required and how to plan an appropriate instructional design (ID) project by providing guidance for performance analysis, instructional needs assessment, and project planning. The analysis that occurs as a part of the Define process is different from that which occurs as an integral part of the Design process (see Unit 2). This chapter also introduces planning for four functions that are essential to the Deployment of the instructional system you design.

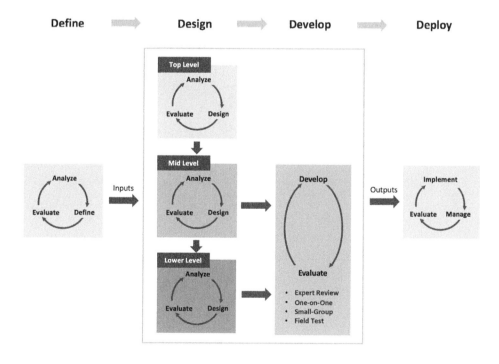

Our Holistic 4D Model of ID.

2   Define Your Project

Pre-Instructional Design

Overview

Performance analysis, instructional needs assessment, and project planning are critical activities that should be initiated before an instructional designer or instructional design (ID) team enters into the ID process. This chapter provides information about each of these critical activities and what goes into planning for your ID project. Further, this chapter introduces four system functions, including management, support, delivery, and evaluation, and provides guidance on how to plan for each of the four system functions.

Performance Analysis

Performance analysis was developed to address organizational needs regarding inadequate performance of employees. However, it can be adapted to address aspects of individual human development, such as an individual's performance as a citizen, a parent, or a reader. First, we offer guidance for addressing organizational needs. Then we comment on adaptations to address individual needs.

Performance analysis, sometimes called performance assessment (Piskurich, 2015) or front-end analysis (Dick, Carey, & Carey, 2014), is often conducted to identify organizational performance problems and to decide what kinds of interventions can best address them. Performance analysis may include:

- A performance gap analysis
- A performance opportunity analysis
- Identification of instructional and non-instructional interventions

Performance Gap Analysis

A performance gap analysis aims to identify: the performance gap (that is, the difference between the desired performance and the current performance); the causes of that gap; and interventions needed to overcome the gap (see Figure 2.1).

Performance Opportunity Analysis. Sometimes the performance gap is between what is and what could be – it is founded on possibilities rather than problems. This form of gap analysis, often referred to as Performance Opportunity Analysis, is conducted to identify areas to improve what is already good performance (Piskurich, 2015). An analysis

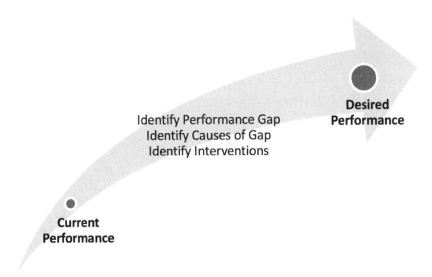

Identify Performance Gap
Identify Causes of Gap
Identify Interventions

Desired Performance

Current Performance

Figure 2.1 The Concept and Purpose of Performance Gap Analysis.

of what top performers do that distinguish them from average performers can provide insights into ways to further improve employee performance.

An example of this approach may be found in Tom Gilbert's article "The Science of Winning," (*Training Magazine*, August 1988) in which he analyzes the performance of the legendary Paul "Bear" Bryant of the University of Alabama who built a reputation as the "best ever" football coach, with six national championships and 323 wins. Gilbert knew Bryant well, through personal conversation, through his public pronouncements when interviewed, and through observation of his performance as coach. What Bryant said was typical of what most coaches say ("inspire them – give them great leadership – show them how much you care"), but what he did was to observe and record the performance of his players (on videotape) and use exemplary performance as examples to emulate and typical performance (containing typical errors) as a basis for corrective feedback. Bryant was an expert in performance gap/opportunity analysis. Marilyn Gilbert, who also knew Bryant, updated her husband's article in 2003. The subtitle of this version "says it all": *Wherein We Observe Paul "Bear" Bryant Build A Winning Team – But Not the Way He Said He Did.* This version of the article (Gilbert & Gilbert, 2003) may be accessed online at: https://eppicinc.files.wordpress.com/2007/11/the-science-of-winning-tom-and-marilyn-gilbert.pdf.

Regardless of the kind of performance gap, the three major categories of causes of the gap (Piskurich, 2015) are:

- Organizational/environmental problems
- Motivational/attitude problems
- Knowledge/skill deficits.

ID is mostly concerned with knowledge/skills deficits, which can be addressed by instruction. Other (non-instructional) interventions are needed to address organizational/environmental causes and motivational/attitude problems.

Table 2.1 Essential Questions for Performance Gap Analysis

Goal	Questions
To Identify the Performance Gap	• What does excellent performance look like? • How are the employees currently performing? • What is the gap between the desired performance and the current performance? • What should the employees be doing differently, stop doing, or start doing?
To Identify the Causes of the Gap	Organizational/environmental problems • Are the employees clear on performance standards and expectations? • Do they have tools and resources needed for effective performance? • Do they receive timely and constructive feedback on their performance? • Do the organizational structure and systems support effective performance? • Do they receive appropriate incentives for desired performance? • Are there negative consequences for poor performance? • Is workload distributed fairly? • Are there any organizational or environmental problems that prevent them from working effectively or efficiently? Motivational/attitude problems • Do they have adequate commitment for their job? • Are they motivated to meet or exceed the performance expectations? Knowledge/skills deficits • Do they have the knowledge and skills needed for effective performance? • Have they been properly trained on the task or job? • Do they receive accurate and up-to-date information in a timely manner? • Are their skills outdated?
To Select Appropriate Solutions	• What non-instructional interventions are needed to address the performance gaps? • Are instructional interventions necessary? • Can instructional interventions augment other performance interventions?

So, how can you do a performance gap analysis? Table 2.1 offers some questions to guide this kind of analysis.

We highly recommend conducting an expert-review type of formative evaluation of the results of the performance analysis. See Chapter 10 for guidance.

Identification of Instructional and Non-Instructional Interventions

Instructional interventions. When a performance problem or gap has been identified as being caused by a knowledge and skills deficit, an *instructional needs assessment* is conducted (see "Instructional Needs Assessment" below) to identify the major instructional goals (instructional needs). However, in most cases, one or more non-instructional interventions are needed in combination with training or education. For example, conducting training without repairing faulty equipment will not solve the problem; it will only exhaust resources. In addition, many non-instructional interventions require instruction as part of their implementation. Therefore, instructional designers need to work with human

Table 2.2 Motivation Killers and Motivators

What Causes and Destroys Motivation in Organizations?	
Motivation Killers	1. Act in a way that is perceived as dishonest, hypocritical, or unfair 2. Provide vague, impossible, and constantly changing performance goals 3. Impose arbitrary and unnecessary rules, policies, and work processes 4. Support constant competition among everyone in the organization 5. Point out people's mistakes and criticize them for errors
Motivators That Work for Everyone	1. Help people develop levels of self-confidence in their work skills 2. Create a positive emotional environment at work 3. Ask people to accept and value their own performance goals
Team Motivation Strategies	1. Foster mutual respect among teammates 2. The team must believe weaker members are working hard to improve 3. Require team members to collaborate with others 4. Hold individual team members accountable 5. Direct the team's competitive spirit outside the team and the organization

performance technologists or others to develop an instructional program that augments other performance interventions (Piskurich, 2015).

Non-instructional interventions. When the performance gap is attributed to organizational or environmental problems (e.g., poor equipment) or motivational/attitude problems (e.g., lack of motivation), non-instructional interventions should be used. Performance technology (PT) looks at the factors affecting workplace behavior. PT interventions address both individual and organizational factors that impact performance. Non-instructional interventions may include job redesign, culture change, facilities and tool design, job aids, incentive and feedback systems, organizational communications, and organizational design, to name a few. Non-instructional interventions are often beneficial in combination with instructional interventions (Chyung, 2008; Gilbert, 1978; Harless, 1975; Kaufman, 2000; Kaufman, Rojas, & Mayer, 1993; Mager & Pipe, 1997; Romiszowski, 1981; Rossett, 2009).

Motivational programs or interventions can provide the initiative and lead us to use our knowledge and skills to enhance our performance. Clark (2006) identified five major motivation killers, three motivators that work for everyone, and five team motivation strategies (see Table 2.2). They provide practical insights into how to increase work motivation at the individual and team levels. Another effective way to increase work motivation is to provide financial incentives. A variety of incentive and compensation programs, such as monetary and non-monetary rewards, vacations, and career opportunities, can be effective non-instructional interventions.

Another common example of non-instructional interventions is electronic performance support systems (EPSS), which are self-contained, online environments that support job performance on an as-needed basis (Brown, 1996). While conventional training is usually isolated from the performer's workplace, an EPSS is integrated into the performer's workplace. EPSS is a good solution for enhancing performance when experts are not available. Further, EPSS can be particularly useful for performers who prefer a self-directed style of learning (Brown, 1996). Finally, ergonomics should be considered to create a safe and productive work environment. Ergonomic interventions can be used to decrease physical and mental stressors and increase comfort and safety (Kearney & Smith, 1999).

EXAMPLE OF PERFORMANCE GAP ANALYSIS

The picture below shows a "problem" with a quadricycle.

This is a tough problem to solve just from the information available in the picture. But let's do our best to define some more or less probable causes. If inspection were to reveal that the drive train of the quad bike broke due to metal fatigue of some key component or wear in the bearings, one may ask whether there is a procedure in place for regular checking and maintenance, repair, or replacement of these components. If not, we have a potential work-organization cause. If the appropriate routine procedures are in place, were they followed completely and correctly? If not, why not?

The answers to these questions may lead us in several directions: (1) training interventions if we verify that the mechanics lack essential knowledge or skills to perform the procedures; (2) motivational interventions if we verify that they "just don't care"; (3) other forms of organizational or environmental interventions if we verify that despite knowing what should be done (and when) and despite possessing the necessary knowledge, skills, and motivation, some key tasks were this time overlooked or improperly executed. But we lack essential information.

Bottom line: performance gap analysis should be done through observation of the performers performing – in this case, the team that prepares and maintains the quad bikes and not only the bike and rider during the race. The picture we analyzed only indicates that there is a problem to solve. Let's do our gap analysis in the workshop where the mechanics work. Remember Tom Gilbert's story about "Bear" Bryant.

We highly recommend conducting an expert-review type of formative evaluation of the results of the analysis of the instructional and non-instructional interventions. See Chapter 10 for guidance.

Instructional Needs Assessment

Purpose

An instructional designer enters into the needs assessment process once a determination has been made that instruction is a necessary intervention for a performance gap. An instructional needs assessment is often referred to as a *training needs assessment, learning needs assessment*, *needs analysis*, or *discrepancy analysis*. The purpose of this kind of assessment is to generate the instructional goals for an ID project (Dick, Carey, & Carey, 2014; Kaufman et al., 1993; Witkin & Altschuld, 1995). A typical instructional needs analysis takes the results of the performance gap analysis and attempts to provide information that will help answer the following questions:

- What knowledge, skills, and/or attitudes do the learners need to address the performance gap?
- How important is each of the knowledge, skills, and attitudes you identified? Which training needs should be given priority if you can't afford to address them all?
- What are the "orienting" and "transfer" contexts like? Tessmer and Richey (1997) define the orienting context as preexisting conditions, such as learners' prerequisite skills, attitudes toward instruction, and organizational culture regarding instruction; and they define transfer context as the real-world conditions in which the learner will use the knowledge, skills, and attitudes. In Chapter 4 we will also discuss the instructional context – the context within which the instruction takes place.

A tremendous amount of money, time, and resources is often spent on unnecessary training that does not solve performance problems. An instructional needs assessment enables instructional designers to adequately define the scope of the ID project based on data and to avoid spending resources on unnecessary or unimportant areas by identifying and prioritizing the training needs that address the performance gap.

Instructional Needs Assessment Process

This assessment is often conducted in five phases:

1. Gather preliminary data
2. Plan the instructional needs assessment
3. Collect the data
4. Identify and prioritize training needs
5. Prepare a needs assessment report

Table 2.3 describes these five phases.

We highly recommend conducting an expert-review type of formative evaluation of the results of the instructional needs assessment. See Chapter 10 for guidance.

ID Project Planning

What Is ID Project Planning?

In this section, we describe the nature of an ID project, project management, ID project management, the project management process, and the ID project planning process.

What is an ID project? According to the Project Management Institute (2009), a project is:

> a temporary endeavor undertaken to create a unique product, service, or result. The temporary nature of projects indicates that a project has a definite beginning and end. The end is reached when the project's objectives have been achieved or when the project is terminated because its objectives will not or cannot be met, or when the need for the project no longer exists. (p. 3)

Table 2.3 Five Phases of an Instructional Needs Assessment

Phase	Activity
Phase 1: Gather Preliminary Data	Given the results of the performance gap analysis, obtain information about the perceptions of the client and key stakeholders associated with the problem or opportunity, regarding the performance gap. Also, obtain information about any ethical concerns associated with the instructional needs assessment (if applicable), management's views about the purpose and goals for the assessment, and the attitudes of learners and other stakeholders toward the assessment.
Phase 2: Plan the Instructional Needs Assessment	Develop a work plan to ensure the assessment stays on target. The planning phase involves determining (1) the purpose of the assessment, (2) the target audience, (3) the types of data to be collected about the audience, (4) the methods for collecting data (sources and collection methods), and (5) the personnel, resources, and tools needed to collect the data. The final step of the planning phase is (6) to develop data collection instruments. Common data collection techniques include interviews, observations, focus-group meetings, questionnaires, and review of documents or artifacts (e.g., strategic plans, personnel requirements, job descriptions).
Phase 3: Collect the Data	Collect assessment data. Careful consideration of the sample size and distribution is needed when collecting data, since it is impossible to collect data from the entire audience in most, if not all, situations. Data should be collected from a representative sample of the audience.
Phase 4: Identify and Prioritize Training Needs	Analyze and interpret the collected data. The output of the analysis is a prioritization of instructional needs. Needs can be prioritized using a variety of criteria – including the number of people impacted, the cost, the frequency, and timeliness – and developing a ranking scale. Define the instructional goals based on the data, the ID resources available, and the instructional resources that can be afforded when the instructional system is deployed. You may not have enough resources to address the lowest priority training needs.
Phase 5: Prepare a Needs Assessment Report	Prepare an instructional needs assessment report to help managers, decision makers, and stakeholders make the appropriate decisions about what to teach. The following four sections should be included in a final report: 1. The purpose of the assessment 2. Description of the assessment process (how it was conducted and who was involved) 3. Results – critical instructional needs and a prioritization of the identified needs 4. Instructional goals that identify who needs instruction and what instruction is needed

An ID project involves the execution of five key activities – analysis, design, development, implementation, and evaluation – but they are not strictly sequential. Analysis and design should be done together (just-in-time analysis), formative evaluation should be done frequently throughout the ID project, and implementation should be considered throughout the ID project.

The Holistic 4D Model (see Figure 1.7 and the remaining chapters in this book) is a fairly complete description of how these five key activities may be sequenced and performed during an ID project, showing how they are embedded in the overall project – preceded by Project Definition (which includes performance gap analysis and instructional needs assessment) and followed by Deployment (which includes implementation and summative evaluation).

What is project management? Project management (PM) is both an art and a science. The science consists of a set of processes using a systematic methodology for planning and executing a project. The art consists of "soft skills," including leadership, problem solving, and managing resources and expectations. Successful PM is the art of bringing together tasks, resources, and people needed to accomplish the project's goals (Kerzner, 2009; Lewis, 2011; Randolph & Posner, 1988).

What is ID project management? ID projects vary in size and complexity from creating a job aid for a simple task to developing an interactive e-learning curriculum for globally distributed employees. Some ID projects involve only one instructional designer, while other projects may require a large team of many instructional designers, media developers, subject-matter experts, and other professionals. Instructional designers play different PM roles in different ID contexts (e.g., organizations, projects). In some small-scale ID projects, for example, instructional designers may play multiple roles, including the project manager role. On the other hand, large ID teams often include a project manager or a project coordinator, which allows instructional designers to focus on designing instruction.

What is the PM process? Ensuring the effective flow of a project throughout its lifecycle is the key to successful project management. The PM process is composed of five phases (Project Management Institute, 2009).

1. *Initiating* includes actions to begin a project.
2. *Planning* includes defining the scope of the project, developing a strategic plan, and beginning to assemble priority lists and to plan team needs. This phase also addresses and clarifies the project goals and customer's expectations, and it identifies the resources necessary to achieve those goals within timeline and budgetary constraints.
3. *Executing* includes coordinating the right people and right resources to carry out the project plan and produce deliverables that meet the customer expectations.
4. *Monitoring and controlling* measures progress toward achieving project goals, monitors deviation from the plan, and takes corrective action to match progress with plans and expectations.
5. *Closing* includes formalizing acceptance of the project and bringing it to a well-documented end.

The activities within each phase are a series of actions directed toward either defining or producing a specific result. The information required in each PM activity can be customized to fit the particular project environment. Each PM phase's outputs often become inputs to another PM phase. These activities are iterative in nature, which requires continuous updating of the plan during the lifecycle of the project. Table 2.4 presents the activities according to the Project Management Body of Knowledge (PMBOK).

Guidance for ID Project Planning

Managing an ID project, whether large or small, can be a major undertaking. Instructional designers or ID project managers can apply PM activities and tools to successfully manage any ID project. In this chapter, we offer guidance on the first two phases of ID PM – initiating and planning. We also provide some guidance for formatively evaluating the ID process.

Initiating phase. The initiating phase begins with a validated instructional needs assessment report outlining the instructional needs. First, the instructional designer or project manager needs to identify all stakeholders affected by the ID project, document relevant information regarding their interests, and establish the project charter (or contract),

Table 2.4 PM Process Activities from the PMBOK Guide (from Project Management Institute, 2009)

Phase	Definition	Activities/Products
1. Initiating	Authorize the project	1. Develop project charter 2. Identify stakeholders
2. Planning	Define and refine the objectives; select the best alternative courses of action to attain objectives	1. Collect requirements 2. Define scope 3. Define activities 4. Prepare milestone chart 5. Sequence activities 6. Estimate activity duration 7. Estimate activity resources 8. Develop schedule 9. Estimate costs 10. Determine budget
3. Executing	Coordinate people and other resources to carry out the plan	1. Direct/manage execution 2. Acquire project team 3. Manage project team 4. Manage stakeholders' expectations 5. Conduct procurements
4. Monitoring & Controlling	Ensure objectives are met; monitor and measure progress regularly to identify variances so necessary corrective action can be taken	1. Monitor & control project work 2. Control schedule 3. Oversee budget/funding 4. Perform quality assurance 5. Communicate progress 6. Mitigate risks 7. Administer procurements
5. Closing	Formalize project or phase acceptance and bring it to an orderly end	1. Close project or phase 2. Close procurements

which formally authorizes the ID project. The project charter documents the instructional need, defines the initial requirements and expectations, and gives the project manager the authority to apply resources to the project work.

Planning phase. The planning phase entails gathering information to produce an ID PM plan. The purpose of this plan is to focus the project manager and team on systematically identifying, tracking, and documenting all of the project requirements. The plan should generally address the project management elements shown in Table 2.5. Whatever planning format is required for the project, it should start with the two outputs from the initiating phase – the project charter and the list of stakeholders/sponsors. Planning activities should address both instructional and non-instructional interventions and should be completed before developing any new instruction or revising any existing instruction. Planning should identify potential problems or difficulties that the project may encounter. A useful tool for identifying such issues is the **SWOT** (Strengths – Weaknesses – Opportunities – Threats) method of analysis. Another useful tool, based on systems-thinking, is the **CIPP** (Context – Input – Process – Product) method for "troubleshooting" issues in complex systems. This can be used both for evaluating problems in existing systems and for initial diagnosis to predict potential sources of problems. These tools may be used in combination, one complementing the other. Finally, planning should also consider any of your adaptations to the Holistic 4D Model, and you should expect to revise the plan at the end

Table 2.5 Elements of an ID PM Plan

Element	Description
Team Formation	Decide who should be on the team and the roles and responsibilities of each.
Stakeholders	State the details of the stakeholders.
Target Audience & Goals	Describe the intended learners and goals of the education or training.
Scope	Define what the ID project contains, summarizing all the work required to successfully complete the instruction.
References	Identify all necessary policies, guidance, and directives applicable to the instruction.
Constraints & Assumptions	Identify all known or potential problems or issues and assumptions that could arise during the ID process (e.g., resources, manpower, security, safety, environmental issues).
Project Management Strategies	Determine the way the team will work (decision-making process, frequency of meetings to discuss project progress, methods of communication and reporting, etc.).
Definition and Sequence of ID Activities	Determine specific activities and interactivity dependencies that must be performed to produce various project deliverables.
Timeline and Resources	Create an ID project timeline identifying activity sequences, durations, and resource requirements.
Estimated Costs	Determine an approximation of (1) the costs for the ID process and (2) the costs of implementing instruction (resources, people, equipment, infrastructure).
Budget	Establish a cost baseline for allocated funds and resources for the ID process and for implementing the instruction.
ID Process Evaluation	Develop an evaluation plan to improve process quality throughout the ID process (see below for more details).
Other Considerations	Produce written plans that detail how to execute, monitor, and control each of the activities of the ID process: analysis/design, development, implementation, and evaluation. Plan for the ID project closing processes, during which all project activities will be evaluated and documented for lessons learned to finalize the project. Consider the effects of the ID project on the organization.

of the top-level, the mid-level, and the lower-level ADE process. A template for an ID PM plan is shown in Figure 2.2.

ID process evaluation. Process evaluation is one of the key elements of the ID PM Plan. A project manager or instructional designer should plan for process evaluation to ensure that the ID process is of high quality. Process evaluation, for which we provide guidance in Chapter 10, focuses on enabling instructional developers to improve their ID process as it unfolds. A preliminary evaluation plan should be created during the planning phase, and it should be updated throughout all phases of the ID process. A process evaluation plan may contain such information as:

- How the ID activities will be evaluated
- Who will conduct the evaluations
- When to conduct the evaluations
- Evaluation schedule constraints

PM Plan: [ID Project Title]

1. Clients & Stakeholders

2. Target Audience

3. Project Goal & Scope

4. Project Timeline & Process
   - Start Date:
   - End Date:

No.	ID Activities	Deliverables	Duration	Start Date	End Date	Status

5. Resources & Constraints

6. Budget

7. Project Team Members

Name	Roles	Responsibilities

8. PM Strategies & Meeting Schedules
   - Decision-Making Process
   - Frequency of Meetings
   - Methods and Tools of Communication
   - Meeting Schedule

Date	Time	Location/Tool	Objectives & Attendees

9. ID Process Evaluation Plan

Figure 2.2 Template for an ID PM Plan.

- Who will be interviewed for each activity being evaluated
- Other data sources for each activity being evaluated
- How the results should be documented
- How problems should be resolved

Everyone conducting an activity in any phase should constantly seek to collect data about what is working well, what is not working well, and how to improve it. The process evaluation plan should be updated periodically to include new or revised information, such as:

- Changes in the evaluation plan for the next phase
- Rationale for changes made to the evaluation plan
- Lessons learned about the evaluation process during the latest evaluations

It is usually beneficial to conduct an expert-review type of formative evaluation (with expert project managers) of the project management plan. See Chapter 10 for guidance.

Figure 2.3 Four System Functions.

Planning the Instructional-System Functions

Planning the instructional-system functions needs to occur as soon as you or your ID team completes the ID PM plan. Figure 2.3 shows the four top-level functions of the instructional system – management, delivery, support, and evaluation – all of which take place simultaneously.

Delivery is the function whereby instruction is brought to the learner, such as instructor-led or online instruction.

Support is the function of maintaining all parts of the system (e.g., instructor professional development, technology support). The importance of the support function in the instructional system cannot be over-emphasized. A well-designed course may fall short of the training goal without the right support components or systems being in place for the education or training intervention(s).

Management, sometimes called administration, is the function of directing or controlling instructional operations, such as assigning individuals to certain tasks associated with an instructional program, acquiring, installing, and maintaining equipment and materials, hiring and managing staff, coordinating day-to-day operations of an instructional system, and maintaining records. Competent management is the key to an effective instructional system. Management has the overall responsibility for ensuring that all components of the system are fully integrated and compatible.

Evaluation of all system functions is conducted periodically to ensure efficiency and effectiveness of the operational instructional system. It is important to periodically evaluate all the functions as long as the instructional system is operational. Both formative and summative evaluation are important.

The functions are permanent organizational functions that provide critical operational support for any education and training programs. Managers (aka administrators) and instructors may perform these system functions at any time, in any order, and as often as necessary during the lifetime of an instructional program. The outer three functions are inextricably linked by operational evaluation that takes place continuously throughout all the other functions of the total instructional system to achieve an improved instructional program.

Each of the four functions is brought into the planning process to adjust the ID PM plan to ensure that all instructional system functions are taken into consideration. Some of the products generated from this planning include:

- Preliminary direction on the type of delivery system or methods
- Operations constraints and day-to-day operations requirements
- Instructional resource requirements
- Plans for acquisition of equipment and facilities
- Selection and preparation of instructors
- Operational evaluation strategies
- And so forth

Table 2.6 shows the activities for which you should plan for each of the four system functions.

Table 2.6 Planning Activities for the System Functions

Management
Description: Directs and controls all aspects of the instructional process.
Planning Activities – Plan how to:
1. **Direct and control** all aspects of the instructional process.
2. **Organize, schedule, and monitor** resources, such as personnel, equipment, facilities, and funds.
3. **Coordinate** the instructional system operation and support.
4. **Maintain records**, such as personnel and instructional equipment.
5. **Evaluate** the effectiveness and efficiency of each element in the instructional system.
6. **Report** the status and progress of the operation of the instructional system.

Support
Description: Provides for and maintains the system on a day-to-day and long-term basis.
Planning Activities – Plan how to:
1. **Supply** equipment, parts, and materials.
2. **Provide** student support, such as processing students "in" and "out" of their training or education programs (including resident and non-resident training/education venues).
3. **Provide** staff support, such as leave processing and maintenance of personnel programs.
4. **Maintain** equipment and facilities.
5. **Construct** instructor aids, instructional aids, and facilities.
6. **Provide** funding and services.

Delivery
Description: Provides means by which instruction is made available to students.
Planning Activities – Plan how to:
1. Ensure that instructional delivery takes place as planned, including instructional staff for use and evaluation of the selected delivery method(s).
2. Make instruction available to learners and give them access to whatever delivery method is utilized.

Evaluation
Description: Provides feedback and other information for the total instructional system.
Planning Activities – Plan how to:
1. Gather feedback data through formative and summative operational evaluations.
2. Analyze, report, and use the data.

Where Are We?

In this chapter we have discussed the following:

- Performance analysis, including performance gap analysis, performance opportunity analysis, and identification of instructional and non-instructional interventions
- Instructional needs assessment to identify the instructional goals for the project
- Project planning, including the nature of an ID project, project management, ID project management, the ID project management process, and ID project planning
- Planning the four functions of an instructional-system – management, support, delivery, and evaluation

When you have finished developing the PM plan for your ID project, you are almost ready to start working on the project. But first, it is important to review some theory and address some major considerations for designing instruction. These are the topics of Chapters 3 and 4.

Exercises

Here again we offer suggestions for a teacher using this book as a textbook in a course, to help the students understand more deeply the contents of this chapter. We suggest that you organize students into an even number of teams of about three students each, to choose an ID project to work on throughout the course. However, these exercises can be done individually by any reader who wants to deepen their understanding and skills.

1. Help each team to choose a project "client" for a very simple project.
2. Have each team conduct a performance gap analysis, perform an instructional needs assessment, develop an ID project plan, and develop a systems function plan. This must be a very simple project (simple performance gap and instructional need) to be feasible to complete during the course.
3. Have each team offer suggestions for improvement for one or two other teams before you review and provide feedback to the students.

References

Brown, L.A. (1996). *Designing and developing electronic performance support systems*. Newton, MA: Digital Press.

Chyung, S.Y. (2008). *Foundations of instructional and performance technology*. Amherst, MA: HRD Press, Inc.

Clark, R.E. (2006). Motivating individuals, teams, and organizations. In J. Pershing (Ed.), *Handbook of human performance technology: Principles, practices, and potential* (3rd ed., pp. 478–497). San Francisco, CA: Pfeiffer.

Dick, W., Carey, L., & Carey, J.O. (2014). *The systematic design of instruction* (8th ed.). Boston, MA: Pearson.

Gilbert, T.F. (1978). *Human competence: Engineering worthy performance*. New York, NY: McGraw-Hill.

Gilbert, T.F., & Gilbert, M. (2003). The science of winning: Wherein we observe Paul "Bear" Bryant build a winning team – But not the way he said he did. Retrieved from https://eppicinc.files.wordpress.com/200 7/11/the-science-of-winning-tom-and-marilyn-gilbert.pdf.

Harless, J.H. (1975). *An ounce of analysis (is worth a pound of objectives): A self-instructional lesson* (3rd ed.). Falls Church, VA: Harless Performance Guild.

Kaufman, R.A. (2000). *Mega planning: Practical tools for organizational success*. Thousand Oaks, CA: Sage Publications, Inc.

Kaufman, R.A., Rojas, A.M., & Mayer, H. (1993). *Needs assessment: A user's guide*. Englewood Cliffs, NJ: Educational Technology Publications.

Kearney, L., & Smith, P. (1999). Workplace design for creativity. In H. Stolovich & E. Keeps (Eds.), *Handbook of human performance technology* (2nd ed., pp. 464–482). San Francisco, CA: Jossey-Bass Pfeiffer.

Kerzner, H. (2009). *Project management: A systems approach to planning, scheduling, and controlling* (10th ed.). Hoboken, NJ: John Wiley & Sons.

Lewis, J.P. (2011). *Project planning, scheduling & control: The ultimate hands-on guide to bringing projects in on time and on budget* (5th ed.). New York, NY: McGraw-Hill.

Mager, R.F., & Pipe, P. (1997). *Analyzing performance problems, or, you really oughta wanna: How to figure out why people aren't doing what they should be, and what to do about it* (3rd ed.). Atlanta, GA: Center for Effective Performance.

Piskurich, G.M. (2015). *Rapid instructional design: Learning ID fast and right* (3rd ed.). Hoboken, NJ: John Wiley & Sons, Inc.

Project Management Institute. (2009). *A guide to the project management body of knowledge* (PMBOK Guide – 5th ed.). Retrieved from http://dinus.ac.id/repository/docs/ajar/PMBOKGuide_5th_Ed.pdf.

Randolph, W.A., & Posner, B.Z. (1988). *Effective project planning and management: Getting the job done.* Englewood Cliffs, NJ: Prentice-Hall.

Romszowski, A.J. (1981). *Designing instructional systems: Decision making in course planning and curriculum design.* London: Kogan Page. (Reprinted 1990, 1996).

Rossett, A. (2009). *First things fast: A handbook for performance analysis.* San Francisco, CA: Pfeiffer.

Witkin, B.R., & Altschuld, J.W. (1995). *Planning and conducting needs assessments: A practical guide.* Thousand Oaks, CA: Sage Publications.

Unit 2

Design

This unit begins with the most important consideration for designing instruction – theories of learning and instruction (see Chapter 3). They provide guidance for selecting instructional methods that determine the effectiveness, efficiency, and appeal of your instruction. Then Chapter 4 describes nine other major considerations to improve the quality of your instruction and the efficiency of your ID process.

These two chapters are followed by detailed guidance for designing instruction, integrated with just-in-time analysis activities and immediate formative evaluation activities (analysis-design-evaluation – ADE cycles). Chapter 5 addresses top-level ADE to create a fuzzy vision of the instruction, including a top-level view of the content, sequence,

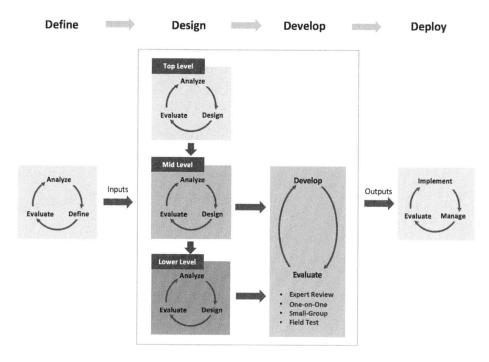

Our Holistic 4D Model of ID.

and instructional methods. Then Chapter 6 addresses mid-level ADE to provide the next level of clarity about the vision, including the mid-level content, sequence, objectives, assessments, instructional methods, and media for both task expertise and topic expertise. Chapters 7 and 8 address lower-level ADE to provide the final level of clarity about the vision, including content, sequence, and instructional methods, based on resources and existing instruction, for both task expertise and topic expertise. Chapters 5–7 indicate when to do formative evaluation and revision during those analysis and design activities.

3   Considerations for Design

Theories of Learning and Instruction

Overview

Instructional design (ID) should be grounded in theories of learning and instruction. In order to provide an overview of basic theories of learning and instruction, this chapter first describes five major *categories of learning* that are helpful for selecting instructional methods: (1) memorizing, (2) understanding, (3) applying skills, (4) applying higher-order thinking skills, and (5) acting on attitudes and values. Then, it summarizes three types of *learning theories*: (1) behavioral, (2) cognitive, and (3) constructivist. Further, this chapter explains what *instructional theory* is, how it is different from learning theory, and why it is important. A summary of some of the well-known instructional theories is also provided.

Categories of Learning

There are many purposes and ways of categorizing learning. For designing instruction, the focus is on categories that require differences in instructional methods. In real-life performances, these types of learning are integrated, but they are learned differently. For those who are familiar with the taxonomies of Bloom (Anderson et al., 2000; Bloom, Engelhart, Furst, Hill, & Krathwohl, 1956), Gagné (1985), Ausubel (1968), J.R. Anderson (1983, 1996), and/or Merrill (1983), Reigeluth (Reigeluth & Moore, 1999) has synthesized from those taxonomies the most useful categories for designing instruction. The synthesis identifies four major categories that are particularly helpful for selecting instructional methods for the cognitive and motor domains of learning: (1) memorize, (2) understand, (3) apply skills, and (4) apply higher-order thinking skills (see Table 3.1).

Unlike with Gagné's and Anderson's taxonomies, it is helpful to distinguish between memorization and understanding, because each requires very different methods of instruction. Conversely, it is not very helpful to distinguish among analysis, synthesis, and evaluation because those higher-order skills require very similar methods of instruction. Another important kind of learning is attitudes and values from the affective domain. Despite the importance of the affective domain, less research has been done to identify methods of instruction for the types of learning in the affective domain. The five kinds of learning are briefly summarized next, but more in-depth descriptions and examples are provided in Chapter 8.

Memorize information. Memorization entails acquiring the ability to recognize or recall information. Some of the most common kinds of memorization include associations (a simple stimulus and response, such as a picture of an aircraft and its name) and verbal chains (such as a poem or a Miranda rights statement to be read to someone being

Table 3.1 Taxonomies Identifying Four Major Kinds of Learning

Bloom	Gagné	Ausubel	Anderson	Merrill	Synthesis
Knowledge	Verbal information	Rote learning	Declarative knowledge	Remember verbatim	Memorize information
Comprehension		Meaningful learning		Remember paraphrased	Understand relationships
Application	Intellectual skill		Procedural knowledge	Use a generality	Apply skills
Analysis Evaluation Synthesis	Cognitive strategy			Find a generality	Apply higher-order thinking skills

placed under arrest), but one can also memorize visuals, sounds, spatial relationships, and muscle movements.

Understand relationships. Understanding entails learning the relationships among concepts. Concepts are objects, events, or ideas. In most cases, instances can be classified as either belonging or not belonging to the category represented by the concept. This is a skill, rather than an understanding. For example, "fraction" is a concept. Classifying numbers as being or not being a fraction is a skill. Some concepts are difficult to classify, like "atom." While the ability to classify is desired for many concepts, sometimes it is important for the learner to understand rather than be able to classify a concept, as in the case of "atom." There are two major kinds of understanding: conceptual and theoretical understanding (Reigeluth, 1980). These are the major elements of a schema.

- *Conceptual understanding.* Conceptual understanding entails learning descriptive relationships among concepts. There are different dimensions of conceptual understanding that are based on different kinds of conceptual relationships, including superordinate, coordinate, subordinate, analogical, experiential, and others. There are many different dimensions of understanding for any given concept.
- *Theoretical understanding.* Theoretical understanding entails learning change relationships among concepts, including cause-effect relationships and natural-process relationships. *Causal* relationships, often called causal models, can have multiple causes for an effect and multiple effects for a cause. They can also exist in chains of causes and effects, and each relationship is more often probabilistic (the cause will not always have a given effect) than deterministic (the cause always has a given effect). Learning complex causal models is essential for developing many kinds of expertise. *Natural-process* relationships are the ordered events that comprise a natural process. A natural process is different from a procedure in that it is not a set of steps intended to achieve a goal; rather it is a set of events that occur naturally in the world, like the life cycle of a flowering plant or the phases of the moon.

Apply skills. Application entails acquiring the ability to perform a skill (physical and/or cognitive). Three kinds of cognitive skills include *concept-classification* (such as identifying numbers that are fractions and those that are decimals), *procedure-using* (such as adding fractions), and *principle-using* (such as predicting the effects of a one-fifth reduction in the production of oranges in the United States). Each of these three kinds of skills arrays on a continuum from purely *routine skills*, whose performance does not vary from one situation to another, to *transfer skills*, whose performance varies greatly from one situation to another and therefore requires the ability to generalize. Transfer skills are often called complex cognitive skills.

Apply higher-order skills. Higher-order learning includes the top three levels of Bloom's taxonomy (analysis, synthesis, and evaluation) and their various configurations in metacognitive skills (sometimes called metaskills), including critical thinking, learning strategies, and self-direction. This kind of skill is distinguished from domain-specific skills (subject-area skills) because it takes much longer to learn and needs to be applied across a broader range of domains. Metacognitive skills are configured into the complex skills of adapting, monitoring, and correcting the use of individual skills in complex performances that integrate cognitive, perceptual, and motor processes. Difficulty in learning a higher-order thinking skill depends on the number of component higher-order skills involved.

Act on attitudes and values. A value is the importance a person attaches to something, such as honesty and consideration for others, and is difficult to change. An attitude is the way a person's values are manifested. Put another way, a value is associated with a collection of attitudes. Typically, values are changed by changing related attitudes gradually over time. Attitude change entails a person moving from one point on a continuum to another. For example, attitudes about sexual harassment fall on a continuum from being strongly against it to being strongly disposed to it. An attitude has three components: affective, cognitive, and psychomotor (Kamradt & Kamradt, 1999). To change an existing attitude, all three components should be moved by manageable stages in the desired direction. If any one component lags much behind the other two components, attitude change is unlikely to occur. Each component requires different instructional methods. It is easier to create new attitudes than to change existing attitudes. What Romiszowski (1981) refers to as interactive skills and reactive skills also fall largely into this category with some cognitive and physical components.

Of course, there are other kinds of learning in the affective domain. Krathwohl, Bloom and Masia (1964) categorized this domain into five stages of affective learning: receiving, responding, valuing, organizing, and characterizing. Common categories in this domain include attitudes, values, morals, ethics, emotions, intrapersonal skills, interpersonal skills, and more. Social and emotional learning (SEL) has received increasing attention since about 2000. These kinds of affective learning are very complex, and research is far from conclusive on how best to foster them. Therefore, in this book we only address attitudes and values.

In real life, the types of learning are integrated. This integration can be accomplished through project-based (or task-based) learning whereby authentic tasks are performed, requiring use of all the various types of learning they encompass. Guidance for designing each of these kinds of learning is offered in Chapter 8.

Learning Theories

Learning theory is the body of principles proposed by psychologists and educators to explain how people acquire skills, knowledge, and attitudes. Learning theories are descriptive. They describe how learning occurs. Types of learning theories (often called theoretical approaches) include (1) **behavioral theories**, such as classical conditioning theory and reinforcement theory; (2) **cognitive theories**, such as information processing theory, schema theory, and social interaction theory; and (3) **constructivist theories**, such as cognitive constructivism, social constructivism, and constructionism. While these three types are useful, it is important to understand that the boundaries among them can be fuzzy, and that some learning theories – and most instructional theories – have elements from two or even all three types.

Behavioral Theory

Behavioral theories focus on observable events and therefore do not attempt to explain what goes on in the mind. The two major kinds of behavioral theories are classical conditioning theory and reinforcement theory, but there are other kinds of behavioral theories as well.

Classical conditioning theory. This theory was proposed by a Russian physiologist, Ivan Pavlov. Classical conditioning (also known as respondent conditioning) occurs when a stimulus (e.g., food) already elicits a response (e.g., salivation) from a person, and a new stimulus (e.g., a bell) is paired with the existing stimulus (e.g., food) until it alone elicits the same response (Pavlov, 1897/1902; Watson, 1924). A person salivates when presented with delicious food. If a bell is rung each time the food is presented, eventually the bell alone will cause the person to salivate.

Reinforcement theory. Reinforcement (or operant conditioning or instrumental conditioning) takes place when the learner makes an association between a stimulus or cue and the desired behavior. When the behavior is followed by a reward or removal of a punishment, it is reinforced. Learning occurs as learners become able to distinguish among stimuli and respond to them in accordance with the way they were previously reinforced (Skinner, 1953, 1965; Thorndike, 1911, 1921).

Behavioral theories are primarily relevant for lower levels of learning, such as emotional responses (e.g., extinguishing a fear response to spiders) and memorizing information.

Cognitive Theory

Cognitive theories focus on what is going on in the learner's mind. Three major kinds of cognitive theory are the information processing theory, schema theory, and social cognitive theory, but there are also many other cognitive learning theories, such as attribution theory (Weiner, 1972), cognitive load theory (Sweller, 1994), gestalt theory (Wertheimer, 1923), metacognitive theory (Flavell, 1985), situated cognition (Brown, Collins, & Duguid, 1989), and stage theory of cognitive development (Piaget, 1952), among others.

Information processing theory. Information processing theory says that the learner's brain has internal structures that select and process incoming material, store and retrieve it, use it to produce behavior, and receive and process feedback on the results. A number of cognitive processes are involved in learning, including the "executive" functions of selective perception, short-term storage, semantic encoding, long-term storage, retrieval, response organization, and performance (Atkinson & Shiffrin, 1968; Craik & Lockhart, 1972; Gagné, 1985).

Schema theory. Knowledge is thought to be stored as schemata and as part of propositional networks. A schema is a structured set of memory elements (concepts, propositions, images, and attitudes) representing a large set of meaningful information pertaining to an event or object (Anderson & Spiro, 1977; Bartlett, 1932; Piaget, 1952; Rumelhart, 1980). For an event, such as a preflight check or preventive maintenance procedure like checking the oil in your car, a schema may take the form of a script (a kind of story or scenario that organizes information). For an object, such as an automobile, house, or chair, a schema may take the form of a frame (a structure that looks like a table or matrix into which different kinds of information fit). Regardless of type, a schema contains information on features of the object or event. These features, called slots, are filled in by the learner when encountering new information that relates to the schema in a process called assimilation. When inconsistencies are found between a schema and new information, the schema is modified in a process called accommodation. Sometimes the inconsistencies are so great that a massive change in the schema is required. That massive change is called restructuring.

Social cognitive theory. This theory, sometimes called social learning theory, says that learning and consequent changes in behavior take place as a result of interaction between the learner and the environment, primarily through observing and imitating the actions of others (Bandura, 1977, 1986). Behaviors are modeled either by other people or symbolically. The environment demonstrates the consequences of the modeled behaviors (elements of behaviorist theory), and the learner cognitively processes the observed behaviors and consequences and changes his or her own behavior appropriately. The cognitive processes include attention, retention, motor responses, and motivation. Techniques for achieving learning (which are instructional theory rather than learning theory) include direct modeling and verbal instruction. Behavior, personal factors, and environmental events all operate together to produce learning.

Constructivist Theory

Constructivist theory proposes that people learn by actively constructing their knowledge and skills, primarily through experience, reflection on their experience, observation of experience, and discussion of experience. Three major kinds of constructivist theory include cognitive constructivism, social constructivism, and constructionism, but there are other constructivist theories, or varieties of these theories, as well, such as anchored instruction (Bransford, Sherwood, Hasselbring, Kinzer & Williams, 1990), cognitive apprenticeship (Collins, Brown, & Newman, 1988), cognitive dissonance (Festinger, 1962), communities of practice (Wenger, 1998), and social development theory (Vygotsky, 1978, 1986), among others.

Cognitive constructivism. This kind of constructivism proposes that people learn primarily by doing and that skills learned are "situated" in the context in which they are learned, meaning that transfer of those skills to unfamiliar contexts is difficult (Dewey, 1933; Lave & Wenger, 1990; Perry, 1999; Piaget, 1952). Furthermore, in order to not become "inert knowledge," they should be learned and practiced within a broader context.

Social constructivism. This theory proposes that individual learning occurs through the construction of shared meaning in a group (Palincsar, 1998; Vygotsky, 1978, 1986). It addresses a group's development of a "small culture" with shared artifacts. Collaborative learning and small-group discussion are instructional methods that are aligned with social constructivism. So are communities of practice (Wenger, 1998).

Constructionism. Building upon Jean Piaget's constructivist theory, constructionist theory agrees that knowledge is actively constructed by learners rather than transmitted by a teacher (Papert, 1993a, 1993b). However, constructionism takes the notion of individual knowledge construction one step further by adding the idea of "learning-by-making." It proposes that learners learn best when they are actively engaged in the construction of concrete and meaningful artifacts that can be shared with others (Harel & Papert, 1991). Constructionist theory emphasizes that the construction of concrete artifacts "in the world" can support the construction of knowledge "in the head," whereas Piaget's constructivist theory focuses on the construction of knowledge in the learner's head.

Instructional Theories

What is an instructional theory? How is it different from learning theory? An instructional theory or instructional-design theory is "a theory that offers explicit guidance on how to better help people learn and develop" (Reigeluth, 1999, p. 5). While learning theory is about natural processes by which learning occurs, instructional theory is about what should be done to help those natural processes take place (Reigeluth, 1999). Instructional theory is prescriptive, whereas learning theory is descriptive. Instructional theory identifies methods of instruction (ways to facilitate learning) and their situations (when and when not to use those methods).

Learning theory explains why an instructional method works in a given situation, and it can be used to derive new methods of instruction, but it is of very little help to instructional designers. Instructional theories are more directly and easily applied to ID problems since they describe specific methods and situations for their use, rather than describing what goes on inside a learner's head when learning occurs.

To be useful to instructional designers, instructional theory must offer guidance about which instructional methods to use when. These are called instructional methods and instructional situations, respectively (Reigeluth & Carr-Chellman, 2009a). Here are some characteristics of each:

- Instructional situations
  - Values about various aspects of the instruction (based on philosophy, not data)
    - About learning goals – opinions about what should be taught
    - About priorities – opinions about the relative importance of effectiveness, efficiency, and appeal for the instruction
    - About methods – opinions about which methods are best
    - About power – opinions about who should be given the power to decide about learning goals, priorities, and methods
  - Conditions
    - Content – the nature of what is to be learned
    - Learner – the nature of the learner
    - Learning environment – the nature of the learning environment
    - ID constraints – the nature of constraints on the ID process
- Instructional methods
  - Scope of a method – the amount of instruction with which a method deals
    - Continuum from macro through meso to micro
  - Generality of a method – the breadth of instructional situations in which a method should be used
    - Continuum from universal to local
  - Precision of a method – the level of detail of the description of a method
    - Continuum from highly precise to very vague
  - Power of a method – the amount a method contributes toward the attainment of its learning goal
    - Continuum of probability from 0.0 (no power) to 1.0 (absolute power)
  - Consistency of a method – the reliability with which a method contributes its power toward the attainment of its learning goal
    - Continuum from high to low consistency

All instructional theories describe not only the methods, but also the situations in which they should (and should not) be used. Without the situations, all you have is an instructional model, and any instructional model is inappropriate for many situations. Instructional designers look to instructional theories to identify the best methods for helping people learn in different situations. Of all the situational factors, *the kind of learning* (the nature of the content) is the most important consideration for selecting the best instructional methods – much more important than the kind of learner. Learner differences have much more impact on what to learn than how to learn it. The following is a brief summary of four instructional theories. The precision of these descriptions is not sufficient to reveal the situational factors in three of them.

Gagné's Nine Events of Instruction and Hierarchical Sequencing

Gagné (1985) created a nine-step process called the events of instruction, which provides a systematic approach to instruction. Gagné's "nine events of instruction" consist of the following:

1. Gain attention
2. Inform learners of objectives
3. Stimulate recall of prior learning
4. Present the content
5. Provide guidance
6. Elicit performance
7. Provide feedback
8. Assess performance
9. Enhance retention and transfer

Gagné (1985) also proposed a hierarchical sequence for teaching skills. It consists of breaking a complex skill into simpler part-skills, which in turn are broken into their simpler part-skills, and so forth until the skills hierarchy reaches the learners' entry level of knowledge. The sequence is then designed by always teaching simpler part-skills before teaching the larger skills of which they are a part.

Elaboration Theory

The elaboration theory, developed by Reigeluth (1999) and Merrill, aims to help select and sequence content in a way that optimizes attainment of learning goals. This theory offers three major methods: conceptual elaboration sequence, theoretical elaboration sequence, and simplifying conditions sequence.

1. *Conceptual elaboration sequence*: teach broader, more inclusive concepts before the narrower, more detailed concepts that elaborate upon them. Use this approach when the goals call for learning many related concepts.
2. *Theoretical elaboration sequence*: teach broader, more inclusive principles before the narrower, more detailed ones that elaborate upon them. Use this approach when the goals call for learning many related principles and/or heuristics.
3. *Simplifying conditions sequence*: teach a simpler version of a task (that is still fairly representative of all versions) before teaching progressively more complex versions. Use this approach when the goals call for learning a task of at least moderate complexity.

First Principles of Instruction

Merrill (2002) identified five prescriptive principles that are common to various instructional theories (see Figure 3.1). The five "first principles" include:

1. *Problem*: learning is promoted when learners are engaged in solving real-world problems
2. *Activation*: learning is promoted when existing knowledge is activated as a foundation for new knowledge
3. *Demonstration*: learning is promoted when new knowledge is demonstrated to the learner
4. *Application*: learning is promoted when new knowledge is applied by the learner
5. *Integration*: learning is promoted when new knowledge is integrated into the learner's world

4C/ID Model

The four-component ID (4C/ID) model claims that environments for complex learning can always be described in terms of four interrelated blueprint components: learning tasks, supportive information, procedural information, and part-task practice (van Merriënboer, 1997); van Merriënboer, Clark, & de Croock, 2002; van Merriënboer & Kirschner, 2007, 2013).

1. *Learning tasks*: concrete, authentic, whole-task experiences (organized in simple-to-complex task classes)
2. *Supportive information*: supports the learning and performance of non-recurrent aspects of learning tasks
3. *Procedural information*: prerequisite to the learning and performance of recurrent aspects of learning tasks or practice items
4. *Part-task practice*: provides additional practice for selected recurrent constituent skills in order to reach the required level of automaticity

To provide an easy-to-use version of the 4C-ID model, van Merriënboer and Kirschner (2007) developed ten steps to complex learning (see Table 3.2). The ten steps are ID process (not instructional theory) intended for the development of educational or training programs aimed at the acquisition of complex cognitive skills.

Where Are We?

We have described three major considerations that underlie the second D in the Holistic 4D Model – Design. First, the *categories of learning* – memorize information, understand

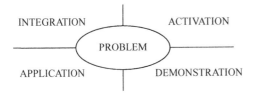

Figure 3.1 First Principles of Instruction.

Table 3.2 Ten Steps to Complex Learning

Blueprint Components of 4C-ID	Ten Steps to Complex Learning
Learning tasks	1. Design learning tasks
	2. Sequence task classes
	3. Set performance objectives
Supportive information	4. Design supportive information
	5. Analyze cognitive strategies
	6. Analyze mental models
Procedural information	7. Design procedural information
	8. Analyze cognitive rules
	9. Analyze prerequisite knowledge
Part-task practice	10. Design part-task practice

Source: van Merriënboer, J.J.G, & Kirschner, P.A. (2007). *Ten Steps to Complex Learning*. Mahwah, NJ: Lawrence Erlbaum Associates.

relationships, apply skills, apply higher-order thinking skills, and act on attitudes and values – are the foundation for designing effective instruction, because each requires different instructional strategies. Furthermore, learning theories provide guidance and rationale for selection of instructional methods for each category of learning. Second, we briefly summarized three types of *learning theories* – behavioral, cognitive, and constructivist theories – for they all are relevant to the design of good instruction. Third, we described *instructional theories*, which differ from learning theories in that they provide direct guidance as to which instructional methods to use when, for each of those different kinds of learning. We briefly summarized the nature of instructional theory, followed by four instructional theories: Gagné's nine events of instruction, elaboration theory, Merrill's first principles, and van Merriënboer's 4C/ID model, but these are only a few of the many instructional theories that provide valuable guidance for ID. Descriptions of some others are provided in the four volumes of *Instructional-Design Theories and Models* edited by Reigeluth and colleagues (Reigeluth, 1983, 1999; Reigeluth, Beatty, & Myers, 2017; Reigeluth & Carr-Chellman, 2009b).

The next chapter (Chapter 4) describes eight other considerations for Design. Then, Chapters 5–8 provide detailed guidance for Design using the considerations in Chapters 3 and 4. The remaining chapters address Develop and Deploy.

Exercises

Here again we offer suggestions for a teacher using this book as a textbook in a course, to help the students understand more deeply the contents of this chapter. We suggest that you keep the same teams of about three students each to continue to work on their ID projects throughout the course. However, these exercises can be done individually by any reader who wants to deepen their understanding and skills.

1. Have each team categorize several of the types of learning that will possibly be important for its project.
2. Have each team offer suggestions for improvement for the categorizations of one or two other teams before you review and provide feedback to the students.

3. Have a whole-class, synchronous discussion of the differences between learning theories and instructional theories and the ways in which each is useful.

References

Anderson, J.R. (1983). *The architecture of cognition.* Cambridge, MA: Harvard University Press.

Anderson, J.R. (1996). *The architecture of cognition.* Mahwah, NJ: Lawrence Erlbaum Associates.

Anderson, L.W., Krathwohl, D.R., Airasian, P. W., Cruikshank, K.A., Mayer, R.E., Pintrich, P.R., … Wittrock, M.C. (2000). *A taxonomy for learning, teaching, and assessing: A revision of Bloom's taxonomy of educational objectives.* New York, NY: Pearson, Allyn & Bacon.

Anderson, R.C., & Spiro, R.J. (1977). *Schooling and the acquisition of knowledge.* Hillsdale, NJ: Lawrence Erlbaum.

Atkinson, R.C., & Shiffrin, R.M. (1968). Human memory: A proposed system and its control processes. *Psychology of Learning and Motivation, 2,* 89–195.

Ausubel, D.P. (1968). *Educational psychology: A cognitive view.* New York, NY: Holt, Rinehart & Winston.

Bandura, A. (1977). *Social learning theory.* New York, NY: General Learning Press.

Bandura, A. (1986). *Social foundations of thought and action: A social cognitive theory.* Englewood Cliffs, NJ: Prentice-Hall.

Bartlett, F.C. (1932). *Remembering: A study in experimental and social psychology.* Cambridge, England: Cambridge University Press.

Bloom, B.S., Engelhart, M.D., Furst, E.J., Hill, W.H., & Krathwohl, D.R. (Eds.). (1956). *Taxonomy of educational objectives, the classification of educational goals. Handbook I: Cognitive domain.* Harlow, Essex, England: Longman.

Bransford, J.D., Sherwood, R.D., Hasselbring, T.S., Kinzer, C.K., & Williams, S.M. (1990). Anchored instruction: Why we need it and how technology can help. In D. Nix & R. Sprio (Eds.), *Cognition, education, and multimedia: Exploring ideas in high technology.* Hillsdale, NJ: Erlbaum Associates.

Brown, J.S., Collins, A., & Duguid, P. (1989). Situated cognition and the culture of learning. *Educational Researcher, 18*(1), 32–42.

Collins, A., Brown, J.S., & Newman, S.E. (1988). Cognitive apprenticeship. *Thinking: The Journal of Philosophy for Children, 8*(1), 2–10.

Craik, F.I., & Lockhart, R.S. (1972). Levels of processing: A framework for memory research. *Journal of Verbal Learning and Verbal Behavior, 11*(6), 671–684.

Dewey, J. (1933). *How we think.* Lexington, MA: Heath.

Festinger, L. (1962). *A theory of cognitive dissonance* (Vol. 2). Stanford, CA: Stanford University Press.

Flavell, John H. (1985). *Cognitive development.* Englewood Cliffs, NJ: Prentice Hall.

Gagné, R.M. (1985). *The conditions of learning and theory of instruction.* New York, NY: Holt, Rinehart and Winston.

Harel, I., & Papert, S. (1991). Software design as learning environment. In I. Harel & S. Papert (Eds.), *Children designers: Interdisciplinary constructions for learning and knowing mathematics in a computer-rich school* (pp. 41–85). Norwood, NJ: Ablex.

Kamradt, T.F., & Kamradt, E.J. (1999). Structured design for attitudinal instruction. In C.M. Reigeluth (Ed.), *Instructional-design theories and models: A new paradigm of instructional theory* (Vol. II, pp. 563–590). Mahwah, NJ: Lawrence Erlbaum Associates.

Lave, J., & Wenger, E. (1990). *Situated learning: Legitimate peripheral participation.* Cambridge, UK: Cambridge University Press.

Merrill, M.D. (1983). Component display theory. In C.M. Reigeluth (Ed.), *Instructional-design theories and models: An overview of their current status* (Vol. I). Hillsdale, NJ: Lawrence Erlbaum Associates.

Merrill, M.D. (2002). A pebble-in-the-pond model for instructional design. *Performance Improvement, 41*(7), 39–44.

Palincsar, A.S. (1998). Social constructivist perspectives on teaching and learning. *Annual Review of Psychology, 49,* 345–375.

Papert, S. (1993a). *Mindstorms: Children, computers, and powerful ideas* (2nd ed.). New York, NY: Basic Books.

Papert, S. (1993b). *The children's machine: Rethinking schools in the age of the computer.* New York, NY: Basic Books.

Pavlov, I.P. (1897/1902). *The work of the digestive glands.* London: Griffin.

Perry, William G. (1999). *Forms of ethical and intellectual development in the college years.* San Francisco, CA: Jossey-Bass Publishers.

Piaget, J. (1952). *The origins of intelligence in children.* New York, NY: International University Press.

Reigeluth, C.M. (1980). *Meaningfulness and instruction: Relating what is being learned to what a student knows.* New York, NY: Syracuse Univ., NY. School of Education.

Reigeluth, C.M. (1983). *Instructional-design theories and models: An overview of their current status.* Hillsdale, NJ: Lawrence Erlbaum Associates.

Reigeluth, C.M. (Ed.). (1999). *Instructional-design theories and models, Vol. 2. A new paradigm of instructional theory* (Vol. II). Mahwah, NJ: Lawrence Erlbaum Associates.

Reigeluth, C.M. (1999). The elaboration theory: Guidance for scope and sequence decisions. In C.M. Reigeluth (Ed.), *Instructional-design theories and models: A new paradigm of instructional theory* (Vol. II, pp. 425–453). Mahwah, NJ: Lawrence Erlbaum Associates.

Reigeluth, C.M. (1999). What is instructional-design theory and how is it changing? In C.M. Reigeluth (Ed.), *Instructional-design theories and models: A new paradigm of instructional theory* (Vol. II, pp. 5–29). Mahwah, NJ: Lawrence Erlbaum Associates.

Reigeluth, C.M., Beatty, B.J., & Myers, R.D. (Eds.). (2017). *Instructional-design theories and models, Volume IV: The learner-centered paradigm of education.* New York, NY: Routledge.

Reigeluth, C.M., & Carr-Chellman, A.A. (2009a). Understanding instructional theory. In C.M. Reigeluth & A.A. Carr-Chellman (Eds.), *Instructional-design theories and models: Building a common knowledge base* (Vol. III, pp. 3–26). New York, NY: Routledge.

Reigeluth, C.M., & Carr-Chellman, A.A. (Eds.). (2009b). *Instructional-design theories and models: Building a common knowledge base* (Vol. III). New York, NY: Routledge.

Reigeluth, C.M., & Moore, J. (1999). Cognitive education and the cognitive domain. In C.M. Reigeluth (Ed.), *Instructional-design theories and models: A new paradigm of instructional theory* (Vol. II, pp. 51–68). Mahwah, NJ: Lawrence Erlbaum Associates.

Romiszowski, A.J. (1981). *Designing instructional systems: Decision making in course planning and curriculum design.* New York, NY: Nichols Publishing.

Rumelhart, D.E. (1980). The building blocks of cognition. In R.J. Spiro, B.C. Bruce & W.F. Brewer (Eds.), *Theoretical issues in reading comprehension* (pp. 33–58). Hillsdale, NJ: Lawrence Erlbaum.

Skinner, B.F. (1953). *Science and human behavior.* New York, NY: Macmillan.

Skinner, B.F. (1965). The science of learning and the art of teaching. *Harvard Educational Review, 24*(2), 86–97.

Sweller, J. (1994). Cognitive load theory, learning difficulty, and instructional design. *Learning and Instruction, 4*(4), 295–312.

Thorndike, E.L. (1911). *Animal intelligence: Experimental studies.* New York, NY: Macmillan.

Thorndike, E.L. (1921). *Educational Psychology, Volume II: The Psychology of Learning.* New York, NY: Teachers College Columbia University.

van Merriënboer, J.J.G. (1997). *Training complex cognitive skills: A four-component instructional design model for technical training.* Englewood Cliffs, NJ: Educational Technology Publications.

van Merriënboer, J.J.G., Clark, R.E., & de Croock, M.B.M. (2002). Blueprints for complex learning: The 4C/ID-model. *Educational Technology Research and Development, 50*(2), 39–64.

van Merriënboer, J.J.G., & Kirschner, P.A. (2007). *Ten steps to complex learning.* Mahwah, NJ: Lawrence Erlbaum Associates.

van Merriënboer, J.J.G., & Kirschner, P.A. (2013). *Ten steps to complex learning: A systematic approach to four-component instructional design* (2nd ed.). New York, NY: Routledge.

Vygotsky, L.S. (1978). *Mind in society: The development of higher psychological processes.* Cambridge, MA: Harvard University Press.

Vygotsky, L.S. (1986). *Thought and language.* Cambridge, MA: MIT Press.

Watson, J.B. (1924). *Behaviorism.* New York, NY: People's Institute Publishing Company.

Weiner, B. (1972). Attribution theory, achievement motivation, and the educational process. *Review of Educational Research, 42*(2), 203–215.

Wenger, E. (1998). *Communities of practice: Learning, meaning and identity.* Cambridge, UK: Cambridge University Press.

Wertheimer, M. (1923). Laws of organization in perceptual forms. First published as Untersuchungen zur Lehre von der Gestalt II. *Psycologische Forschung, 4*(1), 301–350. Translation published in Ellis, W. (1938). *A source book of Gestalt psychology* (pp. 71–88). London: Routledge & Kegan Paul.

4   Other Considerations for Design

Overview

In this chapter we offer nine additional major considerations for making good decisions about designing instruction in all different contexts, and all eight are important elements of our Holistic 4D Model introduced in Chapter 1 and elaborated in considerable detail in the rest of this book. Design is concerned with both *what* to teach (which we call "content" to refer to everything one teaches, such as information, skills, attitudes, habits, emotional development, ethics, and so forth) and *how* to teach it. The nine additional major considerations for designing instruction are:

1. Task vs. topic expertise
2. What to analyze
3. Just-in-time analysis
4. Subject-matter experts
5. Rapid prototyping
6. Creating a design document
7. Instructional approaches
8. Motivational strategies
9. Media selection

1. Task vs. Topic Expertise

Some people have placed great emphasis on the distinction between education and training, while others have been skeptical that it is an important difference. Those who see a clear distinction argue that training focuses on improving the learner's performance of a job (or of specific tasks which are parts of that job), whereas education focuses on improving the learner's understanding or knowledge of a subject (or of specific topics which are component parts of that subject). Others argue that most worthwhile learning activities of any complexity involve the learner in acquiring *both* knowledge and skills – the understanding of topics which are relevant to a given situation, problem, or challenge and the ability to use this understanding in the performance of relevant tasks (Romiszowski, 1981, 1986).

There is some truth to both these viewpoints. Research has shown that these two major kinds of learning outcomes – or expertise – require very different kinds of instructional content and sequencing: task expertise and topic expertise[1] (Reigeluth, 1999b).

---

1   "Expertise" is used here to denote a kind of learning outcome (or kind of knowledge or skill). Becoming an expert in a task requires a different kind of learning from becoming an expert in a topic.

Task expertise is goal-oriented knowledge. It is knowledge about how to accomplish a goal, usually called a skill or higher-order thinking skill. It is sometimes called productive knowledge because it entails performing a task. Examples are shown in Table 4.1 and are contrasted with related areas of topic expertise.

In contrast, **topic expertise** is general knowledge – it is descriptive rather than productive. It focuses more on understanding than doing. For example, understanding what a recession is constitutes a small piece of topic expertise (but entails a lot more than being able to state the definition of recession), whereas knowing how to get an economy out of a recession is task expertise. Examples related to topic expertise are shown in Table 4.1.

Task expertise is typically thought of as being developed through **training**, while topic expertise is typically thought of as being developed through **education**, but not always. Math skills, writing skills, and higher-order cognitive skills are a few kinds of task expertise that are generally considered within the realm of education. And understanding of many topics is important for task expertise, such as the principles of macroeconomics for getting an economy out of a recession or learning theory for teacher development. Hence, task and topic expertise must often both be developed together.

Of course, these two kinds of expertise are interrelated and even interdependent. Expertise in physics is largely topic expertise (but also involves some task expertise), whereas expertise in engineering, which is strongly related to physics, is largely task expertise (but also involves some topic expertise). Similarly, expertise in biology is primarily topic expertise (with some task expertise), while expertise in medicine, which is strongly related to it, is primarily task expertise (with some topic expertise). The same is true for chemistry and chemical engineering, and for learning theory and instructional theory. For example, schema theory proposes how people's knowledge is organized within their heads and how new knowledge is acquired through assimilation, accommodation, and restructuring. It does not describe what methods of instruction to use to help people learn through assimilation, accommodation, or restructuring – that is instructional theory. Therefore, expertise in schema theory is mostly topic expertise.

Romiszowski (1981) describes different processes for task analysis and topic analysis, and Reigeluth (Leshin, Pollock, & Reigeluth, 1992; Myers & Reigeluth, 2017) describes different instructional strategies for task and topic expertise, both of which we incorporate in the Holistic 4D Model (see Chapters 5–7).

2. What to Analyze

What kinds of information should be collected and analyzed during the ID process? Typically, after the Define phase (a performance analysis and instructional needs assessment as described in Chapter 2), designing effective instruction requires the analysis of content, learners, context, and resources, but these should **not** all be done before doing any design activities (see Major Consideration #3).

Table 4.1 Examples of Topic Expertise and Task Expertise

Topic Expertise	Task Expertise
Biology	Medicine
Physics	Engineering
Learning theory	Instructional theory

Content

Content analysis is the process of defining the content to include in the instruction, including both task analysis for task expertise and topic analysis for topic expertise. Although content analysis is considered the most critical step in the instructional design process (Jonassen, Tessmer, & Hannum, 1999), it is often poorly done. In fact, it appears to be one of the most difficult and challenging activities for novice instructional designers. We provide detailed guidance for analyzing content in Chapters 5, 6, and 7.

Learners

The main goal of learner analysis is to identify all learner characteristics, abilities, and experiences that might influence the selection of instructional content and methods. Conducting an analysis of the target learners allows you to base the instruction on their current skills, knowledge, and attitudes. This increases the likelihood that the instruction will include all content that should be taught and will not include content that should not be taught. Consequently, learner analysis should be integrated with content analysis.

Many characteristics or traits differentiate learners (e.g., age, gender, ethnicity, education, language skills, previous experiences, interests, computer skills, etc.). Heinich, Molenda, Russell, and Smaldino (1999) suggested that instructional designers initially consider three categories of learner characteristics:

- General characteristics: age, gender, ethnicity, education, language skills, work experience, interests.
- Specific entry competencies: prerequisite knowledge, skills, and attitudes that learners must possess to benefit from the instruction.
- Learning styles: traits that refer to how learners approach learning tasks and process information and thereby influence which instructional methods will work well for each learner. Due to a lack of research evidence, there is considerable controversy about which learning styles influence how much learners benefit from any given instructional method – and, indeed, whether any do (Khazan, 2018).

Additional characteristics of learners include, but are not limited to, motivation, attitude toward the subject, previous or current work experience, interests, reading ability, language or cultural differences, physical characteristics (e.g., physical fitness, weight, disabilities), computer skills, and specific motor skills.

It is not helpful to analyze every type of learner characteristic, because relatively few of them influence what kind of instruction will work best. Therefore, the most important decisions in initiating a learner analysis concern (a) which learner characteristics to identify and (b) how to collect the necessary data. Guidance for this is offered in Chapters 5–8. Learner characteristics typically influence the motivational design of instruction and the selection of examples that are both familiar and interesting to the learner.

Contexts

The purpose of a context analysis is to identify environmental factors that will influence the design and delivery of instruction. You need to identify the factors that place limitations or constraints on your design, as well as the factors that facilitate the design and delivery. There are two major kinds of contexts: instructional and transfer. In Chapter 2, we stated that Tessmer and Richey (1997) distinguished between orienting context and transfer context. They defined the orienting context as preexisting conditions, such as learners' prerequisite skills, attitudes toward instruction, and organizational culture regarding instruction. We find it helpful to talk in terms of content, learner, and resource analyses rather than the lump term "orienting context analysis." We also believe it is important to analyze the instructional context, as well as the transfer context.

Instructional context. Learning and instruction do not take place in a vacuum. They are influenced by some environmental factors over which the designer has little control. Therefore, you should identify the environmental factors so you can design instruction that fits the constraints of the instructional environment. The environmental factors to consider depend on design situations. When designing classroom instruction or training, for example, you might need to consider such environmental factors as lighting, noise, temperature, seating, table arrangements, equipment (e.g., projectors, tools), scheduling, and meeting times. On the other hand, when designing online instruction, you should consider other types of factors, including Internet access, computers, and software tools available, keeping in mind that the organization offering the instruction may be able to arrange for the availability of such things at the learners' locations. Synchronous online instruction requires consideration of still other factors. And blended instruction typically requires consideration of all those types of factors. Factors that a designer can control should be considered as methods, not context. Instructional context influences how to teach much more than what to teach.

Transfer context. Analyzing a transfer context, or performance environment (the context in which the new learnings will be used, such as the work context for corporate training), is important, especially when the goal of instruction or training focuses on the improvement of performance or the application of newly learned knowledge and skills in both familiar and new performance situations. For example, in the early stages of designing instruction for technicians, one should analyze whether the workshop equipment and tools available in the schools or training centers are sufficiently similar to, and compatible with, those currently used in the relevant real-world context where the learners will work once they qualify. New technologies often result in the instructional context falling way behind the realities of the respective transfer context. This may pose some challenges for your ID project. Transfer context influences what to teach far more than how to teach it.

Resources

Resource analysis is conducted to identify the resources needed and available, as well as resource constraints, for both the ID process and the instructional context. In a large ID team, the project manager is typically in charge of resource analysis, but instructional designers should have a good understanding of the resources available for instructional design. Keep in mind that the design of instruction, whether an extensive amount, like an entire curriculum, or a smaller amount, like a half-day workshop, is limited by many resource constraints. The ID process should be carefully planned to fit these resource limits. Here are some critical questions to ask during resource analysis:

- How much time and money do we have for the ID process and products?
- What prior content analyses and existing instructional resources can we adopt or adapt?
- What human resources do we need to design (and/or adapt) and create the instruction?
- What types of equipment, facilities, or tools can we select for the ID process, given the budget?

- What types of instructional media (e.g., advanced technologies) can we include in the product (instructional system), considering the development personnel and resources available?

The importance of asking and seeking realistic answers to such questions is illustrated by studies of the resources used by real-world ID projects. Studies such as those published by the Association for Training and Development (Kapp & Defelice, 2009; Defelice, 2018), Chapman (2010), and the eLearning Guild (2002) report data on hundreds of projects, involving several hundred instructional designers and developers who, together, were responsible for producing many thousands of hours of instruction, delivered in various formats. The common criterion of measurement used in these reports was the total time, in hours, of all those involved in the project, to design and develop one hour of instruction. Table 4.2 is our summary of this large data base, organized in terms of average time and the range of reported time investment to design, develop, and evaluate all components for four typical instructional system categories. Projects report widely different amounts of time invested per hour of instruction produced, but they are remarkably consistent in terms of **how many times more time** was needed for successively more sophisticated and technologically advanced instructional solutions. The simplest of e-learning instruction tends to require about twice the time investment of conventional, instructor-led training; interactive multimedia instructional systems typically require up to four times more time; and full use of the latest educational technologies could need over ten times the time investment.

Resource analysis is done mostly at the beginning of the design phase because it cannot really be done until the performance analysis and instructional needs analysis have been completed. However, it should be periodically updated throughout the rest of the ID project.

3. Just-in-Time Analysis

Traditionally, the ID process calls for completing all the analysis before beginning the design. However, as design decisions are made, they narrow the subsequent design decisions and therefore the information needed (analysis) to make those decisions. For example, the choice of a kind of instructional sequence, such as a procedural sequence, narrows the kind of content analysis that is needed, in this case a procedural analysis (which identifies the steps in a procedure and the order those steps are performed in). If you do all the analysis before any design, much of the information collected goes unused and additional analysis is often needed.

Table 4.2 Typical Time Investment in Instructional Design and Development Projects

Hours of ID Per Hour of Instruction: A Review of Typical Case Studies	*Average*	*Range*
Instructor-led – including front end analysis, design, SME reviews, lesson plans, handouts, workbooks, PowerPoint presentations, slides, etc.	40 hrs./hr.	22–82 hrs./hr.
Self-instructional, minimally interactive, offline or online – including the above plus quality graphics, test questions, simple audio or video, etc.	80 hrs./hr.	49–125 hrs./hr.
Interactive multimedia – including any of the above plus online tests, exercises, simulations and liberal use of audio, video, animations, etc.	180 hrs./hr.	127–267 hrs./hr.
Highly interactive "state-of-the-art" multimedia – including complex simulations and games, use of virtual reality, "Second Life," avatars, etc.	490 hrs./hr.	217–716 hrs./hr.

Therefore, the ID process can be much more efficient and effective by doing most of the analysis "just in time" when it is needed, especially when you have easy access to subject-matter experts (see Major Consideration #4 next). This avoids performing unnecessary analysis and not conducting analysis that is needed. Also, just-in-time analysis greatly enhances the rapid prototyping process (see Major Consideration #5).

4. Subject-Matter Experts (SMEs)

Table 4.1 mentions "SME reviews" as one essential component of instructional design and development. What exactly is the function of the subject-matter expert in this process? In most cases, instructional designers work with content in which they are not experts. Therefore, it is necessary to interview one or more people who are experts in the content. Careful selection of SMEs is crucial because many experts aren't really experts. Interview situations vary depending on the locations and availability of SMEs. Ideally, you will have face-to-face meetings with SMEs, but if that is not feasible, you will have to communicate with them with conference calls, video conferences, and such – and you are likely to use email frequently either way. In terms of the number of SMEs, some large ID projects involve numerous experts, while simple ID projects may involve only one (or preferably two, to address idiosyncrasies).

When possible, you should have SMEs as part of your development team to facilitate frequent contact. In most cases, you must get all the information you need in a very limited time. Therefore, you should seek other sources of subject-matter expertise before interviewing the expert. Collect previous instructional materials, conduct a web search, and/ or review available resources to learn all you can about the content. Otherwise, it will take longer for you to understand your experts during the interviews. Keep in mind that not all experts can verbalize the task well. Most experts are often not consciously aware of all the knowledge they possess (called "tacit knowledge"), so you may find newer experts to be more aware of the knowledge they possess and the difficulties learners face. In any event, it is crucial to develop good questions to elicit such knowledge. Table 4.3 provides some general tips for the interviews.

Working with SMEs effectively also demands some interactive or interpersonal skills on the part of the instructional designer. One skill which helps to ensure that the designer correctly and fully understands the SME's contributions, even if they are not clearly expressed

Table 4.3 Tips for Interviews with Subject-Matter Experts (SMEs)

Timing	Tips
Before the Interview	• Research the subject matter • Ask for any previous materials on the content • Develop interview questions
During the Interview	• Listen actively • Take notes • Help SMEs articulate their knowledge • Seek clarification when necessary • Control the flow of the interview • Record the interview
After the Interview	• Review your notes and draft an initial content outline while your memory is fresh • Schedule a follow up interview as necessary • Confirm the accuracy of your analysis

at first, is "echoing." The designer, before moving on to a further step in the interview, repeats what the SME has just said, but using different words, sentence structures, or examples. The SME then has to confirm or correct the designer's version. In echoing what was said by the SME, the designer will often prompt the SME into clarifying, correcting or otherwise improving what was said previously. In addition, especially if it is impossible to record a given conversation, the use of echoing gives the designer extra time to make notes on what was said before moving on.

Echoing is also useful when SMEs are for some reason unable or unwilling to "open up" and "tell the whole story." This may happen because the SMEs, due to their level of expertise, just do not appreciate what aspects of the task are likely to be difficult for novices to understand or perform – they omit aspects which to them seem too obvious to be worth mentioning. It may also happen because the SME imagines that some aspects are already known and understood by the designer. Sometimes it happens when the SME is busy and so is keen to complete the interview as fast as possible and get back to other activities. And, most seriously, it happens if SMEs feel that "revealing all" in some way devalues their expertise, or even threatens their position in the organization. In this case, the skilled analyst can use echoing in a way that conveys apparent misunderstandings, thus intentionally adopting a position of inferiority. Reluctant SMEs will then usually "open up" and "reveal all" to demonstrate their superiority.

Sometimes you might serve as both the instructional designer and SME. Even in that case, it is recommended that you find another content expert to review your content analysis results, primarily to validate the accuracy and completeness of your content selection.

5. Rapid Prototyping

Rapid prototyping (RP) is an approach to the ID process that quickly produces a working model (prototype) of the instruction for review and modification before creating the full-blown version of the instruction (Batane, 2010; Desrosier, 2011; Jones & Richey, 2000; Pham & Dimov, 2003; Tripp & Bichelmeyer, 1990). There are some similarities between RP and agile software development (Allen & Sites, 2012; Schwaber & Beedle, 2002).

There are three major benefits of RP:

a. It helps ensure that instruction will be well aligned with the learners and their needs, because the instruction can be tried out with sample learners before most of it is fully designed and developed.
b. It helps ensure that instruction will be well aligned with the client or owner of the need, because they will have an opportunity to review the prototype before the instruction is fully developed.
c. It typically shortens the overall development time and lowers development costs, because revisions can be made early on before the expensive production process occurs. Prototype revisions can also guide the design of other parts of the instruction, reducing the need for extensive revisions.

We propose that there are two basic approaches to RP: quantitative reduction and qualitative reduction of the instruction. In **quantitative reduction**, you create a prototype that is one representative part of the whole instruction. You might design and develop one module of a 14-module course, or test an even smaller component, such as one content artifact (reading, video, etc.) representing other similar artifacts. In **qualitative reduction**, you create a prototype that is a "quick and dirty" version of the entire instruction. You might create a paper version of computer-based instruction before eventually programming it with graphics and video. Of course, there is also a **combination approach** that does both – a qualitative reduction on the representative part from a quantitative reduction.

In all cases, the creation of the prototype is followed by formative evaluation (trying out the prototype with some learners who are representative of the target population) and client review. Then revisions are made in the prototype before full-blown production (in the qualitative approach) and before designing and developing other parts of the whole instruction (in the quantitative approach).

6. Creating a Design Document

A design document is a "blueprint" or written description of the instructional system. Developing a design document is one of your major responsibilities, especially if you work on large-scale ID projects in a team consisting of multiple professionals. Similar to a blueprint of a house, a design document should specify what the instruction or training (the building) will be like. Your design document will gradually expand from a fuzzy vision of the instruction in the early stages of the design process, to detailed specifications in the final stages. It is also helpful to include some information from your analysis and evaluation activities in the document, making it an Analysis-Design-Evaluation (ADE) document. Sample templates are provided for each stage of development of this document in Chapters 5–8.

The ADE documents become your guide as you continue to develop your instruction. You can also create a client version to serve as a contract and vehicle of communication between your design team and your client (even if it is a client within your organization). It is very important to clearly describe your instructional design so that your design team members and clients can easily understand and visualize your instruction, but you may want to remove the analysis and evaluation parts of the ADE document and use language and a level of detail that is tailored to that audience.

7. Instructional Approaches

Our digital-age society needs people who can take initiative, think critically and creatively, and solve complex problems. Despite the changes in societal systems, our current paradigm in education and training is still based on standardization, conformity, and compliance (Reigeluth & Karnopp, 2013). Like the mass production of industrial-age manufacturing, standardized education entails teaching a large group of learners the same content in the same amount of time and seeks valid comparisons of learners with each other, which was an important need in the industrial age. Learners are expected to sit down, be quiet, listen to the instructor, and do what they are told to do. Corporate training has been quicker than educational systems to transform from standardized, time-based, teacher-centered instruction to personalized, competency-based, learner-centered instruction, but there are currently more than 500 schools throughout the USA that have made this transformation, as well as dozens of post-secondary institutions.

The paradigm of instruction should change from standardization to customization (including adaptive learning), from passive to active learning, and from teacher-centered to learner-centered instruction (Reigeluth, 1999b; Reigeluth & Karnopp, 2013, 2020). Learner-centered instruction is the only way to maximize every learner's learning and meet their needs in the digital age (Reigeluth, Myers, & Lee, 2017). Given that learner-centered methods are almost always preferable to teacher-centered methods, and, given that most readers are all too familiar with teacher-centered methods, we do not provide guidance for teacher-centered ones in this book.

Learner-centered instruction aims to foster the learning of all learners by focusing equally on individual learners and learning (McCombs & Whisler, 1997). It also focuses on developing real-world skills, such as higher-order thinking, problem solving, and decision-making skills, in addition to content knowledge (Bransford, Brown, & Cocking, 2000; McCombs & Whisler, 1997; Reigeluth, 1994). Based on a comprehensive literature review, we identified the following six characteristics of LCI (An, 2012; An & Reigeluth, 2011):

- Personalized and customized learning
- Social and emotional support
- Self-regulation (or self-direction)
- Collaborative learning experiences
- Authentic learning experiences
- Assessment for learning, integrated with instruction

There are several different LCI approaches, including competency-based learning, learning by doing, case-based instruction, and other approaches.

Competency-Based Learning

Typically, education and training have been provided "with time as the constant" and amount of learning as the variable. This does not promote consistently high levels of learning and performance. In competency-based learning, learning is the constant, and amount of time is variable – whatever is needed to really learn what's important. Therefore, learners move forward only when they have mastered the content (and as soon as they have mastered the content), rather than when a predetermined amount of time has passed (Block, 1971; Bloom, 1968, 1984; Carroll, 1963; Kulik, Kulik, & Bangert-Drowns, 1990). Given that different people learn at different rates, the mastery approach means that you should either customize the pace of instruction (vary the timeframe), or you should allow faster learners to spend less time on the instruction (within a given timeframe). Online learning is well suited to using customized pace and competency-based learning, but all too often online instruction fails to realize this potential.

Learning by Doing

Learning by doing is often used as an umbrella term for learner-centered approaches that emphasize experiential learning, including problem-based learning, project-based learning, inquiry-based learning, task-centered instruction, and maker-based learning.[2]

Problem-based learning (PBL). In the 1960s, PBL was first developed in medical education in response to learners' poor clinical performance that resulted from the

---

2   In Chapter 3, we made a distinction between learning theories and instructional theories. Based on that distinction, the term, "problem-based learning" should not be understood to offer guidance about instructional methods for learning through problem solving. The proper term is "problem-based instruction." However, popular usage of PBL has been to designate guidance about instruction, so we use PBL in this book instead of the more technically correct PBI. The same applies to project-based learning, inquiry-based learning, and maker-based learning.

overemphasis on memorization of factual knowledge in traditional health science education (Barrows, 1986; Barrows & Tamblyn, 1980). PBL has become a primary instructional method in medical education throughout the world, and it has also been widely adopted by other disciplines (e.g., nursing, education, business administration, and architecture) and for different learning levels (e.g., K-12 education, higher education, and corporate training).

Unlike traditional (teacher-centered) instructional methods, PBL begins with the presentation of an authentic problem, which is complex, ill-defined, ill-structured, and open-ended. The problem is chosen based on what content is important to learn, and learners no longer passively receive content from the teacher. Instead, they actively engage in self-directed learning and collaborative inquiry and research to identify learning issues and develop a viable solution to the problem (Barrows, 2000; Hmelo-Silver, 2004; Savery, 2006, 2009; Savery & Duffy, 1995). If designed and implemented effectively, PBL can promote in-depth understanding of content, foster self-directed learning, higher-order thinking, problem-solving, and collaboration skills, and can provide an engaging and enjoyable learning environment for both learners and teachers (Albanese & Mitchell, 1993; Barrows & Tamblyn, 1980; Coles, 1985; Newble & Clarke, 1986; Norman & Schmidt, 1992; Vernon & Blake, 1993).

By comparing and contrasting the findings of the meta-analytical research on the effectiveness of PBL, Strobel and van Barneveld (2009) found that PBL is significantly more effective than traditional instruction for long-term knowledge retention, performance improvement, and satisfaction of learners and teachers, whereas traditional approaches are more effective for short-term retention. Furthermore, with appropriate scaffolding (e.g., just-in-time tutorials), PBL can be a fairly efficient method for learner-centered instruction, partly due to enhanced learner motivation accelerating the learning.

Project-based learning. Project-based learning is similar to problem-based learning in that it uses authentic, real-world tasks and takes a learner-centered approach. In fact, problem based learning and project-based learning are often used as synonyms. However, project-based learning is different from problem-based learning in that it focuses more on the creation of end products or artifacts rather than on solving a problem. In project-based learning, learners are usually provided with specifications for a desired end product, and the expected outcomes drive and shape the learning process (Blumenfeld et al., 1991; Buck Institute for Education, 2012; Savery, 2006). In more open-ended learning environments, learners are encouraged to design their own projects, including developing specifications for end products.

Inquiry-based learning (IBL). IBL is a learner-centered approach that begins with a question, like "Where does the white go when snow melts?" Tapping into learners' natural curiosity, it actively involves learners in questioning, investigation, knowledge creation, discussion, and reflection. In IBL, learners search for and evaluate information, use the information to answer questions, and create new knowledge through the inquiry and research process. Like problem- and project-based learning, IBL requires higher-order thinking, such as analysis, synthesis, and evaluation, and fosters real-world skills, such as critical thinking and problem solving. While IBL has been extensively used in science education, it can be applied to all areas of learning (Bateman, 1990; Bruce & Davidson, 1996; Lee, 2004; Prince & Felder, 2006).

Task-centered instruction (TCI). TCI is a learner-centered approach that prescribes the use of the following five elements (Francom, 2017; Merrill, 2002, 2007):

- Learning tasks
- Activation
- Demonstration/modeling

- Application
- Integration/exploration

TCI stems from several theories and models, including first principles of instruction (Merrill, 2002, 2007), the four-component instructional design model (van Merriënboer, 1997; van Merriënboer & Kirschner, 2007, 2013), elaboration theory (Reigeluth, 1979, 1999a), and cognitive apprenticeship (Brown, Collins, & Duguid, 1989; Collins, Brown, & Holum, 1991). Similar to other learner-centered approaches, TCI focuses on the application and transfer of knowledge to realistic contexts by having learners apply their knowledge and skills to complete whole tasks, often real-world tasks. However, unlike pure PBL, it aims to make learning more efficient and increase the chances that learners gain target concepts and skills through demonstration and modeling (Collins et al., 1991; Francom, 2017; Merrill, 2002, 2007).

Maker-based learning. Maker-based learning, or learning by making, is rooted in constructionism, which suggests that learners learn best when they are actively engaged in the construction or creation of concrete and meaningful artifacts (Harel & Papert, 1991; Papert, 1980). In maker-based learning environments, learners learn by making physical artifacts that are personally meaningful and valuable. Learning through doing, learning situated within a community, and self-directed learning are highly valued (McKay & Glazewski, 2017).

Case-Based Instruction (CBI)

The use of cases in teaching and learning began at Harvard Law School in the 1870s, and the instructional method is routinely used in schools of law, medicine, and business (Lynn, 1999). Although case-based instruction is generally considered a learner-centered instructional method, cases can be used in teacher-centered instruction (e.g., lectures). According to Jonassen (2004), cases can be used in three different ways:

- Cases can function as exemplars, exemplifying problem-solving practices in direct teaching
- Cases can function as instructional support during problem-solving activities
- Cases can be used to represent problems to learners to be solved

Therefore, whether CBI is learner-centered depends on how it is implemented. In learner-centered CBI, learners analyze complex, authentic case studies of historical or hypothetical situations that involve problem solving and decision making. The cases should be authentic and representative of situations and dilemmas that are likely to be faced by professionals. Unlike the problems used in PBL, however, cases tend to be relatively well-structured and provide rich contextual details (Lundeberg, Levin, & Harrington, 1999; Lynn, 1999; Prince & Felder, 2006).

Other Approaches

Scenario-based eLearning. By using realistic scenarios that mimic real-world work situations or challenges, scenario-based eLearning provides an authentic and engaging context for instruction that has some elements of learning by doing and allows learners to learn from their mistakes by providing feedback on their decisions. Scenario-based learning is well suited to teach soft skills such as leadership, communication, conflict resolution, and problem-solving skills. Scenarios are typically presented as interactive animations with vector-based graphics or still images, and sometimes in a video format. Some scenario videos are created with real actors, while others are developed using static images. In order to create emotionally engaging scenarios, it is important to have a good storyline and use characters, images, and backgrounds that are industry specific and relatable to learners (Gutierrez, 2015; Pappas, 2015).

Self-paced eLearning. Learners are allowed to work at their own pace within certain parameters. Self-paced training is usually implemented in an eLearning format. With self-paced eLearning, learners can learn and update their knowledge and skills at times and places convenient to them. Also, self-paced instruction is very effective for ensuring mastery by all learners.

Flipped classroom. A flipped classroom reverses the traditional classroom in that learners review instructional content (e.g., online lectures) prior to class, and class time is used to engage learners in meaningful, learner-centered tasks that may have traditionally been considered homework. The flipped classroom approach has been used at all grade levels (K-16) (Bergmann & Sams, 2012; Brame, 2013; Lage, Platt, & Treglia, 2000; Strayer, 2007), but it can also be used in teacher-centered instruction.

Game-based training. More and more organizations are using games to better train their employees. Games have been increasingly used in K-16 education as well. While many games don't involve learning by doing in simulated authentic contexts, a well-designed game can enhance learner engagement, provide situated learning experiences and authentic practice in thinking and working in specific roles and contexts, and foster real-world skills (An & Bonk, 2009; Gee, 2005; Myers & Reigeluth, 2017; Shaffer, Squire, Halverson, & Gee, 2005), in which case it is truly a form of learning by doing.

Gamification. Gamification (Garris, Ahlers, & Driskell, 2002; Kapp, 2017, 2012; Salen, 2008) refers to the use of game elements or mechanics to motivate people to achieve their goals. Gamification is often used to change behaviors, develop skills, and drive innovation. Although gamification has tremendous potential, it is suffering from growing pains. Gartner predicted that 80% of gamified efforts will fail due to poor design (Burke, 2014). Chou (2015) argues that gamification is so much more than points, badges, and leaderboards and requires sophisticated design. His gamification framework, called Octalysis (see next section), provides research-based guidelines and tips for gamification.

Social learning takes place in most, if not all, learner-centered approaches, usually in the form of small collaborative teams. Also, it is important to keep in mind that combinations of approaches are often used in a given ID project. In a learner-centered approach that involves learning-by-doing, it is usually better to organize instruction around authentic tasks or projects that engage learners in learning-by-doing. More is said about this in chapters 5 and 6.

8. Motivational Strategies

As you well know, motivation plays a significant role in learning. What strategies will you use to motivate your learners? Keep in mind that extrinsic motivators (usually rewards of various kinds) reduce intrinsic motivation in learners (Ryan & Deci, 2000). It is typically better to use intrinsic motivators, especially if you want the learners to continue learning after the instruction is over. You should develop specific motivational strategies when designing instruction. Learning by doing is one powerful motivational strategy. The following are some others you might want to consider.

Needs theory. McClelland's (1987) needs theory identifies three fundamental human needs (or motivators): achievement, affiliation, and power. Need for achievement can be addressed by using competency-based education. Mastering a competency provides a powerful sense of achievement that motivates most learners. Need for affiliation can be addressed by using collaborative learning, primarily in the form of team-based projects. Working with teammates can be a powerful motivator for most learners. Finally, need for power can be addressed through self-directed learning – allowing learners to choose goals, projects, scaffolding, assessments, and reflection. Empowerment is a powerful motivator for most learners.

The Attention, Relevance, Confidence, and Satisfaction (ARCS) model. The ARCS model, developed by John Keller, defines four major components of motivation: Attention, Relevance, Confidence, and Satisfaction. These components are the result of a synthesis of the research on human motivation. Further, the ARCS model provides a set of strategies to use to enhance the motivational appeal of instruction for each of the four components (Keller, 1983, 1987, 2010). Table 4.4 summarizes the ARCS components and strategies.

Self-determination theory (SDT). Self-determination theory was developed by Deci and Ryan (1985). As a theory of motivation, it distinguishes between intrinsically motivated behaviors, which are performed out of interest and satisfy the innate psychological needs for competence and autonomy, and extrinsically motivated behaviors, which are executed because they are instrumental to some separable consequence.

- Intrinsically motivated behaviors are the prototype of self-determined behavior.
- Extrinsically motivated behaviors can vary in the extent to which they represent self-determination. They can become more self-determined through internalization and integration.

Table 4.4 ARCS Components and Strategies

Category	Strategies
Attention	A1 Perceptual arousal – use novelty and surprise to gain interest
	A2 Inquiry arousal – stimulate curiosity by posing challenging questions or problems
	A3 Variability – vary instructional methods and media
Relevance	R1 Goal orientation – provide the objectives and utility of the instruction, and either present goals or have learners define them
	R2 Motive matching – use instructional strategies that match learner motives and values
	R3 Familiarity – make the materials familiar by providing concrete examples and analogies related to the learners' backgrounds and/or experiences
Confidence	C1 Learning requirements – make learners aware of learning and performance requirements
	C2 Success opportunities – enhance learners' beliefs in their competence by providing multiple, challenging experiences that increase learning success
	C3 Personal control – use strategies that allow personal control whenever possible, and provide feedback that attributes success to personal effort
Satisfaction	S1 Intrinsic reinforcement – encourage and support intrinsic enjoyment of the learning experience
	S2 Extrinsic rewards – use verbal praise, real or symbolic rewards, and incentives
	S3 Equity – make performance requirements consistent with stated expectations, and use consistent standards for all learners' tasks and accomplishments

In the context of education, SDT suggests that learning environments can facilitate intrinsic motivation by supporting the needs for the following essential elements (Ryan & Deci, 2000):

- Competence (e.g., optimal difficulty of challenges and feedback)
- Relatedness (e.g., learners' feeling respected by the teacher or trainer)
- Autonomy (e.g., choices and self-direction)

Octalysis. Yu-Kai Chou (2015), a well-known gamification expert, views gamification as a human-focused design process that focuses on human feelings and motivations as opposed to function-focused design that focuses on efficiency (e.g., getting the job done quickly). Based on extensive gamification research and study, Chou developed a gamification framework called Octalysis, originally as a model for the design of games for entertainment. However, Chou argues that the model can be used to design motivational experiences of various types, including learning experiences.

The Octalysis framework consists of the following eight core drives:

Core Drive 1: epic meaning and calling
Core Drive 2: development and accomplishment
Core Drive 3: empowerment of creativity and feedback
Core Drive 4: ownership and possession
Core Drive 5: social influence and relatedness
Core Drive 6: scarcity and impatience
Core Drive 7: unpredictability and curiosity
Core Drive 8: loss and avoidance

As Chou pointed out, gamification places the most emphasis on human motivation. His Octalysis framework provides a number of research-based motivational strategies. Indeed, the eight "core drives" should be understood as eight powerful motivators which may lead one to participate and get involved in the game – the "game of learning" among others.

9. Media Selection

Media selection is an important part of the design process, along with the design, development, and production of the selected media. However, it is helpful to understand that media typically influence efficiency and appeal, not effectiveness, of the instruction (Clark, 1983, 1985). "The message, not the medium, is what teaches" (Romiszowski, 1988, p. 60).

Fortunately, media selection has become increasingly more flexible due to the convergence of media in a single digital system. Not long ago, designers often had to choose between such alternatives as print, radio, TV, film, and computer. Now, all of these alternatives and other new media are available on a digital device, often at a no or lower cost than through means available at the time. This makes it possible to combine and alternate among media, so designers are not so restricted as before. In addition, there are now numerous social media that promote social interaction and collaboration and allow learners to become knowledge creators and producers (Brown & Adler, 2008; Downes, 2005; Richardson, 2009). Consequently, you do not need to commit to certain media so early in the design process.

At the top level of design, there are two major questions to address. One is what would be *feasible*? Criteria include:

- affordable/available (considering both capital costs and operating costs)
- cost-effective
- administratively feasible and
- practically feasible (for learners and teachers).

This is media selection by rejection (Romiszowski, 1988). The other question is what would be *ideal*? Criteria include:

- ideal for the content (given the affordances needed – e.g., based on the nature of the performance, tools needed, and so forth)
- ideal for the instructional methods (given the affordances needed – e.g., interaction, discussion, motion, color, and such)
- ideal for the learners (given any special characteristics – e.g., poor reading skills, physical disabilities, and so forth and
- ideal for the teachers (given their media skills, media preferences, teaching logistics, and such).

This is media selection by optimization (Romiszowski, 1988).

At the mid-level of design, it is helpful to consider the following questions:

- What sensory channels are required by the content: hearing (audio), seeing, (still or motion visuals), or touching (tactile)?
- What learner performance and instructor feedback capabilities are needed?
- What preferences do learners have for particular media?
- Who needs to control the media: teacher or learner?
- What collaboration capabilities should the media have: none (for individual use) or many (for collaborative use)?
- What other capabilities (e.g., content creation and sharing capabilities) should the media have to facilitate learner-centered instruction?
- How easy should it be to modify the content and/or instructional methods?

During the selection process, it helps to understand that some media characteristics are essential, such as audio for music instruction and motion visuals for manual skills, and some are optional, because they are attractive or address learner or teacher preferences but do not have significant impact on learning. Selection decisions should be made on all three levels of design, but early decisions limit later decisions, so you should typically delay the decisions as long as possible (Romiszowski, 1988). While we provide some guidance for media selection on all three levels of design (see Chapters 5–7), you can find much more useful guidance (though somewhat dated) in Romiszowski (1988).

Where Are We?

This chapter has described nine major considerations to take into account when designing instruction, in addition to categories of learning, learning theories, and instructional theories briefly described in Chapter 3. Particularly important are the two kinds of expertise discussed in this chapter: task expertise and topic expertise. Different ID processes

Table 4.5 ADE Process for Task Expertise and Topic Expertise (Differences Are in **Bold**)

	Task Expertise	*Topic Expertise*
Top Level Ch. 5	1. Select and sequence top-level content 2. Plan high-level instructional methods 3. Formatively evaluate and document the top-level design	1. Select and sequence top-level content 2. Plan high-level instructional methods 3. Formatively evaluate and document the top-level design
Mid Level Ch. 6	1. Identify and sequence **versions of each task** 2. Identify variations within each **version** and create designer objectives 3. Formatively evaluate the findings 4. Develop the learner objectives for each **version** 5. Design learner assessments for each **version** 6. Design the ways that learning by doing will be accomplished for each **version** 7. Select media in general for the **version** 8. Formatively evaluate and document the results	1. Identify and sequence **applications of each topic** 2. Identify variations within each **application** and create designer objectives 3. Formatively evaluate the findings 4. Develop the learner objectives for each **topic** 5. Design learner assessments for each **topic** 6. Design the ways that learning by doing will be accomplished for each **topic** 7. Select media in general for the **application** 8. Formatively evaluate and document the results
Lower Level Ch. 7	1. Select and sequence the organizing content for each **version of the task** 2. Select and classify the supporting content for each **version** 3. Sequence the supporting content for each **version** 4. Evaluate and document the findings 5. Identify resource requirements, availability, and existing instruction for each **version** 6. Revise and elaborate the instruction and assessments for each **version** 7. Formatively evaluate the ADE document 8. Begin developing the implementation plan, and update the project management plan	1. Select and sequence the organizing content for each **topic** 2. Select and classify the supporting content for each **topic** 3. Sequence the supporting content for each **topic** 4. Evaluate and document the findings 5. Identify resource requirements, availability, and existing instruction for each **topic** 6. Revise and elaborate the instruction and assessments for each **topic** 7. Formatively evaluate the ADE document 8. Begin developing the implementation plan, and update the project management plan
Ch. 8	Detailed guidance is provided for Lower-Level Step 6: Revise and Elaborate the Instruction and Assessments for Each Version/Topic. It includes instructional strategies for: • Remembering information • Understanding relationships • Applying skills and higher-order skills • Acting on attitudes or values	

are required for these two kinds of expertise. The next three chapters provide guidance to design instruction for both task expertise and topic expertise for top-level design (Chapter 5), mid-level design (Chapter 6), and lower-level design (Chapters 7 and 8). Table 4.5 provides a summary of the design process for each kind of expertise. The activities are numbered within each level to facilitate cross-referencing, but please keep in mind that, while the activities are loosely done in a sequence, there is a lot of looping back to earlier activities and simultaneous performance of some activities.

Develop and Deploy are addressed in Chapters 9–12.

Exercises

Here again we offer suggestions for a professor using this book as a textbook in a course, to help the students understand more deeply the contents of this chapter. We suggest that you keep the same teams of about three students each to continue to work on their ID projects throughout the course. However, these exercises can be done individually by any reader who wants to deepen their understanding and skills.

1. Have each team prepare a report that describes:
    *   Whether task expertise or topic expertise should be the dominant content for its project
    *   The target learners, contextual factors, and resources for its project (on a preliminary, general level)
    *   Who will be the SME for its project
    *   How important motivational strategies will be for its target learners
2. Have each team offer suggestions for improvement for the report of one or two other teams before you review and provide feedback to the students
3. Have a whole-class, synchronous discussion of the pros and cons of
    *   Just-in-time analysis
    *   Each kind of rapid prototyping (qualitative reduction and quantitative reduction)
    *   Learner-centered versus teacher-centered instruction

References

Albanese, M.A., & Mitchell, S. (1993). Problem-based learning: A review of literature on its outcomes and implementation issues. *Academic Medicine, 68*(1), 52–79.

Allen, M., & Sites, R. (2012). *Leaving ADDIE for SAM: An agile model for developing the best learning resources.* Alexandria, VA: ASTD Press.

An, Y. (2012). Learner-centered technology integration. In V.C.X. Wang (Ed.), *Encyclopedia of e-leadership, counseling and training.* Hersey, PA: IGI Global.

An, Y., & Bonk, C.J. (2009). Finding that SPECIAL PLACE: Designing digital game-based learning environments. *TechTrends, 53*(3), 43–48.

An, Y., & Reigeluth, C.M. (2011). Creating technology-enhanced, learner-centered classrooms: K-12 teachers' beliefs, perceptions, barriers, and support needs. *Journal of Digital Learning in Teacher Education, 28*(2), 54–62.

Barrows, H.S. (1986). A taxonomy of problem-based learning methods. *Medical Education, 20*(6), 481–486.

Barrows, H.S. (2000). *Problem-based learning applied to medical education.* Springfield, IL: Southern Illinois University School of Medicine.

Barrows, H., & Tamblyn, R. (1980). *Problem-based learning: An approach to medical education.* New York, NY: Springer.

Batane, T. (2010). Rapid prototyping for designing and delivering technology-based lessons. In M. Orey, S.A. Jones, & R.M. Branch (Eds.) *Educational media and technology yearbook* (Vol. 35, pp. 45–55). New York, NY: Springer US.

Bateman, W. (1990). *Open to question: The art of teaching and learning by inquiry.* San Francisco, CA: Jossey-Bass.

Bergmann, J., & Sams, A. (2012). *Flip your classroom: Reach every student in every class every day.* Washington, DC: International Society for Technology in Education.

Block, J.H. (1971). *Mastery learning: Theory and practice.* New York, NY: Holt, Rinehart and Winston, Inc.

Bloom, B.S. (1968). Learning for mastery. *Evaluation Comment, 1*(1), 1–12.

Bloom, B.S. (1984). The 2 sigma problem: The search for methods of group instruction as effective as one-to-one tutoring. *Educational Researcher, 13*(6), 4–16.

Blumenfeld, P., Soloway, E., Marx, R., Krajcik, J., Guzdial, M., & Palincsar, A. (1991). Motivating project-based learning: Sustaining the doing, supporting the learning. *Educational Psychologist, 26*(3&4), 369–398.

Brame, C. (2013). *Flipping the classroom.* Vanderbilt University Center for Teaching. Retrieved from https://wp0.vanderbilt.edu/cft/guides-sub-pages/flipping-the-classroom/.

Bransford, J.D., Brown, A.L., & Cocking, R.R. (2000). *How people learn: Brain, mind, experience, and school.* Washington, DC: National Academy Press.

Brown, J.S., & Adler, R.P. (2008). Minds on fire: Open education, the long tail, and learning 2.0. *EDUCAUSE Review, 43*(1), 17–32.

Brown, J., Collins, A., & Duguid, P. (1989). Situated cognition of learning. *Educational Researcher, 18*(1), 32–42.

Bruce, B.C., & Davidson, J. (1996). An inquiry model for literacy across the curriculum. *Journal of Curriculum Studies, 28*(3), 281–300.

Buck Institute for Education. (2012). *What is PBL?* Retrieved from http://www.bie.org/about/what_is_pbl.

Burke, B. (2014). *Gamify: How gamification motivates people to do extraordinary things.* Brookline, MA: Bibliomotion.

Carroll, J.B. (1963). A model of school learning. *Teachers College Record, 64*(8), 723–733.

Chapman, B. (2010). How long does it take to create learning? [Research Study]. Published by Chapman Alliance LLC. Retrieved from www.chapmanalliance.com.

Chou, Y. (2015). *Actionable gamification: Beyond points, badges, and leaderboards.* Fremont, CA: Octalysis Media.

Coles, C.R. (1985). Differences between conventional and problem-based curricula in their students' approaches to studying. *Medical Education, 19*(4), 308–309.

Collins, A., Brown, J.S., & Holum, A. (1991). Cognitive apprenticeship: Making thinking visible. *American Educator, 15*(3), 6–11, 38–39.

Deci, E.L., & Ryan, R.M. (1985). The general causality orientations scale: Self-determination in personality. *Journal of Research in Personality, 19*(2), 109–134

Defelice, R. (2018). *How long to develop one hour of training: Updated for 2017.* Retrieved from https://www.td.org/insights/how-long-does-it-take-to-develop-one-hour-of-training-updated-for-2017.

Desrosier, J. (2011). Rapid prototyping reconsidered. *Journal of Continuing Higher Education, 59*(3), 135–145.

Downes, S. (2005). E-learning 2.0. eLearn magazine. Retrieved from http://www.elearnmag.org/.

Francom, G.M. (2017). Principles for task-centered instruction. In C.M. Reigeluth, B.J. Beatty & R.D. Myers (Eds.), *Instructional-design theories and models: The learner-centered paradigm of education* (Vol. IV, pp. 65–92). New York, NY: Routledge.

Garris, R., Ahlers, R., & Driskell, J.E. (2002). Games, motivation, and learning: A research and practice model. *Simulation and Gaming, 33*(4), 441–467.

Gee, J.P. (2005). Good video games and good learning. *Phi Kappa Phi Forum, 85*(2), 33–37.

Gutierrez, K. (2015). *A 5-step plan to create your own scenario-based elearning course.* Retrieved from https://www.shiftelearning.com/blog/a-5-step-plan-to-create-your-own-scenario-based-elearning-course.

Harel, I., & Papert, S. (1991). Software design as learning environment. In I. Harel & S. Papert (Eds.), *Children designers: Interdisciplinary constructions for learning and knowing mathematics in a computer-rich school* (pp. 41–85). Noorwood: Ablex.

Heinich, R., Molenda, M., Russell, J.D., & Smaldino (1999). *Instructional media and technologies for learning* (6th ed.). Upper Saddle River, NJ: Prentice H.

Hmelo-Silver, C.E. (2004). Problem-based learning: What and how do students learn? *Educational Psychology Review, 16*(3), 235–266.

Jonassen, D.H. (2004). *Learning to solve problems: An instructional design guide.* San Francisco, CA: Jossey-Bass.

Jonassen, D.H., Tessmer, M., & Hannum, W.H. (1999). *Task analysis methods for instructional design.* Mahwah, NJ: Lawrence Erlbaum Associates.

Jones, T.S., & Richey, R.C. (2000). Rapid prototyping methodology in action: A developmental study. *Educational Technology Research and Development, 48*(2), 1042–1629.

Kapp, K.M. (Ed.). (2012). *The gamification of learning and instruction: Game-based methods and strategies for training and education.* New York, NY: Pfeiffer.

Kapp, K.M. (2017). Gamification designs for instruction. In C.M. Reigeluth, B.J. Beatty & R.D. Myers (Eds.), *Instructional-design theories and models, Volume IV: The learner-centered paradigm of education* (Vol. IV, pp. 351–383). New York, NY: Routledge.

Kapp, K.M., & Defelice, R.A. (2009, August 31). *Time to develop one hour of training.* Retrieved from the Association for Talent website https://www.td.org/Publications/Newsletters/Learning-Circuits/Learning CircuitsArchives/2009/08/Time-to-Develop-One-Hour-of-Training.

Keller, J.M. (1983). Motivational design of instruction. In C.M. Reigeluth (Ed.), *Instructional-design theories and models: An overview of their current status* (pp. 386–434). Hillsdale, NJ: Lawrence Erlbaum.

Keller, J.M. (1987). Development and use of the ARCS Model of instructional design. *Journal of Instructional Development, 10*(3), 2–10.

Keller, J.M. (2010). *Motivational design for learning and performance.* New York, NY: Springer.

Khazan, O. (2018). *The myth of 'learning styles'.* Retrieved from https://www.theatlantic.com/science/archive/2018/04/the-myth-of-learning-styles/557687/.

Kulik, C.-L. C., Kulik, J.A., & Bangert-Drowns, R.L. (1990). Effectiveness of mastery learning programs: A meta-analysis. *Review of Educational Research, 60*(2), 265–299. doi:10.3102/00346543060002265.

Lage, M.J., Platt, G.J., & Treglia, M. (2000). Inverting the classroom: A gateway to creating an inclusive learning environment. *The Journal of Economic Education, 31*(1), 30–43.

Lee, V.S. (Ed.). (2004). *Teaching and learning through inquiry: A guidebook for institutions and instructors.* Sterling, VA: Stylus.

Leshin, C.B., Pollock, J., & Reigeluth, C.M. (1992). *Instructional design strategies and tactics.* Englewood Cliffs, NJ: Educational Technology Publications.

Lundeberg, M., Levin, B., & Harrington, H. (1999). *Who learns what from cases and how? The Research Base for teaching and learning with cases.* Mahwah, NJ: Lawrence Erlbaum Associates.

Lynn, L. (1999). *Teaching and learning with cases: A guidebook.* Chatham House Publishers, Seven Bridges Press, LLC.

McClelland, D. (1987). *Human motivation.* Cambridge, UK: Cambridge University Press.

McCombs, B.L., & Whisler, J.S. (1997). *The learner-centered classroom and school: Strategies for increasing student motivation and achievement.* San Francisco, CA: Jossey-Bass.

McKay, C.S., & Glazewski, K.D. (2017). Designing maker-based instruction. In C.M. Reigeluth, B.J. Beatty & R.D. Myers (Eds.), *Instructional-design theories and models, Volume IV: The learner-centered paradigm of education* (Vol. IV, pp. 145–172). New York, NY: Routledge.

Merrill, M.D. (2002). First principles of instruction. *Educational Technology Research and Development, 50*(3), 43–59.

Merrill, M.D. (2007). First principles of instruction: A synthesis. In R.A. Reiser & J.V. Dempsey (Eds.), *Trends and issues in instructional design and technology* (2nd ed., pp. 62–71). Upper Saddle River, NJ: Merrill/Prentice-Hall.

Myers, R.D., & Reigeluth, C.M. (2017). Designing games for learning. In C.M. Reigeluth, B.J. Beatty & R.D. Myers (Eds.), *Instructional-design theories and models, Vol. IV: The learner-centered paradigm of education* (pp. 205–242). New York, NY: Rougledge.

Newble, D.I., & Clarke, R.M. (1986). The approaches to learning of students in a traditional and in an innovative problem-based medical school. *Medical Education, 20*(4), 267–273.

Norman, G.R., & Schmidt, H.G. (1992). The psychological basis of problem-based learning: A review of the evidence. *Academic Medicine, 67*(9), 557–565.

Papert, S. (1980). *Mindstorms.* New York, NY: Basic Books.

Pappas, C. (2015). *5 Tips to develop effective scenario-based online training.* Retrieved from https://elearningindustry.com/5-tips-to-develop-effective-scenario-based-online-training.

Pham, D., & Dimov, S. (2003). Rapid prototyping: A time compression tool. *Ingenia, 17*, 43–48.

Prince, M., & Felder, R.M. (2006). Inductive teaching and learning methods: Definitions, comparisons, and research bases. *Journal of Engineering Education, 95*(2), 123–138.

Reigeluth, C. M. (1979). In search of a better way to organize instruction: The elaboration theory. *Journal of Instructional Development, 2*(3),8–15.

Reigeluth, C.M. (1994). Envisioning a new system of education. In C.M. Reigeluth & R.J. Garfinkle (Eds.), *Systemic change in education* (pp. 59–70). Englewood Cliffs, NJ: Educational Technology Publications.

Reigeluth, C.M. (1999a). The elaboration theory: Guidance for scope and sequence decisions. In C.M. Reigeluth (Ed.), *Instructional-design theories and models: A new paradigm of instructional theory* (Vol. II, pp. 425–453). Mahwah, NJ: Lawrence Erlbaum Associates.

Reigeluth, C.M. (1999b). What is instructional-design theory and how is it changing? In C.M. Reigeluth (Ed.), *Instructional-design theories and models: A new paradigm of instructional theory* (pp. 1–29). Mahwah, NJ: Lawrence Erlbaum Associates.

Reigeluth, C.M., & Karnopp, J.R. (2013). *Reinventing schools: It's time to break the mold.* Lanham, MD: Rowman & Littlefield Publishing Group.

Reigeluth, C.M., & Karnopp, J.R. (2020). *Vision and action: Reinventing schools through personalized competency-based education.* Bloomington, IN: Marzano Resources.

Reigeluth, C.M., Myers, R.D., & Lee, D. (2017). The learner-centered paradigm of education. In C.M. Reigeluth, B.J. Beatty & R.D. Myers (Eds.), *Instructional-design theories and models: The learner-centered paradigm of education* (Vol. IV, pp. 5–32). New York, NY: Routledge.

Richardson, W. (2009). *Blogs, wikis, podcasts, and other powerful web tools for classrooms* (2nd ed.). Thousand Oaks, CA: Corwin Press.

Romiszowski, A.J. (1981). *Designing instructional systems: Decision making in course planning and curriculum design.* New York, NY: Nichols Publishing.

Romiszowski, A.J. (1986). *Developing auto-instructional materials: From programmed texts to CAL and interactive video.* New York, NY: Nichols Publishing.

Romiszowski, A.J. (1988). *The selection and use of instructional media.* New York, NY: Nichols Publishing.

Ryan, R.M., & Deci, E.L. (2000). Self-determination theory and the facilitation of intrinsic motivation, social development, and well-being. *American Psychologist, 55*(1), 68–78.

Salen, K. (Ed.). (2008). *The ecology of games: Connecting youth, games, and learning.* Cambridge, MA: The MIT Press.

Savery, J. (2006). Overview of problem-based learning: Definitions and distinctions. *Interdisciplinary Journal of Problem-Based Learning, 1*(1). Retrieved from https://docs.lib.purdue.edu/ijpbl/vol1/iss1/3/.

Savery, J.R. (2009). Problem-based approach to instruction. In C.M. Reigeluth & A.A. Carr-Chellman (Eds.), *Instructional-design theories and models: Building a common knowledge base* (Vol. III, pp. 143–165). New York, NY: Routledge.

Savery, J., & Duffy, T. (1995). Problem-based learning: An instructional model and its constructivist framework. In B. Wilson (Ed.), *Constructivist learning environments: Case studies in instructional design* (pp. 135–148). Englewood Cliffs, NJ: Educational Technology Publications.

Schwaber, K., & Beedle, M. (2002). *Agile software development with scrum.* Upper Saddle River, NJ: Prentice Hall.

Shaffer, D.W., Squire, K.R., Halverson, R., & Gee, J.P. (2005). Video games and the future of learning. *Phi Delta Kappan, 87*(2), 104–111.

Strayer, J. (2007). *The effects of the classroom flip on the learning environment: A comparison of learning activity in a traditional classroom and a flip classroom that used an intelligent tutoring system* (Doctoral Dissertation). Retrieved from http://faculty.washington.edu/rvanderp/DLData/FlippingClassDis.pdf ETD Center 1189523914.

Strobel, J., & van Barneveld, A. (2009). When is PBL more effective? A meta-analysis of meta-analyses comparing PBL to conventional classrooms. *The Interdisciplinary Journal of Problem-Based Learning, 3*(1), 44–58.

The eLearning Guild. (2002). *The e-learning development time ratio survey.* Retrieved from http://www.elearning guild.com/pdf/1/time%20to%20develop%20Survey.pdf.

Tripp, S.D., & Bichelmeyer, B. (1990). Rapid prototyping: An alternative instructional design strategy. *Educational Technology Research and Development, 38*(1), 31–44.

van Merriënboer, J.J.G. (1997). *Training complex cognitive skills: A four-component instructional design model for technical training.* Englewood Cliffs, NJ: Educational Technology Publications.

van Merriënboer, J.J.G., & Kirschner, P.A. (2007). *Ten steps to complex learning.* New York, NY: Taylor & Francis.

van Merrienboer, J.J.G., & Kirschner, P.A. (2013). *Ten steps to complex learning* (2nd ed.). New York, NY: Taylor & Francis.

Vernon, D.T, & Blake, R.L. (1993). Does problem-based learning work? A meta-analysis of evaluative research. *Academic Medicine, 68*(7), 550–563.

5 Top-Level Analysis, Design, and Evaluation

Overview

When an instructional needs assessment has indicated a need for some form of instruction and the necessary definition of the ID project has been done (see Chapter 2), it is time to enter the design phase, which goes through three stages: top level, mid level, and lower level. This chapter provides detailed guidance for top-level analysis, design, and evaluation (ADE) for both task and topic expertise.

Top-level instructional design aims to create a "fuzzy vision" of the instruction, including big-picture content, sequencing, and instructional methods for your instruction, offering greater opportunity for creativity and coherence in the instruction. The purpose of the **top-level analysis** is to begin to determine what to teach (given the instructional goals identified in the needs assessment) and how to teach it (big-picture instructional methods). It identifies the general content and structure for the instruction and allows you to create a fuzzy vision of what the instruction should be like. A top-level analysis is *not* required if the major parts and structure of the content have already been identified (e.g., if your project is focused on developing a part of a larger instructional system). Table 5.1 shows the major activities involved in the top-level ADE process, including relevant formative evaluation activities.

As we said in Chapter 1, designing instruction is often like complex problem solving. There are many factors to consider. Suppose that you are designing training to teach employees how to use a new tool. There are many ways to teach how to use a tool, including a job aid, a lecture, a video demonstration, an eLearning course with interactive animations, demonstrations, or practice using virtual reality or augmented reality, and classroom training involving expert demonstrations and hands-on practice opportunities, to name just a few. What is the best way to teach the new tool?

It depends. If the new tool is very simple and easy to use, a job aid might be enough. You must consider your target learners' skills and readiness, for the tool could be easy to use for some people but complex and confusing for others. The learners may already have some of the skills for using the tool. Also, if your target learners have negative attitudes or biases toward the new tool for some reason, you should help them understand why they need to use the tool and how it can be beneficial for their work. There are many factors like these that call for very different instructional designs.

The budget for the ID process and the resources for the instruction are critical factors affecting design decisions in most, if not all, design situations. With very limited budget and resources, for example, you won't be able to design and develop a highly interactive e-learning course, even if one is desired. However, interactive e-learning could be cost effective if your training is targeted for a large number of learners who are globally distributed. Other factors to consider may include the cost and availability of the new tool for use in instruction, instructional resources and staff available, and timeline.

Table 5.1 Top-Level ADE Processes for Task and Topic Expertise

Task Expertise	*Topic Expertise*
1. Select and sequence big-picture task expertise	**1. Select and sequence big-picture topic expertise**
1A.1. Analyze each job to identify its duties	1B.1. Analyze each domain to identify its subjects
1A.2. Analyze each duty to identify its tasks	1B.2. Analyze each subject to identify its topics
1A.3. Design a sequence of duties and tasks	1B.3. Design a sequence of domains and topics

2. Plan big-picture instructional methods

- Make decisions about such things as mastery, learner-centered instruction, pacing, delivery methods and media selection, and templates or course management systems

3. Formatively evaluate, revise, and document the top-level design

- Formatively evaluate the big-picture content and design decisions
- Make warranted revisions
- Document the results

To help you understand and apply the guidance offered in the rest of this book, we provide many examples for different types of topic expertise and different types of task expertise. This allows the reader to perceive the applicability of the instructional design approach and its general principles across different areas of academic subject matter and different professional and job contexts. At the same time, it allows the reader to compare and contrast how these general principles lead to specific design decisions and instructional procedures adapted to the specific needs and characteristics of each project.

1. Select and Sequence Big-Picture Content

Guidance for this activity is different for task expertise than for topic expertise. The differences are explained in the following two subsections of this chapter and are illustrated by examples taken from past instructional design projects. In most courses, both task and topic expertise are involved, but you should select one as the primary focus, even if both seem equally important. If in doubt, we recommend going with task expertise for the overall organization of the course.

1A. Select and Sequence Big-Picture Task Expertise

Task expertise exists on a **scope continuum** from very narrow expertise to very broad or comprehensive expertise. It also can be described on a **description continuum** from very precise (detailed description) to very vague (general description).

On the **scope** continuum, we use the term "job" to refer to the broadest scope. A job is made up of "duties," which in turn are made up of "tasks," each of which typically has several "versions" that are done differently (see Figure 5.1), and both tasks and versions have "subtasks." Please understand that these are relative terms, and what one person considers a "duty," another might consider a "task," and so forth. However, the difference between a version of a task and a subtask is clear. A *version of a task* is one way of doing the real-world task from beginning to end. In contrast, a *subtask* is a part of a task and is not performed in the real world without other parts. This distinction will become clearer in the guidance that follows. Your ID project may only require teaching a single duty or even a

Figure 5.1 Levels of Content for Task Expertise.

single task, in which case you would need to do little or no top-level task analysis, but you may still need other parts of the top-level ADE process.

On the **description** continuum, task expertise is typically described more precisely by either providing greater detail – breaking it down into parts (e.g., subtasks) or describing alternative versions, or both.

1A.1. Analyze Each Job to Identify Its Duties

In the rare case that the task expertise to be taught is of very broad scope (a whole job or even more than one job), you begin by analyzing each job (typically called a job analysis) to identify its duties. (Otherwise, skip this step.) This is usually done by interviewing several experts in the job. Don't be surprised to find different perspectives about the duties from different experts (see Table 5.2 for an example).

1A.2. Analyze Each Duty to Identify Its Tasks

If the task expertise to be taught encompasses one or more duties, you analyze each duty to identify and list the **tasks** that make it up. (Otherwise, skip to Step 2 to plan big-picture instructional methods.) If two tasks are typically conducted together, they are usually considered subtasks of a larger task. At this point, just list tasks (that are not typically conducted together). Be comprehensive in scope but general in description (level of detail). Subtasks will be identified in the lower-level analysis (Chapter 7) as either steps or heuristics. To help distinguish between jobs, duties, and tasks, see Table 5.3. Be sure to list *all* the tasks that should be taught in each duty.

For the *quantitative approach* to **rapid prototyping** (described in Chapter 4), conduct the job analysis for only one job now, and proceed to analyze it on the mid level. For the *qualitative approach*, conduct a top-level analysis for all jobs addressed in the project before moving

Table 5.2 Example of Two Perspectives on Duties for the Job "Elementary School Math Teacher"

Teacher-Centered Perspective on Duties	*Learner-Centered Perspective on Duties*
Decide on a curriculum sequence for math	Decide on a curriculum sequence for math
Choose or create instructional resources	Choose or develop authentic projects
Teach whole-class lessons	Form teams and initiate projects
Prepare tests	Provide just-in-time scaffolding
Grade tests	Monitor and coach learner teams
Report grades	Report skills and concepts mastered

Table 5.3 Example of Job, Duty, and Tasks for Elementary School Math Teacher

Level of Analysis	Example of Content
Job	Teach elementary school mathematics (learner-centered perspective)
Duty	Form teams and initiate projects
Task	Choose members of each team
Task	Introduce a project to the teams
Task	Help each team organize and set its norms

on to the mid-level analysis, to give you a broad sense of how the different jobs, duties, and tasks relate to each other, if at all. (However, most ID projects address only one job, or even just one or two duties in a job, because they are associated with a specific knowledge or performance gap.) Later, this qualitative approach (described in Chapter 4) would likely develop mock-ups of expensive media for product evaluation and revision, before developing the full-blown expensive media products. For the combination approach, conduct the job analysis for only one job now and proceed to analyze it on the mid level.

1.A.3. Design a Sequence of Duties and Tasks

Having identified the duties and their tasks, you should design a sequence for teaching them. Do this by identifying any factors among the duties and their tasks that may make it advantageous to teach one before another. For example, when there is overlap of skills in two tasks, and one of the tasks is simpler or easier to learn than the other, then sequence the simpler/easier one first. For another example, the order in which the duties and/or tasks are performed may be a helpful order for teaching them. Your big-picture sequence design will either be a **linear sequence** of tasks, or a **branching sequence** that offers each learner control over the sequence within the constraints of the branches (such as in digital instruction). The example in Table 5.4 shows a

Table 5.4 Example of a Sequence Design for Duties and Tasks to Be Taught to Elementary School Math Teachers

Sequence of Duties	Sequence of Tasks
1. Decide on a curriculum sequence for math (assuming that's possible in one's school)	1.1 Decide what math content to teach (facts, skills, and understandings)
	1.2 Identify contingency relationships (prerequisite and facilitative relationships)
	1.3 Decide whether to have a single sequence or allow sequencing options, and design the sequence(s)
2. Choose authentic projects	2.1 Decide on project specifications
	2.2 Search project databases for projects that meet those specifications, and choose the best ones for your learners
3. Form teams and initiate projects	3.1 Choose members of each team
	3.2 Introduce a project to the team(s)
	3.3 Help each team organize and set its norms
4. Provide just-in-time scaffolding	4.1 Monitor learner teams
	4.2 Provide learners with just-in-time instruction as needed
	4.3 Provide each team with tips, resources, and/or other support needed just in time
5. Report skills and concepts mastered	5.1 Enter information into an online database
	5.2 Post evidence of mastery to the student's electronic portfolio and link it to the mastery information in the database

procedural sequence[1] for teaching the duties and their tasks in the job of elementary school math teacher.

Once the basic sequence has been determined, **chunk** (combine) the tasks comprising that sequence into units of appropriate size for your instructional situation (e.g., online or face to face). Appropriate size is typically determined by the number of hours of learning time required. Typical terms for these units are course (for a large chunk) and module (for a smaller chunk, typically about ten hours of learning time). While those terms are not appropriate for all instructional systems, we use them out of convenience and familiarity, but please understand that you may find other terms more appropriate for your instructional situation. In most cases, other individuals should be consulted about the sequence and chunks, such as task experts or others your client may recommend. You may need to make adjustments in the size or composition of those chunks later, when you have more information about how long each chunk will take to master. But keep in mind that, if tasks are small, you may want to include two or more of them in one chunk.

Finally, be sure to enter all the results of this step in a top-level ADE document, such as the sample template shown in Table 5.5.[2] Also, you could conduct formative evaluation (described in Step 3) on the results of this step now, but it is usually better to wait until you have finished Step 2 (Plan Big-Picture Instructional Methods), so that you can evaluate content and methods at the same time.

1B. Select and Sequence Big-Picture Topic Expertise

To initiate the design of your instruction, you should make very general decisions about what to teach and how to teach it. Like task expertise, topic expertise exists on a **scope** continuum from very narrow expertise to very broad or comprehensive expertise. It also can be *described* on a **description** continuum from very detailed to very general or vague.

On the **scope** continuum, we use the term "domain" to refer to the broadest scope. A domain is made up of "subjects," which are made up of "topics," which can be further analyzed to ever more narrow levels (see Table 5.6 for examples). Please understand that these are relative terms, and what one person considers a "subject," another might consider a "topic," and so forth. Your ID project may only require teaching a single subject or even a single topic, in which case you would need to do little or no top-level topic analysis, but you may still need other parts of the top-level ADE process.

The **description** continuum is the same for topic expertise as for task expertise (as explained earlier in this chapter).

1B.1. Analyze Each Domain to Identify Its Subjects

In the rare case that the topic expertise to be taught is of very broad scope, you begin by analyzing each domain to identify all its subjects. (Otherwise, skip this step.) This is usually done by consulting expert resources and interviewing several experts in the domain. Don't be surprised to find different perspectives about the subjects from different experts. Try to get them to reach consensus. At this point, just list the subjects.

1B.2. Analyze Each Subject to Identify Its Topics

If the topic expertise to be taught encompasses one or more subjects, you analyze each subject to identify and list the topics that make it up, again by interviewing several domain

---

1   A procedural sequence entails teaching the steps of a procedure in the same order as they are performed in a real-world task.

2   All templates that appear in this book (such as Tables 5.5 and 5.8) are available as MS Word downloads at www.reigeluth.net/holistic-4d.

experts and trying to reach consensus. (Otherwise, skip to Step 2: Plan Big-Picture Instructional Methods). At this point, just list the topics. To help distinguish between domains, subjects, and topics, see Table 5.6. Be sure to list *all* the subjects and topics that should be taught in each domain, but don't identify subtopics yet. Be comprehensive in scope but general in description (level of detail). A rule of thumb is that a domain should only have about five to ten subjects, and a subject should only have about five to ten topics, but of course there are many exceptions to this rule.

For the *quantitative approach* to **rapid prototyping** (described in Chapter 4), analyze only one topic now, and proceed to analyze it on the mid level. For the *qualitative*

Table 5.5 Template for a Top-Level ADE Document for Task Expertise

Top-Level ADE Document for Task Expertise	
Name of Job:	
Name and Sequence of Duties	**Name and Sequence of Tasks**
1.	1.1 1.2 1.3 …
2.	2.1 2.2 2.3 …
…	…
Big-Picture Instructional Methods	
Mastery approach? ☐ Yes ☐ No **Learner-centered?** ☐ Yes ☐ No **Pacing strategy?** ☐ Self-paced ☐ Group pacing ☐ Group lockstep **Initial thoughts about learning by doing:** **Initial thoughts about delivery methods:** **Initial thoughts about templates and course management systems:**	

Table 5.6 Examples of Domains, Subjects, and Topics

Level of Analysis	Example 1	Example 2
Domain	Learning theory	Economics
Subjects	Behaviorism (*see topics below*)	Microeconomics (*see topics below*)
	Cognitivism	Macroeconomics
	Constructivism	International economics
		Development economics
Topics	(*For behaviorism*)	(*For microeconomics*)
	Classical conditioning theory	Supply and demand
	Reinforcement theory	Markets
		Production, cost, and efficiency
		Specialization
		Firms

approach, conduct a top-level analysis for all topics addressed in the project before moving on to the mid-level analysis. Later, this *qualitative approach* would likely entail developing mock-ups of expensive media for product evaluation and revision, before developing the full-blown expensive media products. For the combination approach, conduct the domain analysis for only one domain now and proceed to analyze it on the mid level.

1B.3. Design a Sequence for the Subjects and Topics

Having identified the subjects and their topics, you should design a sequence for teaching them. Do this by identifying any factors among the subjects/topics that may make it advantageous to teach one before another. For example, one topic may build on understandings learned in another topic. Also, when there is overlap of concepts or principles in two topics, and one of the topics is easier to learn than the other, then sequence the easier one first. Often, the historical order in which the knowledge (subjects and topics) was developed is a good indicator of an easy-to-difficult sequence (see Table 5.7). In some cases, it doesn't matter which you teach first. In such cases, it is usually beneficial to allow learners to select their own sequence when possible (such as in online instruction). In such a case, your big-picture sequence design will be a branching sequence that offers each learner control over the sequence within the constraints of the branches, rather than a linear sequence of topics.

Table 5.7 Example of a Sequence Design for Subjects and Topics for the Domain "Learning Theory"

Sequence of Subjects	Sequence of Topics
1. Behaviorism	1.1 Classical conditioning theory
	1.2 Reinforcement theory
2. Cognitivism	2.1 Information processing theory
	2.2 Schema theory
	2.3 Social cognitive theory
3. Constructivism	3.1 Cognitive constructivism
	3.2 Social constructivism
	3.3 Constructionism

Once the basic sequence has been determined, **chunk** (combine) the subjects and topics comprising that sequence into units of appropriate size for your instructional situation (e.g., online or face to face). Appropriate size is typically determined by the number of hours of learning time required. Typical terms for these units are course (for a large chunk) and module (for a smaller chunk, typically about ten hours of learning time). While those terms are not appropriate for all instructional systems, we use them out of convenience and familiarity, but please understand that you may find other terms more appropriate for your instructional situation. In most cases, other individuals should be consulted about the sequence and chunks, such as task experts or others your client may recommend. You may need to make adjustments in the size or composition of those chunks later, when you have more information about how long each chunk will take to master. But keep in mind that, if subjects or topics are small, you may want to include two or more of them in one chunk. You may need to make adjustments in those chunks later, when you have more information about how long each chunk will take to master.

Note that the chunking may vary depending on the level of learning. For example, in a doctoral program, you might choose a large chunk (equivalent to a course) for each subject – one on behaviorism, one on cognitivism, and one on constructivism. Conversely, for a high school curriculum, you might have learning theory as a smaller chunk within a large chunk on psychology.

Finally, be sure to enter all the results of this step in a top-level ADE document, such as the sample template shown in Table 5.8. Also, you could conduct formative evaluation (described in Step 3) on the results of this step now, but it is usually better to wait until you have finished Step 2 so that you can evaluate content and methods at the same time.

2. Plan Big-Picture Instructional Methods

Begin this planning with an analysis of very general information about the target learners:

- How many people are to be taught?
- How geographically dispersed are they?
- What time and timing constraints are they under?
- Can they get together in groups? If so, how large could the groups be?
- Are there limitations regarding such things as age, reading level, and technology skills?

This analysis includes elements of all three kinds of contextual analysis described by Tessmer and Richey (1997) – analysis of the orienting, instructional, and transfer contexts. It provides information to help you plan the big-picture instructional methods, which are a fuzzy vision of the instruction. They include answers to general questions like:

- Will you allow your target learners to move forward only when each has mastered the content – and as soon as each has mastered it?
- Will you use the learner-centered approach, and if so, which form(s) of learning by doing will you use?
- Which pacing strategy will you use?
- Which delivery method and media will you use under your media constraints?
- Will you use a course management system or an existing template for your training?

We offer guidance for these big-picture methods: mastery, pacing, learning by doing, delivery methods and media, and selection of templates and/or course management systems. The guidance for these methods is the same for **both Task and Topic expertise**.

Table 5.8 Template for a Top-Level ADE Document for Topic Expertise

Top-Level ADE Document for Topic Expertise	
Name of Domain:	
Name and Sequence of Subjects	**Name and Sequence of Topics**
1.	1.1 1.2 1.3 …
2.	2.1 2.2 2.3 …
…	…
Big-Picture Instructional Methods	
Mastery approach? ☐ Yes ☐ No **Learner-centered?** ☐ Yes ☐ No **Pacing strategy?** ☐ Self-paced ☐ Group pacing ☐ Group lockstep **Initial thoughts about learning by doing:** **Initial thoughts about delivery methods:** **Initial thoughts about templates and course management systems:**	

Mastery

Typically, education has been done "with time as the constant" (learner progress is based on a fixed, allotted amount of time) and amount of learning as the variable (as indicated by grades on tests). This does not promote high levels of performance. Therefore, whenever possible, you should design instruction in which *learning* is the constant and amount of time is variable – a *mastery approach* or competency or proficiency approach to education or training – whereby learners move forward only when they have mastered the content (and as soon as they have mastered the content), rather than when a predetermined amount of time has passed (Block, 1971; Bloom, 1968, 1984; Kulik, Kulik, & Bangert-Drowns, 1990). Given that different people learn at different rates, the mastery approach means you should either customize the pace of instruction, or you should allow faster learners to spend less time on the instruction and more time on other important matters. Online learning is ideally suited to customized pace and mastery learning.

Learner-Centered or Teacher-Centered Instruction

Whether or not you go with mastery-based instruction and self-pacing, decide whether or not to use *learner-centered instruction*, which includes learning by doing (see Chapter 4), self-pacing, and at least some elements of self-directed learning (Albanese & Mitchell, 1993; Barrows, 1986; Barrows & Tamblyn, 1980; Jonassen, 2011; Kirschner, Sweller, & Clark, 2006; Reigeluth, 2012; Reigeluth & Karnopp, 2013; Savery, 2009). The major alternative is *teacher-centered instruction*, which includes lecture, discussion, tutorial instruction, and others (with or without multimedia) and either group lockstep or group pacing with little or no self-direction. Of course, any of these teacher-centered approaches can be used to provide just-in-time instructional support within the learner-centered approach. This is a time to be creative. Especially if the learners are not likely to be well motivated to learn a topic, think of whether you might be able to organize the instruction around projects of interest to learners, possibly in the form of a game.

Pacing

Pacing is the rate at which learners go through the instructional sequence. Table 5.9 presents several ways to pace the learners' progress.

Table 5.9 Pacing Strategies

Strategy	Description
Group Lockstep	The group moves through the instructional sequence at a predetermined pace, completing the instructional sequence on schedule. Normally, this is the least effective form of pacing, because slower learners may not be able to master the material and faster learners waste time waiting for the group to move on. However, it is often used when there are constraints, such as equipment or facilities that require the learners to flow through the sequence on a schedule to avoid conflicts.
Group Pacing	The group moves through the instructional sequence as a group, at the same rate, but the group may move faster or slower than the predetermined pace depending on the ability and needs of the group as a whole. This is a very easy-to-use method in teacher-centered instruction, but slower learners often are unable to master the material at the group pace, and faster learners miss the opportunity to move on more quickly.
Self-Paced	Learners are allowed to work at their own pace – or their team's pace – through the instructional sequence within certain parameters. This form of pacing is very effective for ensuring mastery by all learners.
Combination Pacing	Any of the above-mentioned forms of pacing may be used in combination in a course. Some of the instruction may be group-paced while other instruction may be self-paced.

Delivery Methods and Media

How will the instruction be delivered to the target learners and where? In this book we use "delivery methods" to refer to big-picture selection of sets of media, such as:

- Online learning (synchronous and/or asynchronous)
- Mobile learning
- Face-to-face instruction
- Blended instruction (both face-to-face and online)

As Piskurich (2015) noted, there is no rule that says you should choose only one delivery method. In fact, many successful instructional programs combine different delivery methods. Learners tend to like some variation (though not too much). One of the most common examples of blending delivery methods is the integration of classroom and online learning, which is often called blended learning or hybrid learning. Blended learning (Horn & Staker, 2015) takes advantage of the strengths of both face-to-face interaction and online learning. There are many ways to blend delivery methods. They include, but are not limited to:

- Classroom and online learning
- Classroom and on-the-job learning
- Classroom learning and job aids
- Synchronous e-learning and asynchronous e-learning
- Self-paced e-learning and job aids
- Any combination of the above

In addition, there are many media options for these delivery methods. Each option has its own advantages and disadvantages. After you make a tentative decision about delivery method, you should do some preliminary thinking about media to use with it. Medium is defined in this book as *any* means by which instruction is implemented with a learner, including humans and real-world objects, as well as different kinds of technology and other materials, to foster learning. In addition to gaining a general understanding of the content and instruction (from Steps 1 and 2), it helps to identify any major constraints on media selection now, because they will likely influence your subsequent design decisions. For this process of selection by rejection, there are several kinds of constraints to consider (Romiszowski, 1988), including:

- Are there some media that you cannot afford? This is a constraint of the funds available for your ID project. Conversely, are there some media that are available, including ones that your client really wants you to utilize?
- Are there some media that are not cost-effective, given the size of your target audience? For example, if you will have a very large number of learners, the extra expense of designing digital media will be more cost-effective in the long run, regardless of what you can afford with your current budget. It would be wise to procure additional funding to end up costing less in the long run.
- Are there some media that are not administratively feasible? There may not be sufficient classroom space for large numbers of learners. Or there may not be enough equipment for learners to work with, such as in hands-on training with heating, ventilation, and air conditioning system (HVAC) repairs.
- Are there some media that are not practically feasible for learners and/or teachers? For example, learners may not have virtual reality headsets, or teachers may not be comfortable or capable of using certain technology systems.

Based on your constraints, you should initially narrow down your media options (selection by rejection) so you can keep them in mind for your mid-level design. Different media will likely be appropriate for different learning needs, so selection of specific media should take place on the mid and lower levels of design. However, it is helpful to counterbalance selection by rejection by also imagining what media might be ideal – selection by optimization (Romiszowski, 1988). As mentioned in Chapter 4, you should consider what might be ideal:

- for the content (given the affordances needed – e.g., based on the nature of the performance, tools needed, and so forth),
- for the instructional methods (given the affordances needed – e.g., interaction, discussion, motion, color, and such),
- for the learners (given any special characteristics – e.g., poor reading skills, physical disabilities, and so forth), and
- for the teachers (given their media skills, media preferences, teaching logistics, and such).

Of course, at this point what might be "ideal" is largely conjecture based on your experience and intuition. This is a time to be creative! But keep in mind that you will have opportunities on Levels 2 and 3 to refine, elaborate, and otherwise change your initial selections.

Templates and Course Management Systems

Determine whether you are required to use, or want to use, a template or pattern for your instruction. Also decide whether the instruction will be delivered on an existing platform (course management or learning management system). If so, note the limitations of the template and/or platform, for they will influence the instructional methods that can be used.

3. Formatively Evaluate, Revise, and Document the Top-Level Design

This is the last major activity at the top level. Irrespective of whether you are dealing with task or topic expertise, you should:

- Formatively evaluate the big-picture content and design decisions with content experts and instructors who are experienced in teaching the content to the target learners, and make warranted revisions (see Chapter 10, Formative Evaluation, for guidance)
- Document the results in the form of a top-level ADE document
- Revise your project management plan

Formative Evaluation and Revision

Instructional solutions which at first appear to be ideal may prove to be inadequate, inappropriate, or just impossible, for a variety of reasons that may spring from a variety of issues:

- Contextual issues (e.g., rejection by teachers, parental opposition, lack of management support)
- Resource issues (e.g., lack of adequate funding, time for development, or ID staff)
- Implementation/usability issues (e.g., lack of necessary study skills, learning time, or other necessary resources on the part of the target learners)
- Distribution/dissemination issues (e.g., inability of the target learners to access and use the instructional system, such as not all the target learners having Internet access)

This list is just a sample of the many sources of potential problems or difficulties that an ID project may encounter. A useful tool for identifying such issues is the SWOT (Strengths – Weaknesses – Opportunities – Threats) methodology of analysis (Helms & Nixon, 2010; Jackson, Joshi, & Erhardt, 2003). Another useful tool, based on systems-thinking, is the CIPP (Context – Input – Process – Product) methodology for troubleshooting issues in complex systems (Stufflebeam, 2003; Stufflebeam & Zhang, 2017). This can be used both for evaluating problems in existing systems and for initial diagnosis to predict potential sources of problems.

Your formative evaluation cannot involve tryouts with learners yet because the design decisions are too general, so among the options described in Chapter 10, you should conduct an **expert review** with content experts and, especially for large projects, instructional experts by means of a walk-through exercise to enhance appropriateness, accuracy, effectiveness, and appeal. It is usually beneficial to choose experts who have experience teaching your content to your target learners, for they tend to have both kinds of expertise. Also, get input from the experts on what changes they think would likely improve the content and design, and either make revisions during the walk-through exercise, or as soon as possible after it. Please see Chapter 10 for guidance on expert review.

Top-Level ADE Document

Your top-level ADE document should be prepared as you proceed through Steps 1 and 2 of the top-level ADE process and revised as soon as possible during or after your formative evaluation and revisions. As already explained in Chapter 4, a design document is a "blueprint" or written description of the instructional system. Tables 5.5 and 5.8 present templates for top-level ADE documents for task expertise and topic expertise, respectively. We encourage you to improve on these templates according to your particular needs and working styles.

Project Management Plan

Perhaps one of the most important activities during your top-level ADE process is to see how others have addressed similar instructional needs. There is no benefit to be gained from "reinventing the wheel" if there already exists a wheel that works well. But even if an existing design is not perfect in all respects, it is often much more cost-effective to **redesign** (adapt) what exists than to start from scratch. The time to review and evaluate existing designs is early in the design process – during the top-level phase of ADE. With a "fuzzy" idea of how best to design the needed instruction, you can review instruction previously developed for the same or similar instructional needs and adopt, adapt, or reject what is available before embarking on a totally fresh (and more expensive) ID endeavor. Consequently, you should revise your project management plan (developed with guidance in Chapter 2) based on any appropriate instruction you have found.

Where Are We?

You have previously completed the Define activities in which your instructional needs analysis revealed a need for some form of instruction and your project planning created the foundation for the rest of your ID project (Chapter 2). This chapter has offered guidance for conducting a top-level ADE for both task and topic expertise, based on the major considerations described in Chapters 3 and 4. This guidance should result in a top-level ADE document similar to the ones shown in Tables 5.5 and 5.8, which include selection and sequencing of the major "chunks" of the content and the selection of big-picture instructional methods.

Table 5.10 ADE Process for Task Expertise and Topic Expertise (Differences Are in **Bold**)

	Task Expertise	Topic Expertise
Top-Level Ch. 5	1. Select and sequence big-picture content 2. Plan big-picture instructional methods 3. Formatively evaluate and document the top-level design	1. Select and sequence big-picture content 2. Plan big-picture instructional methods 3. Formatively evaluate and document the top-level design
Mid-Level Ch. 6	1. Identify and sequence **versions of each task** 2. Identify variations within each **version** and create designer objectives 3. Formatively evaluate the findings 4. Develop the learner objectives for each **version** 5. Design learner assessments for each **version** 6. Design the ways that learning-by-doing will be accomplished for each **version** 7. Select media in general for the **version** 8. Formatively evaluate and document the results	1. Identify and sequence **applications of each topic** 2. Identify variations within each **application** and create designer objectives 3. Formatively evaluate the findings 4. Develop the learner objectives for each **topic** 5. Design learner assessments for each **topic** 6. Design the ways that learning-by-doing will be accomplished for each **topic** 7. Select media in general for the **application** 8. Formatively evaluate and document the results
Lower-Level Ch. 7	1. Select and sequence the organizing content for each **version of the task** 2. Select and classify the supporting content for each **version** 3. Sequence the supporting content for each **version** 4. Evaluate and document the findings 5. Identify resource requirements, availability, and existing instruction for each **version** 6. Revise and elaborate the instruction and assessments for each **version** 7. Formatively evaluate the ADE document 8. Begin developing the implementation plan, and update the project management plan	1. Select and sequence the organizing content for each **topic** 2. Select and classify the supporting content for each **topic** 3. Sequence the supporting content for each **topic** 4. Evaluate and document the findings 5. Identify resource requirements, availability, and existing instruction for each **topic** 6. Revise and elaborate the instruction and assessments for each **topic** 7. Formatively evaluate the ADE document 8. Begin developing the implementation plan, and update the project management plan
Ch. 8	Detailed guidance is provided for Lower-Level Step 6: Revise and elaborate the instruction and assessments for each version/topic. It includes instructional strategies for: • Remember information • Understand relationships • Apply skills and higher-order skills • Act on attitudes or values	

Now it is time to add some more detail to this fuzzy vision of your new instructional system. The next chapter (Chapter 6) provides guidance for conducting a mid-level ADE for both task and topic expertise, again based on the major considerations described earlier. Chapters 7 and 8 complete the ADE process with guidance for lower-level ADE. Finally, Develop and Deploy are addressed in Chapters 9–12. The whole ID process is again summarized in Table 5.10.

Exercises

Here again we offer suggestions for a professor using this book as a textbook in a course, to help the students understand more deeply the contents of this chapter. We suggest that you keep the same teams of about three students each to continue to work on their ID projects throughout the course. However, these exercises can be done individually by any reader who wants to deepen their understanding and skills.

1. Have each team prepare a top-level ADE document for their project. Given the intentionally narrow scope of each project, this will likely be a very small ADE document. For what you consider to be the best ADE documents, we suggest you get written permission from the students to use them as examples in the next offering of your course.
2. Have each team offer suggestions for improvement of the ADE document of one or two other teams before you review and provide feedback to the students.
3. Have a whole-class, synchronous discussion of the pros and cons of a top-level ADE process, including any difficulties or challenges they faced during the process and what changes to the process might have helped. You can also have them discuss when top-level ADE is critical or unnecessary. We would love to get your suggestions for improvement.

References

Albanese, M.A., & Mitchell, S. (1993). Problem-based learning: A review of literature on its outcomes and implementation issues. *Academic Medicine, 68*(1), 52–79.

Barrows, H.S. (1986). A taxonomy of problem-based learning methods. *Medical Education, 20*(6), 481–486. doi:10.1111/j.1365-2923.1986.tb01386.x.

Barrows, H.S., & Tamblyn, R.M. (1980). *Problem-based learning: An approach to medical education.* New York, NY: Springer.

Block, J.H. (1971). *Mastery learning: Theory and practice.* New York, NY: Holt, Rinehart and Winston, Inc.

Bloom, B.S. (1968). Learning for mastery. *Evaluation Comment, 1*(1), 1–12.

Bloom, B.S. (1984). The 2 sigma problem: The search for methods of group instruction as effective as one-to-one tutoring. *Educational Researcher, 13*(6), 4–16.

Helms, M.M., & Nixon, J. (2010). Exploring SWOT analysis – where are we now? A review of academic research from the last decade. *Journal of Strategy and Management, 3*(3), 215–251.

Horn, M.B., & Staker, H. (2015). *Blended: Using disruptive innovation to improve schools.* San Francisco, CA: Jossey-Bass.

Jackson, S.E., Joshi, A., & Erhardt, N.L. (2003). Recent research on team and organizational diversity: SWOT analysis and implications. *Journal of Management, 29*(6), 801–830.

Jonassen, D.H. (2011). *Learning to solve problems: A handbook for designing problem-solving learning environments.* New York, NY: Routledge.

Kirschner, P.A., Sweller, J., & Clark, R.E. (2006). Why minimal guidance during instruction does not work: An analysis of the failure of constructivist, discovery, problem-based, experiential, and inquiry-based teaching. *Educational Psychologist, 41*(2), 75–86.

Kulik, C.-L. C., Kulik, J.A., & Bangert-Drowns, R.L. (1990). Effectiveness of mastery learning programs: A meta-analysis. *Review of Educational Research, 60*(2), 265–299. doi:10.3102/00346543060002265.

Piskurich, G.M. (2015). *Rapid instructional design: Learning ID fast and right* (3rd ed.). Hoboken, NJ: John Wiley & Sons, Inc.

Reigeluth, C.M. (2012). Instructional theory and technology for a post-industrial world. In R.A. Reiser & J.V. Dempsey (Eds.), *Trends and issues in instructional design and technology* (3rd ed., pp. 75–83). Boston, MA: Pearson Education.

Reigeluth, C.M., & Karnopp, J.R. (2013). *Reinventing schools: It's time to break the mold.* Lanham, MD: Rowman & Littlefield Publishing Group.

Romiszowski, A.J. (1988). *The selection and use of instructional media: For improved classroom teaching and for interactive, individualized instruction* (2nd ed.). New York, NY: Nichols Publishing.

Savery, J.R. (2009). Problem-based approach to instruction. In C.M. Reigeluth & A.A. Carr-Chellman (Eds.), *Instructional-design theories and models: Building a common knowledge base,* (Vol. III, pp. 143–165). New York, NY: Routledge.

Stufflebeam, D.L. (2003). The CIPP model for evaluation. In D.L. Stufflebeam & T. Kellaghan (Eds.), *International handbook of educational evaluation* (pp. 31–62). Berlin: Springer.

Stufflebeam, D.L., & Zhang, G. (2017). *The CIPP evaluation model: How to evaluate for improvement and accountability.* New York, NY: Guilford Publications.

Tessmer, M., & Richey, R. C. (1997). The role of context in learning and instructional design. *Educational Technology Research and Development, 45*(2), 85–115.

6   Mid-Level Analysis, Design, and Evaluation

Overview

Having identified the big picture about what to teach and how to teach it in your top-level analysis, design, and evaluation (ADE) process (Chapter 5), you have a more creative and meaningful context within which to gather more detailed information about what to teach and how to teach it for each task and/or topic listed. **Mid-level** analysis and design aims to provide the next level of clarity about the vision for each task or topic, including not only a more detailed selection of content and its sequence, but also objectives, assessments, and instructional methods.

Table 6.1 presents a summary of the steps involved in performing the second level of the ADE process. Once more, we note that, although the same steps are performed in both cases (task expertise and topic expertise), there are certain differences in the way some of them should be performed for each. The points of difference are identified in the table and are explained in the following sections of this chapter.

Keep in mind that mid-level ADE processes are not linear processes. You are encouraged to use this model flexibly rather than trying to complete the steps in a linear manner. It may be beneficial to perform some of these steps simultaneously and/or recursively, based on your professional judgment. You may skip the first three steps for some small-scale ID projects. During later steps, you will likely revise the outputs of earlier steps.

Two terms you may not be familiar with in this table are designer objectives and learner objectives. Objectives serve two purposes: to help instructional designers design good instruction (herein called designer objectives) and to help learners learn (herein called learner objectives). Each kind of objective needs different types of information to be most useful. One kind of objective does not fit both purposes. Therefore, we offer guidance for developing both kinds of objectives: designer and learner.

It is also important to keep in mind that on the mid level, you are designing instruction for each individual task or topic. Table 6.2 is a reminder of the levels of content.

1. Identify and Sequence Major Content for Each Task or Topic

This step is done differently for task and topic expertise. If your content has equal amounts of task and topic expertise, you may design a holistic sequence separately for each kind of content, and then merge the two sequences by adjusting each to fit well with the other. If the content is not close to equal amounts, then view the lesser one as supporting content that will be plugged into the sequence of the other (see guidance in Step 3.2, Adjust the Size of the Learning Session, in Chapter 7).

Table 6.1 Mid-Level ADE Process for Task and Topic Expertise

A. Task Expertise	B. Topic Expertise
1A. Identify and sequence versions of each task	**1B. Identify and sequence applications of each topic**
1A.1. Identify simplifying conditions for each task	1B.1. Identify applications of each topic
1A.2. Identify versions of each task	1B.2. Classify each topic as primarily conceptual or theoretical understanding
1A.3. Design a simple-to-complex or branching sequence of versions	1B.3. Design a tentative sequence of applications
2A. Identify variations within each version, and create designer objectives for the version	**2B. Identify variations within each application, and create designer objectives for the application**
2A.1. List all important kinds of variations for each version	2B.1. List all important kinds of variations for each application
2A.2. Categorize the difficulty of each variation	2B.2. Categorize the difficulty of each variation

3. Formatively evaluate the findings
- Review and validate the results of Steps 1 and 2 with experts

4. Develop learner objectives for each version or application
- Develop demonstration objectives (or abstract objectives)

5. Design appropriate kinds of learner assessments for the version or application
- Criterion-referenced vs. norm-referenced assessments
- Performance vs. predictive assessments
- Characteristics of assessments
- Develop assessments

6A. Design the ways learning-by-doing will be accomplished for each version	**6B. Design the ways learning-by-doing will be accomplished for each application**
6A.1. Decide about the project environment and number of projects	6B.1. Design a scenario for each variation of each application
6A.2. Design the scenario for each project	6B.2. Develop details of the application for each scenario
6A.3. Develop details of the project for each scenario	

7. Select media in general for the version or application
- Types of media
- Rules for media selection

8. Formatively evaluate your designs and revise your project management plan
- Formatively evaluate and revise your designs with experts
- Update your project management plan

Table 6.2. Levels of Content

Task Expertise	Topic Expertise
Job	Domain
Duty	Subject
Task	Topic

1A. For Task Expertise: Identify and Sequence Versions of Each Task

This book advocates not only a holistic approach to instructional design and task analysis, but also a holistic instructional sequence. This stands in contrast to the traditional, fragmented, hierarchical sequence pioneered by Robert Gagné. That approach advocates breaking a complex task down into progressively simpler component skills (called prerequisite skills) until you reach the level of skills that learners already possess. Then the instructional sequence works its way up from the simpler components (prerequisites) to progressively broader and more complex components until, finally, at the end of the instruction, the learner gets to learn and perform a complete task. This approach is in direct conflict with schema theory's understanding that meaningful learning is assimilated into a mental model, which provides a meaningful context for what is being learned, and consequently requires a holistic sequence. But prerequisites do exist. So, how can you design a holistic sequence without ignoring the need to teach prerequisites first?

The solution lies in recognizing that all complex tasks have different versions, which range from relatively simple to very complex. For example, the task of driving a car (which we are designating as a unit of instruction) has a variety of versions, including driving with a standard versus automatic transmission, driving in heavy traffic versus no traffic, driving in bad weather versus good weather, and much more (hill starts, parallel parking, and so forth). So, you can begin the sequence of instruction on a task with the simplest real-world version of the task (unless the learner has already mastered it), and restrict the prerequisites to those that are relevant for that simple version (Reigeluth, 1999, 2007). Research has shown that people learn better with such a holistic sequence (Anderson, Osborn, & Tierney, 1984; West & Kellett, 1981; Widmayer, 2004). Furthermore, the versions of a task represent the full range of expertise that should be taught for the task, and different versions have different content that needs to be taught, so analyzing the versions of a task is key to deciding *what to teach* as well as for designing a good instructional sequence. If there is not much variation within the task, then you may only need to teach one or two versions.

1A.1. Identify Simplifying Conditions for Each Task

Work with a task expert to identify the simplest real-world version of the task that is fairly representative of the task as a whole. This is stated as a behavior, together with the conditions that distinguish that version from all other real-world versions (called *simplifying conditions*). Table 6.3 shows an example.

Ask the task expert what conditions call for the task to be performed differently from other versions of the task. (In the lower-level ADE process, the task expert will identify the knowledge that an expert needs to perform each version of the task.)

1A.2. Identify Versions of Each Task

Work with the task expert to identify each of the progressively more complex versions of the task up to the level of complexity required by the instructional need. This is usually done by removing one of the simplifying conditions at a time. Table 6.4 shows an example.

Table 6.3 Example of a Simplest Real-World Version

For the task, "drive a motor vehicle," the simplest real-world version might be "drive a small, automatic-transmission car in good weather with no traffic, a familiar simple route, and no need to parallel park or start up on a hill."

Table 6.4 Example of More Complex Real-World Versions

In the car driving example, more complex versions include: drive on an unfamiliar complex route, drive in bad weather conditions, drive with parallel parking required, starting up on a hill, drive a larger vehicle, drive with a standard transmission and clutch, and all likely combinations of these conditions.

1A.3. Design a Simple-to-Complex or Branching Sequence of Versions

In general, the order in which you identified the versions of the task should be a good simple-to-complex sequence for teaching the versions, because you identified the simpler versions before the more complex versions (Reigeluth, 1992, 1999, 2007; Reigeluth & Rodgers, 1980). However, versions of a complex task are seldom related linearly; they usually have branching relationships whereby several versions could be learned immediately after a given version has been learned. Arranging versions in a branching sequence allows more flexibility (learner control) in the instructional sequence, which is particularly beneficial for online instruction, and takes little additional effort. Table 6.5 shows an example.

The learner could be allowed to choose the sequence of those versions based on her or his interests, or the critical or more difficult versions could be taught first, because once mastered, the learner could be required to occasionally drive under those (previously mastered) conditions while learning to handle each new condition, thereby overlearning those critical or difficult versions.

While you could formatively evaluate your sequence design at this point, it is usually better to do so after you have completed Step 2 (Identify Variations and Create Designer Objectives), because it is more efficient to evaluate the sequence at the same time as the variations and designer objectives.

For rapid prototyping. If you are using a *quantitative approach* to rapid prototyping (see Chapter 4), you only do the above for one task, and then move on through the rest of the ID process, including formative evaluation and revision, before coming back to repeat the process for each additional task. Otherwise, conduct a mid-level analysis for all tasks addressed in your ID project before moving on. In the latter case, you can still do a *qualitative approach* to rapid prototyping.

1B. For Topic Expertise: Identify and Sequence Applications of Each Topic

The following is a description of how to conduct mid-level analysis and design for topic expertise. You may perform some of the steps concurrently and others sequentially.

Topics can be useful to learners in different ways. It is important to identify those different ways for several reasons:

- To motivate learners by showing a topic's usefulness
- To aid transfer to the variety of applications of the topic that the learner may encounter in the real world
- To identify ways to accomplish learning by doing in the instruction (when appropriate)

1B.1. Identify Applications of Each Topic

You already designed the sequence of topics in the top-level ADE process (Chapter 5). Now, for each topic, work with a subject-matter expert (SME) to identify the important ways it

Table 6.5 Example of a Branching Sequence of Real-World Versions

When teaching the task of driving a car, the simplest version of the task entails automatic shift, no traffic, good weather, easy parking, no slippery roads, small car, and no hill starts. Once that version is mastered, the learner could go to the version that has moderate traffic, or the version that has bad weather, or the version that has parallel parking between two cars, or the version that has slippery roads, and so forth. Those additional versions can be taught in any order.

could be used by the learners. Table 6.6 shows two examples. Look at each use critically to determine if it is appropriate, given the educational requirements and big-picture instructional methods. Then decide on the number of applications you will include to develop learner mastery of the topic. Budgetary or time constraints may prevent you from being able to include the number of applications that would ensure mastery across all important situations. However, the projected costs of lack of full mastery should be weighed against such constraints. In many cases, you should find ways to lift those constraints rather than sacrifice needed competence. And if there is little variation among applications, you may only need one or two.

1B.2. Classify Each Topic as Primarily Conceptual or Theoretical Understanding

For each topic, work with an SME to decide if its applications *primarily* entail using *conceptual understanding*, which is a matter of describing concepts (e.g., person, place, or thing) and their kinds or parts, or *theoretical understanding*, which is a matter of using causal or natural-process relationships to make predictions, give explanations, or develop solutions to problems (see Table 6.7 for examples in biology). Theoretical understanding always requires some conceptual understanding, but even a topic that primarily entails conceptual understanding usually has some important theoretical understanding. The bottom line is that you should decide which is most important. For example, a biology course might focus on students learning the classifications of life: domains, kingdoms, phyla, classes, orders, families, genuses, and species – which is a focus on conceptual understanding. Or the course might focus on the five basic principles of biology: cell theory, gene theory, evolution, homeostasis, and laws of thermodynamics, as shown in Table 6.7.

In the rare case that the two kinds of understanding are of fairly equal importance, you can create a sequence for each kind of content, and then adjust each to merge the two into a single hybrid sequence (Beissner & Reigeluth, 1987). This entails looking for places in each sequence where the concepts line up with related principles and adjusting each sequence so that related concepts and principles line up with each other with minimal detriment to the soundness of either sequence.

1B.3. Design a Tentative Sequence of Applications

For each topic, work with an SME to arrange its applications in an easy-to-difficult sequence, preferably a branching sequence to allow for some learner control. This sequence may be modified after you analyze additional (more detailed) content for the topic in the lower-level ADE process.

Table 6.6 Examples of Applications for a Topic

Example 1	*Example 2*
The topic "supply and demand" could be used to make predictions, give explanations, or solve problems related to goods, services, labor, money, or stocks. It could be used to make decisions about when to buy and sell, who to vote for, and what government policies to support or oppose (e.g., increase the minimum wage or not). It could be used in work settings, home settings, and casual conversations with people.	The topic "reinforcement theory" could be used to make predictions, give explanations, or solve problems related to human motivation and behavior, or animal behavior and training. It could be used to make decisions about either increasing or decreasing given behaviors. And it could be used in work settings, home settings, and other personal interactions.

Table 6.7 Examples of Conceptual versus Theoretical Understanding in Biology[a]

Conceptual Understandings	Theoretical Understandings
Kinds of life	Cell theory
• Kinds of plants (botany)	• Energy flow occurs within cells
o Kinds of trees	• Heredity information (DNA) is
o Kinds of mosses	passed on from cell to cell
o Kinds of vines	
o …	Gene theory
	• Gene transmission
• Kinds of animals (zoology)	• Law of segregation
o Kinds of mammals	• Law of independent assortment
o Kinds of fish	
o …	Evolution
	• Natural selection
• Kinds of fungi	• Genetic variation
o Kinds of yeasts	
o Kinds of molds	Homeostasis
o …	• Homeostatic processes (various)
	• Thermodynamics
• Kinds of bacteria (microbiology)	• Laws of thermodynamics in
o …	biological systems
• Kinds of viruses (microbiology)	
o …	

[a] Based on Bailey (2019).

While you could formatively evaluate your sequence design at this point, it is usually better to do so after you have completed Step 2 (Identify Variations and Create Designer Objectives), because it is more efficient to evaluate the sequence at the same time as the variations and designer objectives.

For rapid prototyping. In a *quantitative approach* to rapid prototyping (see Chapter 4, Section 5), only do this for one topic (or even just one subtopic, depending on scope), and move on with that one topic through formative evaluation and revision before coming back to repeat the process for each additional topic. Otherwise, conduct a mid-level analysis for all topics addressed in your ID project before moving on. In the latter case, you can still do a *qualitative approach* to rapid prototyping.

2. Identify Variations and Create Designer Objectives

There are often variations in the way a version of a complex task is performed and in the way an application of a topic can be used. It is helpful to make design decisions about such variations now because they provide a map that will guide design decisions on the lower level (see Chapters 7 and 8). Similarly, it is helpful to create designer objectives at this point, for the same reason. The guidance here is different for task and topic expertise.

2A. For Task Expertise: Identify Variations within Each Version of a Task, and Create Designer Objectives for the Version

For complex tasks (e.g., driving a motor vehicle), not only are there different versions (e.g., driving with an automatic versus standard gear shift), but there are also many variations in the way a single version is performed. There may be variations in the *behavior* (e.g., passing other vehicles, merging into traffic), variations in the *conditions* of performance (including contextual factors, environmental factors, tools and other resources – e.g., bad weather may be rainy, icy, windy, sun in your face), and variations in *standards* (e.g., arrive as quickly as possible, drive as safely as possible, make the ride as smooth as possible).

2A.1. List All Important Kinds of Variations for Each Version

You must use your judgment to decide which variations are important to include in the instruction. Later, the variations you select will be designed into authentic scenarios for the demonstrations and practice, to enable the learner to master all those kinds of variations. Small variations may not require instruction on each. (See Table 6.8 for examples of variations and Table 6.9 for an example of a scenario.)

2A.2. Categorize the Difficulty of Each Variation

Categorize the difficulty of each variation in relation to the others, using a scale of 1 (easy) to 5 (difficult) (see Table 6.10 for an example). This will allow you to design an easy-to-difficult sequence of those variations later. If the version is easy, all the variations are likely easy. If the version is difficult, there should be variations on all five levels of difficulty. Combinations of the variations indicate the types of real-world *scenarios* that the learner might encounter after the training. See the guidance and example presented in Table 6.11.

This concludes the process of creating a designer objective for a version of the task, but it is in the form of a table instead of a sentence (see Table 6.10 for an example). Its purpose

Table 6.8 Examples of Variations for a Version of the Task

Version: Driving a Standard Shift Vehicle in Light Traffic and Bad Weather	
Variations	*Examples*
Variations in Behaviors	Passing, merging, parallel parking
Variations in Conditions — Contextual factors	Familiarity of the route, complexity of the route, bumpiness of the road, curviness of the road
Environmental factors	Weather: amount of rain, amount of snow, iciness, strength of sun in face
	Distractions: noise inside and outside the car, doing other things while driving
Tools and other resources	Size of the vehicle: small car, large car, small truck, 18-wheeler
	Trailer: yes or no
	Transmission: number of gears, with or without synchromesh
	GPS: yes or no
Variations in Standards	Arrive as quickly as possible versus drive as safely as possible or make the ride as smooth as possible

Table 6.9 Example of an Authentic Scenario

One scenario for the version of driving shown in Table 6.7 (standard shift, light traffic, bad weather) could be: safety is most important; route and destination are familiar; light snow; quiet inside and outside the car; five-speed shift with synchromesh; large car.

Table 6.10 Example of a Designer Objective Showing Difficulty Categorization for Variations of a Version of the Task

Version: Driving a Standard Shift Vehicle in Light Traffic and Bad Weather		
Variations	Factors	Difficulty (1–5)
Variations in Behaviors	Passing	3
	Merging	3
	Parallel parking	5
	Hill start	3–5
Variations in Conditions Contextual factors	Familiarity of the route	1–5
	Complexity of the route	1–5
	Bumpiness of the road	1
	Curviness of the road	1
Environmental factors	Weather:	
	Amount of rain	1–5
	Amount of snow	3–5
	Iciness	5
	Strength of sun in face	3–5
	Distractions:	
	Noise inside and outside the car	1–3
	Doing other things while driving	3–5
Tools and other resources	Size of the vehicle:	
	Small car	1
	Large car	3
	Small truck	3
	18-wheeler truck	5
	Trailer:	
	Yes	5
	No	1
	Transmission:	
	More gears	3
	Without synchromesh	5
	GPS:	
	Yes	1
	No	3
Variations in Standards	Arrive as quickly as possible	3–5
	Drive as safely as possible	1
	Make ride as smooth as possible	3

is to document information that will be helpful to you to design the learner objectives, assessments, and instruction (including authentic projects) for the module. It is not to be presented to the learners, but it is useful for creating the learner objectives later.

2B. For Topic Expertise: Identify Variations within Each Application, and Create Designer Objectives for the Application

2B.1. List All the Important Kinds of Variations for Each Application

Based on the variety of ways the topic could be useful to the learner in the future (analyzed in Step 1), now you should make a list of the different types of situations or contexts in which the topic might be used. During this process, decide on the number of applications

Table 6.11 Designer Objectives: Behaviors, Conditions, and Standards

	Guidance	*Example*
Behaviors	The learner behaviors state what the learners will need to be able to do on the job for this version of the task. Be sure to capture variations in the behavior within the version of the task (for all the conditions). Use action verbs and ensure the capability is observable, measurable, reliable, and verifiable.	• Drive a car • Park a car
Conditions	The conditions identify the simplifying conditions that distinguish this version of the task from other versions, but also the conditions that create variations *within* this version of the task, such as contextual factors, objects, events, human behaviors, words, and/or symbols that are present in the real world for this version of the task. Be sure to list all the ways the conditions can vary for this version of the task. Conditions might include the following: • Is the learner allowed to use a checklist or other job aid? • What kinds of tools/test equipment should the learner be able to use? • What environmental conditions should the learner be able to deal with? • May learners ask questions while performing the learned capability?	• A small car • Good weather • No traffic • A familiar simple route • No need to parallel park • No hill starts
Standards	The standards of performance define the criteria for acceptable performance of this version of the task by the learner. They are stated in such terms as completeness, accuracy requirements, time constraints, performance rates, or qualitative requirements. They identify the measure of proficiency the learners should achieve when they perform the behavior under the specified conditions. The learner's performance results in an output, the quantity or quality of which is compared to the standard of performance. The standards should be the same as those specified for on-the-job performance unless there is a valid reason for setting a different standard.	• No accidents • No close calls (for accidents) • No traffic violations • Smooth clutch work • No grinding of gears

to include in your instruction, which depends on the amount of variation in ways the topic can be applied that are important to the target learners. These are based primarily on variations in *behaviors* for applying topics in the *conditions* under which the topic may be used in the real world. *Standards* of performance could also vary from one application to another. See Table 6.12 for an example.

2B.2. Categorize the Difficulty of Each Variation

Categorize the difficulty of each variation in relation to the others, using a scale of 1 (easy) to 5 (difficult) (see Table 6.13 for an example). This will allow you to design an easy-to-difficult sequence of those variations later. If the topic is easy, all the variations are likely easy. If the topic is difficult, there should be variations on all levels of difficulty. Combinations of the variations indicate the types of real-world *scenarios* that the learner might encounter after the training.

Table 6.12 Example of Important Variations for an Application

For the following application of the topic "supply and demand":
- Make predictions related to proposed government policies

The important variations might include:
- Different kinds of purchasable things addressed by a policy
  - o Goods
  - o Services
  - o Stocks
  - o Money
- Different kinds of policies
  - o Ones related to controlling the price (e.g., increasing the minimum wage)
  - o Ones related to increasing or decreasing the supply (e.g., reducing subsidies to oil producers)
  - o Ones related to increasing or decreasing the demand (e.g., increasing the gasoline tax)
- Different kinds of performances
  - o Deciding how to vote for a candidate or referendum
  - o Convincing a friend to take a position regarding the policy
  - o Discussing the pros and cons of a policy in polite conversation

Table 6.13 Example of a Designer Objective Showing Difficulty Categorization for Variations of an Application

For the variations shown in Table 6.12	*Difficulty*
• Different kinds of purchasable things addressed by a policy	
o Goods	1
o Services	4
o Stocks	3
o Money	5
• Different kinds of policies	
o Ones related to controlling the price	3
o Ones related to increasing or decreasing the supply	4
o Ones related to increasing or decreasing the demand	4
• Different kinds of performances	
o Deciding how to vote for a candidate or referendum	3
o Convincing a friend to take a position regarding the policy	5
o Discussing the pros and cons of a policy in polite conversation	4

Guidelines for developing designer objectives are shown in Table 6.14, along with an example. They constitute the process for creating the designer objective for an application. This kind of objective is not to be presented to the learners. It is intended to guide the instructional designer and will be the foundation for developing the learner objectives, assessments, and instruction (including authentic applications) for each topic. However, it is in the form of a table instead of a sentence (see Table 6.15 for an example and Table 6.24 for a blank template). The form includes a place to indicate whether the topic entails primarily conceptual or theoretical understanding or an equal combination of the two.

Since topics are typically described at different levels of detail (topics, subtopics, subsubtopics), we recommend developing **designer objectives for each level** at which learner assessment will occur. Further, we propose that assessment should always occur at the lowest level, to ensure mastery of all important knowledge and skills. Then, assessment

Table 6.14 Guidelines and Example for Creating Designer Objectives

	Guidelines	*Example for Law of Supply & Demand*
Conditions	The conditions are the range of situations under which each understanding is expected to be used by the learner in the real world.	• A change in the price of a good, service, labor, money, stock, or rent • Information about changes in supply and/or demand
Behaviors	• For concepts: state the dimensions of understanding needed. • For natural-process principles: state the nature of the descriptions needed. • For causal principles: state the nature of the predictions, explanations and/or problem solving needed. • The statements should take a form that aids in developing assessments.	• Explain why the price changed
Standards	These define the criteria for mastery of the topic. The standards should be the same as those needed in the real world.	• Correct on 10 performances in a row
Assessment Instruments	A description of the way in which mastery of the topic will be measured.	• A narrative about the changes, and a short short-answer response

Table 6.15 Form for Listing Designer Objectives for Each Topic

Mid-Level ADE Document for Topic Expertise		
Name of Topic: Law of supply & demand	x	
Number of Applications: 3	□ Conceptual □ Theoretical □ Hybrid	
List of Applications: A. Explain the causes of changes in prices, B. Explain the causes of changes in supply, C. Explain the causes of changes in demand.		
Sequence of Applications: A followed by either B or C		
Name of Application 1: A. Explain causes of changes in prices		
Variations Conditions	*Factors*	*Difficulty (1–5)*
Given …	• A change in the price of a good, service, labor, stock, rent, or money	(Listed in order from 1–5)
	• Information available about changes in supply and/or demand	Both are 3
Behaviors The learner will …	• Explain based on supply as a causal factor	3
	• Explain based on demand as a causal factor	3
Standards To this standard …	Correct on 10 performances in a row	
Learner Assessment As measured by …	A narrative about the changes, and a short-answer response	

at any higher levels, as needed, ensures that learners can combine their lower-level knowledge and skills effectively.

It is helpful to **categorize applications by difficulty** (perhaps on a scale of 1–5) so you can later provide the appropriate level of difficulty to each learner.

3. Formatively Evaluate the Findings

This guidance is the same for both task and topic expertise.

Your formative evaluation still cannot involve tryouts with learners because the design decisions are still too general, so among the options described in Chapter 10 (Formative Evaluation), you should conduct an **expert review** of the results of Steps 1 and 2 with both content experts and, especially for large projects, instructional experts (preferably people who are experts in both the content and teaching it to your target learners) by means of a walk-through exercise. Review and evaluate the sequence (from Step 1) and the variations and designer objectives (from Step 2) with the SMEs to enhance appropriateness, accuracy, effectiveness, and appeal. Also, get input from the experts on what changes they think would likely improve the content and design, and either make revisions during the walk-through exercise, or as soon as possible after it. Refer to your evaluation plan for the project and Chapter 10 for guidance.

Also, for a *quantitative approach* to **rapid prototyping** (described in Chapter 4), when the above is done for the one version of the task or one topic (or even just one subtopic, depending on scope), proceed to the next step. Otherwise, perform this step for all the tasks and topics, and then proceed.

4. Develop Learner Objectives for Each Version or Application

You have already created the designer objectives. Now you can use those to create the objectives that are to be presented to the learners, if you think they would be helpful to the learners at this mid level of the ADE process. Learner objectives can be designed for the full range of scopes of the instruction, from a single comprehensive objective for an entire course, to an objective for each of the hundreds of individual facts, skills, understandings, and attitudes in the course (discussed in Chapter 8). At this mid level of design, you should only design the objectives for whole tasks and versions or whole topics and applications. In lower-level design (Chapters 7 and 8), you will address smaller units of content. At this mid level of design, learner objectives will primarily address learners' ability to combine the smaller bits of content into broader performances of tasks or applications of topics. You should decide whether you think learner objectives are helpful on all four scopes – duty or subject, task or topic, version or application, and single fact, skill, understanding, or attitude – but formative evaluation can help you make this determination in your ID project.

Learner objectives, which are often called instructional objectives, should communicate what *learners* will be able to do upon completion of the instruction (intended outcomes). They should not state what the *instruction* or instructor will do. For example, "to provide practice opportunities" is a description of the instructional process, not a learner objective.

There are two basic forms of learner objectives: those that describe the desired performance, which are *abstract*, and those that demonstrate it, which are *concrete*. Research shows that **abstract objectives** are often not helpful to learning, primarily because they are usually difficult for learners to make sense of. Research has shown that a concrete **demonstration objective**, initially called a "work model" (Bunderson, Gibbons, Olsen, & Kearsley, 1981), is most useful. It entails demonstrating a prototypical performance (a concrete example), usually through a video or live demonstration. Table 6.16 shows examples of both kinds of objectives.

The demonstration objective is a **performance-based** objective that aligns well with performance-based instruction and performance-based assessments. For well-designed instruction, learner objectives serve only to orient the learners to what they should learn,

Table 6.16 Examples of Abstract and Demonstration Objectives for Learners

Abstract Objective	Demonstration Objective
The learner will be able to drive a car in city traffic without an accident	A video of a person driving a car safely in city traffic

Table 6.17 Kinds of Learner Objectives for the Two Major Kinds of Instruction

Learner-Centered Instruction (LCI)*	Teacher-Centered Instruction**
For LCI, you should develop *demonstration objectives*, rather than *abstract objectives*. However, it is also sometimes helpful to tell the learners a few of the most common ways the conditions may vary and the criteria for judging successful performance (standards). In some cases, it may not be feasible or cost-effective to create demonstration objectives, in which case you may choose to create abstract ones. For example, unobservable performances cannot be demonstrated.	If you decided to use this approach, you should still use demonstration objectives if you can, but you may need to resort to abstract objectives. If abstract, they should be designed to not overwhelm the learner with a lot of information to remember. It is not very helpful to say a lot about conditions and standards. Abstract objectives are most effective to the extent that they relate what is to be learned to what the learner already knows. Sometimes it is sufficient to just state the goal, perhaps with one or two conditions and standards. Other times it is also helpful to describe the behaviors or actions the learner will be able to perform to achieve the goal (learned capabilities). All of these were identified in the designer objectives, so now you only need to carefully choose the components that will most concisely aid learning.

* Learner-centered instruction is personalized, self-directed, and self-paced.
** Teacher-centered instruction is standardized, teacher-directed, and group paced.

so you should not provide a lot of details about conditions and standards (Hartley & Davies, 1976). Those details are useful for the designer, but not for orienting the learner.

The nature of the learner objective is usually different for learner-centered than for teacher-centered instruction because performance is typically de-emphasized in the latter (see Table 6.17).

To develop a **demonstration objective**, select a prototypical (simple, common, representative, and real-world) way in which the objective can be demonstrated (from Step 2, Identify Variations and Create Designer Objectives), decide whether the demonstration will be live, video, or descriptive (e.g., a very short story), and identify exactly what will be demonstrated (Bunderson et al., 1981). For unobservable skills, a story that reveals the thinking and decision-making process of the performer can approximate a demonstration objective, but that may not always be sufficiently advantageous compared to an abstract objective. Sometimes it is helpful to tell the learners a few of the most common ways the conditions may vary and the criteria for judging successful performance (standards). For more guidance about this, see the guidance for designing demonstrations in Chapter 8, Instructing.

For an **abstract objective**, you may use up to three parts: the behavior (learned capability), the range of conditions for performance, and the standards the performance should meet (Mager, 1975) – three of the four elements in the designer objective. It is not always helpful to tell the learners what the conditions and standards are. It is recommended to use measurable verbs for abstract objectives (Mager, 1975). The categories of learning

Table 6.18 Measurable Verbs Aligned to the Categories of Learning

Memorize Information	Understand Relationships	Apply Skills	Apply Higher-Order Skills		
Choose	Classify	Apply	Analyze	Argue	Build
Define	Compare	Use	Attribute	Assess	Change
Identify	Describe	Develop	Break down	Check	Compose
Label	Discuss	Show	Categorize	Criticize	Construct
List	Exemplify	Execute	Classify	Critique	Create
Match	Explain	Implement	Compare	Evaluate	Design
Name	Illustrate	Organize	Contrast	Judge	Develop
Recall	Infer	Solve	Differentiate	Prioritize	Formulate
Recognize	Interpret	Prepare	Distinguish	Prove	Generate
Select	Summarize	Modify	Examine	Rank	Invent
Show			Relate	Rate	Plan
Tell				Support	Produce

described in Chapter 3 (memorize information, understand relationships, apply skills, apply higher-order skills, and act on attitudes and values) can be useful for writing measurable objectives. You can use the SMART acronym to aid in evaluating your abstract learner objectives: ensure that they are Specific, Measurable, Achievable, Relevant, and Timely. Table 6.18 provides a list of measurable verbs aligned to the categories of learning.

You could conduct formative evaluation (described in Step 8) of Step 4 now, but it is more efficient to evaluate learner objectives and assessments at the same time.

For a *quantitative approach* to **rapid prototyping** (described in Chapter 4), when the above is done for the one version of the task or one topic (or even just one subtopic, depending on scope), proceed to the next step. Otherwise, perform this step for all the tasks and topics, and then proceed.

5. Design Appropriate Kinds of Learner Assessments for the Version or Application

Criterion-Referenced vs. Norm-Referenced Assessments

There are two basic types of assessments: criterion-referenced and norm-referenced. A criterion-referenced assessment compares learner performance to a predefined standard (criterion) as identified in your designer objective (Cronbach, 1970; Shrock & Coscarelli, 2007). A norm-referenced assessment is designed to yield scores that compare each learner's performance with that of a group (a norm established by performances of all the learners). Norm-referenced assessments are used for selection rather than to ensure mastery. There are some situations where selection (norm-referenced assessment) is appropriate (e.g., training for the Navy Seals), but criterion-referenced assessment is usually more appropriate, since learning is typically more important than sorting learners, as is the case with driving a car.

As with learner objectives, assessments can be designed for the full range of scopes of the instruction, from a single comprehensive assessment for an entire course, to an assessment for each of the hundreds of individual facts, skills, understandings, and attitudes in the course. At this point, you should only design the assessments for **whole tasks and versions** or **whole topics and applications**. In lower-level design (Chapters 7 and 8), you will address smaller units of content. At this mid level of design, you will primarily assess learners' ability to combine the smaller bits of content into broader performances of tasks and applications of topics. Try not to duplicate assessments you will design on the lower level. You may find it helpful, when you are designing the lower-level assessments, to return to these mid-level assessments and adjust them as needed to be comprehensive yet not duplicate the lower-level ones. Also, keep in mind that mid-level assessments can be used for placement purposes in many contexts.

Performance vs. Predictive Assessments

A criterion-referenced assessment typically needs to be different for learner-centered instruction than for teacher-centered instruction. For learner-centered instruction they are usually *performance assessments*, whereas for teacher-centered instruction they are typically *predictive assessments*. However, they sometimes can, and whenever possible should, be performance assessments.

A **performance assessment** is one in which the learner actually does a performance that demonstrates the learner's level of skill or understanding of the issue. The behavior, conditions, and standards should all match those in the real world (as closely as possible), which should be reflected in the designer objective. Many versions of a task involve many different ways of performing the task that ought to be assessed, and many applications of a topic involve many different variations that should be assessed in one or more integrated performances. To best prepare learners for the assessment, practice events should be interchangeable with the performance assessment events (but not repeated in them, for then the learner would only need to remember the practice event being repeated). In fact, it is good to *fully integrate* the assessment with the practice by requiring the learner to perform a certain number of practice events correctly in a row, unaided. The criterion for the number of correct responses in a row should increase as the scope of the task or topic increases (e.g., a small scope might warrant only, say, four correct responses in a row, whereas a large scope might warrant, say, 12 correct responses in a row. For example, assessment for driving a car should include assessments for different sized cars, kinds of transmissions, weather conditions, traffic conditions, kinds of intersections, parking requirements, hill starts, and so forth. Performance assessments must have *content validity*, which is consistency between the assessment and the nature of the performances needed in the real world. This is true in both performance and predictive assessments. Learner objectives and assessments should be consistent with the designer objectives, which should be consistent with the real-world requirements.

Predictive assessments are used when performance assessments are too time consuming or expensive or if it is difficult for a performance to adequately measure mastery of the full breadth of the skills (for a task) or understandings (for a topic). A predictive assessment tests *part* of the content represented by the understandings or skills, and from that it makes a prediction as to whether the learner has mastered the understandings or skills. For example, if a learner could describe the law of supply and demand, there is a better probability that the learner could actually apply that understanding in real-world situations than a learner who could not describe it. Assessments that do not test the actual application of the understandings or skills are valid only to the extent that they accurately predict learner application of the understandings or skills in the real world. For more on predictive validity, see Cronbach & Meehl (1955).

Characteristics of Assessments

There are several characteristics to be considered when developing assessments. These characteristics ensure that the assessments measure what is intended each time they

Table 6.19 Characteristics of Assessments

Characteristic	Definition
Validity (Note: different experts categorize validity somewhat differently)	**Construct validity** – degree to which the assessment measures the content (information, understanding, skill, or attribute) it is intended to measure.
	Content validity – degree to which the assessment measures *all* the content it is intended to measure.
	Criterion-related validity – degree to which the assessment can accurately predict specific criterion variables. It includes **concurrent validity**, which involves assessments administered at the same time, and **predictive validity**, which measures the degree to which the assessment predicts the target performance(s).
	Face validity – degree to which an expert believes the assessment serves its purposes well.
Reliability	Degree to which the assessment yields the same results consistently:
	Test-retest – consistency across two administrations to the same learners.
	Split-halves – consistency across two forms of the same assessment.
Usability	**Assessments** that are easy to administer, score, and interpret and for the learner to take.

are administered. The same applies to practice items. The characteristics are shown in Table 6.19.

Develop Assessments

For guidance on how to develop an assessment (Cohen & Wollack, 2013; Mager, 1997) for each version of the task or each topic, see Table 6.20. When you have finished developing an assessment for the version or application (for a quantitative approach to rapid prototyping) or for all versions and applications (in all other cases), proceed to the next step.

You could conduct formative evaluation (described in Step 8) of Steps 4 and 5 now, but it is more efficient to evaluate learner objectives, assessments, and instruction at the same time.

6. Design the Ways That Learning by Doing Will Be Accomplished

Based on the results of Steps 1–5, you should revise and elaborate your high-level instructional methods from Step 2 in Chapter 5. Additionally, you should design the ways learning by doing will be accomplished (the nature of the projects for task expertise and of applications for topic expertise). Refer to Chapter 4 for information about various learning-by-doing approaches.

6A. For Task Expertise: Design the Ways Learning by Doing Will Be Accomplished for Each Version

You should holistically design the project(s)[1] for each version.

6A.1. Decide about the Project Environment and Number of Projects

Decide what the project environment will be like in general (e.g., real, staged, simulated, or narrated) and whether or not learners will be organized into teams. Regarding **the project**

---

1   Please keep in mind that we use the term "projects" to refer to all cases of learning by doing, such as problems, tasks, inquiries, and applications.

Table 6.20 How to Develop an Assessment for a Whole Version or Topic

For Learner-Centered Instruction*	*For Teacher-Centered Instruction***
Assessments are most effective at measuring learning when they are *performance-based*, meaning that they assess performance of authentic versions of the task. Therefore, the assessment for a version should be similar to the demonstration objective, except that the learner has to *do* it for multiple diverse cases instead of being shown how to do it for just one case or one kind of case. If feasible for your instructional situation (sometimes it is too expensive or time consuming for the extra benefit), develop a performance-based assessment that assesses mastery of the full range of variations in the task – that samples all the equivalence classes – or full range of uses for a topic. Note that the assessment does not have to be separate from the instruction – it could merely require that the learner perform (practice) unaided successfully for a certain number of performances in a row, much like unlocking the next level in a computer game.	Whenever feasible, use performance-based assessment (see Learner-Centered Instruction column). If not feasible, develop a predictive assessment that comes as close to this ideal as possible. For example, you can still present a scenario for a particular performance situation and ask the learners to state how they would perform that version of the task or accomplish that application of the topic. You could even give a multiple-choice test in which they need to select the way they would perform the version or accomplish the application for each part of the process in that scenario. However, there are disadvantages of multiple-choice assessments. Foremost is that the learner performance in such an assessment is seldom an authentic performance (consistent with the real-world performance). This makes it more difficult to assess true expertise. Multiple-choice also typically has a 25% chance that the learner will get it right by luck.

* Learner-centered instruction is personalized, self-directed, and self-paced.
** Teacher-centered instruction is standardized, teacher-directed, and group-paced.

environment, the context in which something is learned influences not only what is learned, but also how well it can be used (transferred) in the future. Learning is situated in the context and gains meaning from that context. If a task is learned in an authentic context, it will be easier to perform in that kind of context. If the version is very complex, the learning load can be eased by removing contextual complexity, but, by the end of the instruction (if not sooner), the project environment should be highly similar to the real-world environment. Regarding **teams**, they should be used when the real-world project involves a team, but also when the interaction among learners can supply learning support through tutoring and feedback. For example, peer tutoring can be very effective and cost-effective for improving learning. Furthermore, collaboration increases motivation for most learners. However, with teams, you must ensure that each individual has mastered the task, not just the team as a whole.

Also, decide **how many projects** are needed for learners to master this version of the task. The number of projects depends on how much variation exists within the version. It is important to make sure the learners can generalize across the variations that will be encountered in the real world. However, sometimes budgetary or time constraints prevent you from being able to include the number of projects that would ensure mastery across all variations. The projected costs of lack of full mastery should be weighed against such constraints. In many cases, you should find ways to lift those constraints rather than sacrifice needed competence.

6A.2. Design the Scenario for Each Project

Use the information from Step 2 above (on the variations you identified in the real-world task) to design the scenarios for (or nature of) easy, medium, and difficult authentic

Table 6.21 Example of a Scenario for Application of a Topic

One of the applications for supply and demand is to make decisions about economic policies for you to support or oppose. One scenario could be to explore the pros and cons of increasing the minimum wage: predict what effects it would have on unemployment – the number of jobs available (supplied) compared to the number of people seeking jobs (demand).

projects for this version of the task (see Table 6.21 for an example). Keep in mind that, although objectives can be classified from easy to difficult, here we are talking about the difficulty of each project within a single (fairly large) objective. If the objective is easy, all the projects will likely be easy. If the objective is difficult, there should be projects on all three levels of difficulty.

A scenario should include the goals of the version of the task, an authentic cover story, the players and their authentic roles, the scenario operations (activities the learners do) and their consequences, the resources (e.g., information, tools, and other resources that are available in the real-world task environment), and any other relevant conditions (e.g., opponents, obstacles, allies, etc.) (Schank, Berman, & Macpherson, 1999; Schank, Fano, Jona, & Bell, 1993).

6A.3. Develop Details of the Project for Each Scenario

Finally, design the remaining details for each project (e.g., tools, resources, instructions, simulations, roles, narratives), keeping in mind your latest designs for the instruction. Try to replicate feedback that would occur in the real-world environment (consequences or effects that naturally result from the learner's actions), but include other kinds of feedback when useful. (See Chapter 8 for more guidance about feedback.)

You could conduct formative evaluation (described in Step 8) of Steps 4–6 now, but you may find it helpful to evaluate learner instruction and media at the same time.

6B. For Topic Expertise: Design the Ways Learning by Doing Will Be Accomplished for Each Application

6B.1. Design a Scenario for Each Variation of Each Application

Design a scenario for each variation (see Table 6.21 for an example), as a meaningful context for the instruction and assessments on the topic. A scenario should include the goals of the application of the topic, an authentic cover story, the players and their authentic roles, the scenario operations (activities the learners do) and their consequences, the resources (e.g., information, tools, and other resources that are available in the real-world task environment), and any other relevant conditions (e.g., opponents, obstacles, allies, etc.) (Schank et al., 1999; Schank et al., 1993).

6B.2. Develop Details of the Scenario for each Variation

For each scenario, develop details (e.g., characters, activities, tools, resources, instructions, simulations, roles, narratives), keeping in mind your latest designs for the instruction. Try to replicate feedback that would occur in the real-world environment (consequences or effects that naturally result from the learner's actions) but include other kinds of feedback when useful. (See Chapter 8 for more guidance about feedback.) Scenarios could be presented in various formats, including text, text and images, animations, and videos with actors. Both authentic and fantasy contexts could be used for scenarios, as long as the nature of the performances is authentic. Think about how your scenarios will be presented to learners while developing details.

You could conduct formative evaluation (described in Step 8) of Steps 4–6 now, but you may find it helpful to evaluate learner instruction and media at the same time.

7. Select Media in General for the Version or Application

On the top level of design, you tentatively selected delivery method(s) and identified media options based on constraints and preferences (selection by rejection and selection by optimization). Given the information and design decisions you have made on this mid level of design, you may wish to modify and tailor your earlier decisions, and you should now consider the best media mix for each version of each task or each application of each topic, taking into account the *types of media* available and *five rules* for media selection, described next.

Types of Media

No single medium is the most appropriate choice for every instructional situation. Selecting the appropriate media ensures that the instruction is provided by the most cost-effective and appealing means possible. This mid-level design activity can be done for each part of the instruction (each variation of a version or application) as you design the ways that learning by doing will be done (in Step 6), rather than waiting until it has all been designed. Be sure to take into consideration the constraints and preferences that you identified in the top-level instructional design (Chapter 5), but in some cases you may want to try to remove one or more of the constraints you identified. For example, you may advocate with your client to increase the budget for more expensive media that you believe will be worth the extra investment.

Many different types of media exist for instruction. Examples of human media range from the classroom instructor, to teaching assistants, peer tutors, and on-the-job coaches; and examples of nonhuman media include study guides, books, hands-on materials, networked computers, mobile devices, and much more. Some of the most common types are shown in Table 6.22. (Note: if copyrighted media are selected, get copyright permission.)

Printed text. This is the most abstract and consequently often the least effective – but also least expensive – medium. To gain meaning from printed text, the learner must be able to read (that is, decode words and comprehend what is written). Learning is more difficult because physical cues are absent. The learner cannot query the author when there is ambiguity in the message. But most significantly, the learner seldom can learn by doing, and when the learner is instructed to do some practice, it is rarely an authentic performance and any feedback provided is rudimentary.

Pictures and text. The addition of still pictures and diagrams to printed text makes the instruction more concrete and consequently more effective but also more expensive. In order to understand text, one often needs to look at a picture or diagram of objects, procedures, processes, or relationships, but the text also helps one to understand the picture or diagram.

Video. Video – in all its various formats, including animations like "explainer videos" – is important when motion is involved, as in the performance of a skill and the observation

Table 6.22 Types of Instructional Media

Media Type	Representative Examples	Advantages	Disadvantages
Humans	Instructors Teaching assistants Fellow learners Experts	Flexible, adaptable to the learner Appeal to learners who like the personal touch Can be role models	Can be expensive May not be engaging
Classroom Aids	Slides Blackboards Whiteboards Overhead projectors Video projectors	Can offer additional affordances, such as visuals and motion, that can increase attention, learning, and emotional impact for learners	Are outdated Require additional equipment, complex setup, and careful coordination during planning, preparation, and use Equipment and production costs are higher Are not interactive
Digital Media	Computers and mobile devices Video (e.g., TV, DVDs) Audio (e.g., radio, podcasts, streaming audio) Interactive white boards Internet Social networks Simulators VR/AR	Present text information, graphic images, streaming videos Interact with learners on individual basis through asking questions and judging responses Maintain record of responses Adapt instruction to needs of learner Control other media hardware Can interface computer and video for learner-controlled programs	Require computers, digital tablets, or smartphones Require essential hardware and software for development and use Incompatibility of hardware and software among various systems
Paper Media	Books Journals Workbooks Worksheets	Include common types of materials Wide variety of applications Simple types are quick to prepare	Sophisticated types are more costly to prepare Require suitable reading ability Are not interactive or dynamic
Hands-On Materials and Authentic Experiences	Equipment or materials Mock-ups Simulators	Provide a greater level of realism and motivation	Can be expensive and difficult to obtain Logistics of use can be a problem

of causal dynamics. It can also better capture emotional aspects of a situation. However, video generally has a linear format, delivery is often at a fixed pace, and it is more expensive to produce than pictures and text. It also removes cues that are available from handling the real equipment. But it can be edited to compress time in a demonstration, and it is typically less expensive than interactive media.

Interactive media. Interactive media (often called multimedia, but some multimedia are not interactive) offer all the benefits of the above media, but they add interactivity. They can register learner performances or responses and judge whether they are correct and even determine the nature of the error or misconception to provide customized feedback to the learner. Other benefits include the capability to pause or "rewind" a demonstration and to retry part of a performance. This choice is more expensive to develop, but it can be less expensive than live instruction and performances with physical objects if a lot of learners will be using the instruction. It can also be less expensive if the objects are very expensive (like airplanes), and it is safer if the performance is hazardous. Immersive technologies – such as virtual reality (VR), augmented reality (AR), and 360 video – make learning more immersive, authentic, interactive, engaging, and personalized. For example, VR allows learners to explore new worlds and new identities otherwise inaccessible to them. And AI-powered chatbots provide powerful ways of enhancing learning. Interactive media also make interaction and collaboration among learners possible.

Physical objects. Situations that involve physical objects are the most concrete and easy to understand because they don't require the translation of symbols. When instruction is done with real objects, all the cues for later performance are typically available. Real objects can be used by instructors in demonstrations to a group of learners, but the learner cannot pause or rewind that demonstration. Physical objects can also be used by the learner to manipulate (practice). Through handling them, the learner gains much information about their size, texture, sturdiness, complexity, and other features, which adds important elements to the learner's schema for the task and aids transfer to real-world situations. However, situations with real objects may be very complex or hazardous, and it may be safer and less expensive to use a simplification in the form of a mock-up or simulation.

Experts. In many situations the most effective medium is an expert, typically working one-on-one with the learner on real problems in a real situation. For example, if the skill to be learned was predicting the effects of changes in educational policy, the ideal situation would seem to be to pair a novice with an expert and have the expert explain the considerations while the novice engages in that exercise, as is typically done in on-the-job training. In such a case, the expert should provide all the appropriate instructional strategies. However, there are some situations in which this is not as efficient or effective as interactive media that allow compression of time, greater safety, opportunity to pause and rewind a demonstration, and opportunity to repeat parts of a task or application of a topic in a simulator (e.g., landings in an airplane or predictions about the effects of changes in prices of goods).

Rules for Media Selection

On the top level, you addressed such constraints as affordability, availability, cost-effectiveness, administrative feasibility, and practical feasibility. You also addressed what might be ideal for the content, instructional methods, learners, and teachers. Given the additional information you now have about both content and instructional methods, you should revisit those media selection decisions and tailor them to your instructional designs for each individual version or topic. We offer the following five rules for such tailoring, adapted from Romiszowski (1988). The first two have to do with media characteristics or **affordances** that make media either suitable or unsuitable for particular instructional situations.

1. Sensory Channel

Use the most appropriate sensory channels for communicating the information to be learned. For example, use audio for music appreciation and video (motion visuals) for bicycle repair.

2. *Performance and Feedback Capabilities*

Given that you expect a certain performance from the learner after the instruction, you should use a medium that provides opportunities to practice that behavior during instruction (e.g., hands-on materials for bicycle repair), with a medium that can assess the quality of the learner response and provide helpful feedback. The **fidelity** of the performance situation to the real-world situation should take learner experience into consideration. It is generally better to begin teaching a novice in a low-fidelity situation, so that the amount of information and "noise" is reduced to a manageable level, thus preventing cognitive overload. As the learner's expertise develops, the fidelity of the learning environment should be progressively increased, to improve transfer to the post-instructional situation. Therefore, you may use very different (less expensive) media early in the instruction than later.

3. *Learner Preferences*

If learners have different preferences for certain media, use several media so each learner can attend to the media that they prefer. For example, some learners may prefer visuals, such as graphics, while others may prefer verbal descriptions.

4. *Cost-Effectiveness*

Consider the cost-effectiveness of each medium, weighing the advantages of each medium in comparison to its costs. Be sure to take into account the cost of developing and/or licensing the instruction for that medium and the cost of using, maintaining, and updating the medium in the instructional setting (e.g., computers and instructor salaries). Multimedia can be expensive to develop and implement (equipment), but it can be less expensive than instructors if there will be a large number of learners over the life of the instruction.

5. *Practical Usage*

Consider how well the media will operate in the learning environment (including the skills and attitudes of the learning guide or teacher, as well as the learner – and note any training that may be needed), and how easily the media can be maintained and updated.

Other Considerations

In addition, it is helpful to consider the following questions:

- Who should *control* the media: teacher or learner?
- What *collaboration capabilities* should the media have: none (for individual use) or many (for collaborative use)?
- What *other capabilities* (e.g., content creation and sharing capabilities) should the media have to facilitate learner-centered instruction?
- How easy should it be to *modify* the content and/or instructional methods?

Finally, based on your decisions about media selection for each version or application, you should estimate **production time and expense** for each version or application. If resources are not sufficient, try to get more, or go with less expensive media, or prioritize versions or applications and drop lower-priority ones. Also, we suggest that this is a good time for you to look for **existing instructional resources** (media) that you could procure (and possibly modify) instead of creating your own.

8. Formatively Evaluate Your Designs and Revise Your Project Management Plan

Formatively Evaluate and Revise Your Designs with Experts

Your formative evaluation still cannot involve tryouts with learners because the design decisions are still too general, so among the options described in Chapter 10 (Formative Evaluation), you should conduct an **expert review** of the results of Steps 4–7 with both content experts and, especially for large ID projects, instructional experts (preferably people who are experts in both the content and teaching it to your target learners) by means of a walk-through exercise. Review and evaluate the learner objectives (from Step 4), learner assessments (from Step 5), methods of learning by doing (from Step 6), and general media selections (from Step 7) with the experts to enhance appropriateness, accuracy, effectiveness, and appeal by getting input from the experts on what changes they think would likely improve the content and design, and either make revisions during the walk-through exercise, or as soon as possible after it. Refer to your evaluation plan for the project and Chapter 10 for guidance.

Record all the important design decisions in your mid-level ADE document, which you should be preparing during each step of the mid-level ADE process and revising during or after your formative evaluation and revisions. Tables 6.23 and 6.24 present templates for mid-level ADE documents for task expertise and topic expertise, respectively. We encourage you to improve on these templates according to your particular needs and working styles.

Update Your Project Management Plan

With a clearer idea of how best to design the needed instruction, you can review instruction previously developed for the same or similar instructional needs and adopt, adapt, or reject what is available before embarking on a totally fresh (and more expensive) ID endeavor. Consequently, you should revise your project management plan (developed with guidance in Chapter 2 and updated in Chapter 5) based on any appropriate instruction you have found or expect to find.

Where Are We?

You had previously completed the top-level ADE for both task and topic expertise, resulting in a top-level ADE document showing the selection and sequencing of the major "chunks" of the content and the selection of high-level instructional methods (Chapter 5). In this chapter, you added some more detail to this fuzzy vision of your new instructional system. This entailed:

1. Identifying and sequencing versions of each task or applications of each topic
2. Identifying variations within each version or application and creating designer objectives
3. Formatively evaluating the results
4. Developing learner objectives
5. Designing appropriate kinds of learner assessments
6. Designing the ways learning by doing will be accomplished for each version or topic
7. Selecting media in general
8. Formatively evaluating and documenting the results

Table 6.23 Template for a Mid-Level ADE Document for Task Expertise (Use One Form for Each Version of the Task)

Mid-Level ADE Document for Topic Expertise		
Name of Task: **Simplifying Conditions:** **Number and List of Versions:** **Sequence of Versions:**		
Name of Version # :		Duplicate from here on for each application
Variations in ...	**Factors**	**Difficulty (1-5)**
Behaviors		
Conditions — Contextual factors		
Environmental factors		
Tools and other resources		
Standards		
Learner Objective (if any at mid level) Kind: ☐ Demonstration ☐ Abstract Description:		
Learner Assessment (if any at mid level) ☐ Criterion-referenced ☐ Norm-referenced Description: ☐ Performance ☐ Predictive		
Learning-By-Doing Teams? ☐ Yes ☐ No Names of projects:		
Media: ☐ Text ☐ Pic's/text ☐ Video ☐ Interactive media ☐ Physical objects ☐ Experts General description:		
Info about formative evaluation:		
Name of Project # :		Duplicate from here on for each application
Project environment: ☐ Real ☐ Staged ☐ Simulated ☐ Narrated Description:		
Scenario for this project:		
Details for this scenario:		

The next chapter (Chapter 7) provides guidance for conducting a lower-level ADE for both task and topic expertise, again based on the major considerations described in Chapters 3 and 4. Chapter 8 completes the ADE process with guidance for the design of tutorials for lower-level design. Finally, Develop and Deploy are addressed in Chapters 9–12. The whole ADE process is again summarized in Table 6.25.

Table 6.24 Template for a Mid-Level ADE Document for Topic Expertise (Use One Form for Each Application of the Topic)

Mid-Level ADE Document for Topic Expertise

Name of Topic:
Kind of Topic: ☐ Conceptual   ☐ Theoretical   ☐ Hybrid
Number of Applications:
List of Applications:

Sequence of Applications:

Name of Application # :	Duplicate from here on for each application

Variations in ...	**Difficulty (1-5)**
Behaviors	
Conditions	
Standards	

Learner Objective (if any at mid level)   Kind: ☐ Demonstration   ☐ Abstract
Description:

Learner Assessment (if any at mid level)   ☐ Criterion-referenced   ☐ Norm-referenced
Description: ☐ Performance   ☐ Predictive

Learning-By-Doing   Teams?   ☐ Yes   ☐ No
Contexts for applying the topic: ☐ Authentic   ☐ Fantasy
Description:

Media: ☐ Text ☐ Pic's/text ☐ Video ☐ Interactive media ☐ Physical objects ☐ Experts
General description:

Info about formative evaluation:

Name of Variation # :	Duplicate from here on for each application

Scenario for this variation:

Details for this scenario:

Exercises

Here again we offer suggestions for a professor using this book as a textbook in a course, to help the students understand more deeply the contents of this chapter. We suggest that you keep the same teams of about three students each to continue to work on their ID projects throughout the course. However, these exercises can be done individually by any reader who wants to deepen their understanding and skills.

Table 6.25 ADE Process for Task Expertise and Topic Expertise (Differences Are in **Bold**)

	Task Expertise	*Topic Expertise*
Top Level Ch. 5	1. Select and sequence top-level content 2. Plan high-level instructional methods 3. Formatively evaluate and document the top-level design	1. Select and sequence top-level content 2. Plan high-level instructional methods 3. Formatively evaluate and document the top-level design
Mid Level Ch. 6	1. Identify and sequence **versions of each task** 2. Identify variations within each **version** and create designer objectives 3. Formatively evaluate the findings 4. Develop the learner objectives for each **version** 5. Design learner assessments for each **version** 6. Design the ways that learning by doing will be accomplished for each **version** 7. Select media in general for the **version** 8. Formatively evaluate and document the results	1. Identify and sequence **applications of each topic** 2. Identify variations within each **application** and create designer objectives 3. Formatively evaluate the findings 4. Develop the learner objectives for each **topic** 5. Design learner assessments for each **topic** 6. Design the ways that learning by doing will be accomplished for each **topic** 7. Select media in general for the **application** 8. Formatively evaluate and document the results
Lower Level Ch. 7	1. Select and sequence the organizing content for each **version of the task** 2. Select and classify the supporting content for each **version** 3. Sequence the supporting content for each **version** 4. Evaluate and document the findings 5. Identify resource requirements, availability, and existing instruction for each **version** 6. Revise and elaborate the instruction and assessments for each **version** 7. Formatively evaluate the ADE document 8. Begin developing the implementation plan, and update the project management plan	1. Select and sequence the organizing content for each **topic** 2. Select and classify the supporting content for each **topic** 3. Sequence the supporting content for each **topic** 4. Evaluate and document the findings 5. Identify resource requirements, availability, and existing instruction for each **topic** 6. Revise and elaborate the instruction and assessments for each **topic** 7. Formatively evaluate the ADE document 8. Begin developing the implementation plan, and update the project management plan

Ch. 8	Detailed guidance is provided for Lower-Level Step 6: Revise and Elaborate the Instruction and Assessments for Each Version/Topic. It includes instructional strategies for:
	  • Remembering information
	  • Understanding relationships
	  • Applying skills and higher-order skills
	  • Acting on attitudes or values	

1. Have each team prepare a mid-level ADE document for their project. Given the intentionally narrow scope of each project, this, too, will likely be a very small ADE document. We expect that for a project in a one-semester course, one to three versions of one task or one to three applications of one topic – depending on the size of the task or topic – will be a reasonable scope. For what you consider to be the best ADE documents, we suggest you get written permission from the students to use them as examples in the next offering of your course.

2. Have each team offer suggestions for improvement for the ADE document of one or two other teams before you review and provide feedback to the students.

3. Have a whole-class, synchronous discussion of the strengths and weaknesses of this mid-level ADE process, including any difficulties or challenges they faced during the process and what changes to the process might have helped. We would love to get your suggestions for improvement.

References

Anderson, R.C., Osborn, J., & Tierney, R.J. (1984). *Learning to read in American schools: Basal readers and content texts*. East Sussex, United Kingdom: Psychology Press.

Bailey, R. (2019). Biology: The study of life. Retrieved from https://www.thoughtco.com/biology-meaning-373266.

Beissner, K.L., & Reigeluth, C.M. (1987). A case study on course sequencing with multiple strands using the elaboration theory. *Performance Improvement Quarterly, 7*(2), 38–61. doi:10.1111/J.1937-8327.1994.TB00624.X.

Bunderson, C.V., Gibbons, A.S., Olsen, J.B., & Kearsley, G.P. (1981). Work models: Beyond instructional objectives. *Instructional Science, 10*(3), 205–215.

Cohen, A.S., & Wollack, J.A. (2013). Handbook on test development: Helpful tips for creating reliable and valid classroom tests. Retrieved from http://testing.wisc.edu/Handbook%20on%20Test%20Construction.pdf.

Cronbach, L.J. (1970). *Essentials of psychological testing* (3rd ed.). New York, NY: Harper & Row.

Cronbach, L.J., & Meehl, P.E. (1955). Construct validity for psychological tests. *Psychological Bulletin, 52*(4), 281–302.

Hartley, J., & Davies, I.K. (1976). Preinstructional strategies: The role of pretests, behavioral objectives, overviews and advance organizers. *Review of Educational Research, 46*(2), 239–265.

Mager, R. (1975). *Preparing instructional objectives* (2nd ed.). Belmont, CA: Fearon-Pitman Publishers, Inc.

Mager, R. (1997). *Measuring instructional results, or, got a match?: How to find out if your instructional objectives have been achieved* (3rd ed.). Atlanta, GA: Center for Effective Performance.

Reigeluth, C.M. (1992). Elaborating the elaboration theory. *Educational Technology, Research and Development, 40*(3), 80–86. doi:10.1007/BF02296844.

Reigeluth, C.M. (1999). The elaboration theory: Guidance for scope and sequence decisions. In C.M. Reigeluth (Ed.), *Instructional-design theories and models: A new paradigm of instructional theory* (Vol. II, pp. 425–453). Mahwah, NJ: Lawrence Erlbaum Associates.

Reigeluth, C.M. (2007). Order, first step to mastery: An introduction to sequencing in instructional design. In F. Ritter, J. Nerb, E. Lehtinen & T. O'Shea (Eds.), *In order to learn, How the sequence of topics influences learning* (pp. 19–40). New York, NY: Oxford University Press.

Reigeluth, C.M., & Rodgers, C.A. (1980). The elaboration theory of instruction: Prescriptions for task analysis and design. *NSPI Journal, 19*(1), 16–26.

Romiszowski, A. J. (1988). *The selection and use of instructional media: For improved classroom teaching and for interactive, individualized instruction* (2 ed.). New York: Nichols Pub.

Schank, R.C., Berman, T.R., & Macpherson, K.A. (1999). Learning by doing. In C.M. Reigeluth (Ed.), *Instructional-design theories and models: A new paradigm of instructional theory* (Vol. II). Mahway, NJ: Lawrence Erlbaum Associates.

Schank, R.C., Fano, A., Jona, M., & Bell, B. (1993). *The design of goal-based scenarios*. Evanston, IL: Northwestern University Press.

Shrock, S.A., & Coscarelli, W.C. (2007). *Criterion-referenced test development: Technical and legal guidelines for corporate training* (3rd ed.). San Francisco, CA: Pfeiffer.

West, L.H., & Kellett, N.C. (1981). The meaningful learning of intellectual skills: An application of Ausubel's subsumption theory to the domain of intellectual skills learning. *Science Education, 65*(2), 207–219.

Widmayer, S.A. (2004). Schema theory: An introduction. Retrieved June 22, 2020 from https://pdfs.semanticscholar.org/47b1/5487db915f62aec7a1f57c6f64c0c1c5234f.pdf.

7 Lower-Level Analysis, Design, and Evaluation

Overview

Having made mid-level design decisions, you have a clearer vision within which to make more detailed design decisions about what to teach and how to teach it for each task or topic you listed. These decisions are shown in Table 7.1.

Again, you must analyze the content to make good decisions about both what to teach and how to teach it. And you must formatively evaluate the design decisions you make. Before we proceed, it is helpful to understand the distinction between "organizing content" and "supporting content."

Organizing and supporting content. Organizing content comprises the basic sequence or structure for teaching a task or topic, somewhat like the skeleton of a body. And we refer to the other kinds of content as "supporting content" because they are plugged into that basic sequence (structure) just in time for when they are helpful to the learner, somewhat like flesh on a skeleton. Kinds of supporting content include information, understandings, skills (including higher-order skills), and attitudes, each of which requires different methods of instruction (see "Categories of Learning" in Chapter 3). Examples of organizing content and supporting content are shown in Table 7.2. Therefore, the major parts of lower-level design include (1) *selecting and sequencing* all the organizing and supporting content and (2) *determining what kind of learning* each entails so that the most effective learner objectives, instruction, and assessment can be designed.

1. Select and Sequence the Organizing Content

Guidance for selecting and sequencing the organizing content is different for:

A. Task expertise and
B. Topic expertise.

1A. For Task Expertise: Select and Sequence the Organizing Content

1A.1. Decide on the Kind of Organizing Content – Procedural or Heuristic – for a Version

First, pick a version of a task from your mid-level analysis, design, and evaluation (ADE) document and consult with subject matter experts (SMEs) to determine the extent to which it is procedural versus heuristic. Some tasks are highly procedural, meaning that experts mainly think in terms of steps as they perform the task. On the opposite extreme are tasks that are highly heuristic, meaning that experts think in terms of principles, rules of thumb, guidelines, causal models, and such, rather than steps. Most tasks are intermediate points along that continuum. The more heuristic a task is, the more complex it is. Complex cognitive skills fall

Table 7.1 Lower-Level Analysis and Design Processes for Task and Topic Expertise

A. Task Expertise	B. Topic Expertise
1A. Select and sequence the organizing content for each version of the task 1A.1. Decide on the kind of organizing content: procedural or heuristic 1A.2. Analyze the version of the task and sequence its organizing content	**1B. Select and sequence the organizing content for each topic** 1B.1. Decide on the kind of organizing content: conceptual or theoretical 1B.2. Analyze the topic and sequence its organizing content

2. Select and classify the supporting content for each version or topic
- Identify all the supporting content down to entry level, and note the kind of learning and criteria for mastery for each

3. Sequence the supporting content for each version or topic
3.1. Add the supporting content to your sequence of organizing content
3.2. Adjust the size of the learning session

4. Formatively evaluate and document the findings
- See Chapter 10

5. Identify resource requirements, availability, and existing instruction for each version or topic
5.1. Estimate resource requirements for implementing the instruction
5.2. Estimate resource requirements for the ID project

6. Revise and elaborate the instruction, media, and assessments for each version or topic
6.1. Select appropriate instructional formats and tailor media selections to each
6.2. Design the scaffolding: coaching and instructing and tailor media selections to each
6.3. Design the motivational support
6.4. Design the assessments

7. Formatively evaluate the ADE document
- See Chapter 10

8. Begin developing the implementation plan, and update the project management plan
- See Chapter 11

far to the heuristic side. Over the past 50 years as society has become ever more complex, tasks in general have fewer procedural elements and more heuristic elements, resulting in a distribution of tasks increasingly skewed to the heuristic side of the continuum.

This distinction is an extremely important one, because instructional designers in the past have often tried to teach heuristic tasks as if they were procedural, teaching steps and overlooking heuristics. The results have been disappointing. The bottom line is that tasks must be analyzed to identify and select *both* procedural and heuristic content for instruction, and the best methods of instruction differ somewhat for the two kinds of content. Note the task, version, and mix of procedural and heuristic elements in your lower-level ADE document (see Table 7.6 for a sample template).

1A.2. Analyze the Version of the Task and Sequence Its Organizing Content

Next, you should analyze the version of the task (its procedural and heuristic elements) to identify what needs to be learned to become an expert in the task. There are two kinds of **procedural tasks** that are analyzed a bit differently: linear and branching. *Linear procedures* are ones that have a single sequence of steps that are always performed in a set order, and

Table 7.2 Examples of Organizing and Supporting Content

Examples of Organizing Content	Examples of Related Supporting Content
Procedural Organizing Content Steps involved in installing software on a new computer	**Concepts**: folders, preferences, input devices **Principles**: effects of different settings on preferences, causes of installation problems and their solutions
Heuristic Organizing Content Heuristics, principles, and causal models involved in managing a project	**Concepts**: kinds of interpersonal conflicts, kinds of project management tools (e.g., Gantt chart) **Principles**: causes of interpersonal conflicts, effects of different management styles

Conceptual Organizing Content
Kinds of life
• Kinds of plants
  o Kinds of trees
  o …
• Kinds of animals
  o Kinds of mammals
  o …
	Concepts: parts of flowering plants, circulatory system
	Procedures: steps for identifying oak trees in winter, steps for dissecting a frog
	Principles: process of reproduction in flowering plants, causes of genetic variations

Theoretical Organizing Content Principles and natural processes related to survival of the fittest • Principles and processes related to natural selection • Principles and processes related to genetic variation	**Concepts**: competitive advantage, niche, kinds of genetic variations **Procedure**: how to count animal populations in the wild

Table 7.3 Examples of Procedural and Heuristic Tasks

Procedural Tasks	Heuristic Tasks
Installing software on a new computer	Managing a project
Solving mathematical equations with two unknowns	Diagnosing cognitive disorders in early childhood

the output of one step is the input for the next step (see Table 7.4). It is rare for a task to be a linear procedure. *Branching procedures* are ones in which different "action steps" are performed under different circumstances, but experts still think in terms of steps rather than heuristics. The different circumstances are indicated in a flowchart by "decision steps," where each choice in that decision leads to a different "branch" of the flowchart (see Figure 7.1). Hence, branching procedures are more complex and more difficult to analyze but should not be confused with heuristic tasks.

Analyze linear procedural tasks. If the version of the procedural task is linear, perform a procedural task analysis (Merrill, 1976) of the version to identify its steps and conduct the first part of a hierarchical task analysis (Gagné, 1968) to break the steps down into sub-steps until the entry level of description of steps is reached. To identify the steps for the task and the entry level of the target learners, it helps to consult an experienced instructor or two – experienced in both the task and teaching it to the target learners. Then, design a procedural sequence by planning to teach the steps in the same order as they are performed.

Table 7.4 Example of a Linear Procedure

How to Make Banana Bread

1. Preheat the oven to 350°F.
2. In a mixing bowl, mash the ripe bananas with a fork until completely smooth.
3. Stir the melted butter into the mashed bananas.
4. Mix in the baking soda and salt.
5. Stir in the sugar, beaten egg, and vanilla extract.
6. Mix in the flour.
7. Pour the batter into your prepared loaf pan.
8. Bake for 50 minutes to 1 hour at 350°F.
9. Remove from oven and let cool in the pan for a few minutes.
10. Remove the banana bread from the pan and let cool completely before serving.
11. Slice and serve.

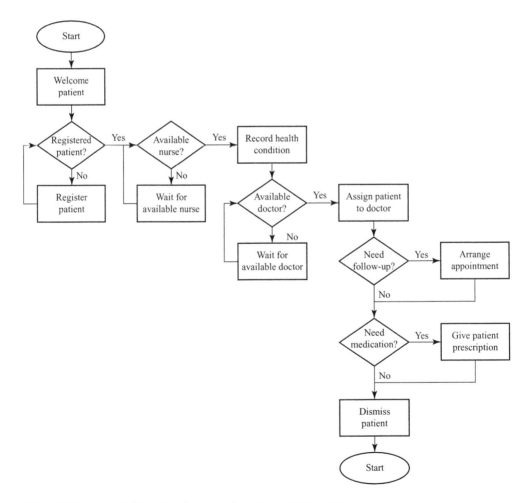

Figure 7.1 Example of a Branching Procedure for a Patient Visit to a Doctor.

Analyze branching procedural tasks. If the version of the procedural task has decision steps and branches, your analysis should result in a flowchart for this version of the task (see Figure 7.1 for an example). Note which steps should be performed sequentially and which can be performed independently of each other. Then design a sequence that teaches the shortest path through the flowchart first, followed by progressively longer paths. You should already have noted the *condition(s)* under which the version should be performed, such as tools, equipment, and materials required to perform the version of the task, and the *standards* of performance that should be achieved. Designing the sequence while the analysis is conducted is usually most efficient.

Analyze heuristic tasks. For heuristic tasks, we recommend the following *heuristic task analysis procedure* (Lee & Reigeluth, 2003; Lee & Reigeluth, 2009) for each version of the task (see examples in Table 7.5 below). Due to the complexity of heuristic tasks, the following are all usually important for the learners to learn.

1. Identify the **goals** for this version of the task under its conditions.
2. Identify all the important **considerations** for attaining each goal. Considerations are the major categories of causal factors that influence performance of the task. If there are more than about seven causal factors for a consideration, it is useful to identify sub-considerations for it.
3. Identify all the important **causal factors** for each consideration (or sub-consideration). A causal factor is something immaterial (as a circumstance or influence) that contributes to producing a result.
4. Analyze each causal factor to identify all **guidelines** (prescriptive principles) that an expert uses to account for this consideration.
5. Identify any **decision rules** an expert uses to combine the guidelines into a *performance model*. (See part of an example in Figure 7.2.) In some cases, these may be obvious enough that they do not need to be taught.
6. Identify **explanations** as to why each of the guidelines works and combine the explanations into *explanatory models*. (See partial example in Figure 7.3.) While not always necessary, explanatory models may provide a depth of understanding that allows the learner to flexibly adapt and improvise when conditions change in the field.
7. Identify a **descriptive model** for any and all objects involved in performing the task. (See partial example in Figure 7.4.) Similarly, while not always necessary, descriptive models provide a depth of understanding that allows the learner to flexibly adapt and improvise when conditions change in the field.

Plan to develop learners' skills and understandings in the following sequence: goals, considerations (and sub-considerations), descriptive models, causal factors, a performance model (guidelines and decisions rules), and explanations (explanatory models). Sometimes it is better to teach explanations with the guidelines, or even have the learners develop the guidelines from the explanations.

Analyze combination tasks. For combination tasks, do *both* procedural and heuristic task analyses: first identify steps at a high level and any sub-steps that represent the way experts think about the task; and then, for each step that experts don't think about in terms of sub-steps, identify guidelines and decision rules in a performance model, explanations in explanatory models (if beneficial), and any relevant descriptive models.

Record this organizing content and its sequence in your lower-level ADE document (see Table 7.6 for a sample template). Also, you could conduct formative evaluation (described in Step 4) on the results of this step now, but it is usually better to wait until you

Table 7.5 Guidance and Example of the Top-Down Approach to Heuristic Task Analysis

Process	Example of a Task: Determine the Media for a Course
1. Identify the **goals** of this version of the task under its conditions.	The media will help the learner to master the objective, will be cost effective, and will fall within the constraints for the course development and implementation.
2. Identify all important **considerations** for attaining each goal. (If there are lots of causal factors for a consideration, then it is helpful to also identify **subcategories** of considerations.)	The budget, skills of personnel available to teach the course, and availability of equipment for the course.
3. Identify all the important **causal factors** for each consideration (or sub-consideration).	The numbers of equipment, scheduling of equipment, alternative uses of equipment and capabilities of equipment.
4. Analyze each causal factor to identify all **guidelines** an expert uses to act on this consideration (or sub-consideration).	For all the above causal factors: • If there is insufficient equipment available for the projected number of learners, do not select that delivery system • If the equipment is not available at all the necessary times, do not select that delivery system • If the equipment is available and would otherwise go unutilized, there may be some pressure to select that delivery system • If the capabilities of the equipment do not meet the instructional requirements, do not select that delivery system Note: these examples are illustrative, not exhaustive, and there may be more than one guideline for a causal factor.
5. Identify any **decision rules** an expert uses to combine the guidelines into a **performance model**.	First, think about the context for delivery of the instruction, and how important digital media might be for that context. Then think about what capabilities are most beneficial for the instructional requirements. Next, if digital media would be best, think about how expensive it would be to (a) use such media and (b) develop the instruction for such media. … (These are just a few of the decision rules.) A *performance model* is a flowchart of this thinking process (including both guidelines and decision rules). A partial performance model is shown in Figure 7.2.
6. Identify specific **explanations** as to why each of the guidelines works and combine the explanations into **explanatory models**.	• Shortage of equipment can increase time for learning and is demotivating for learners • Inaccessibility to equipment when learners need it will increase time for learning and will be demotivating • Underutilization of existing equipment is a waste of scarce resources • If the equipment does not possess the needed affordances for the instructional requirements, learning will be more difficult A partial explanatory model is shown in Figure 7.3.
7. Identify a descriptive model for tools and any other objects involved in performing the task.	There are no objects that one uses to select media for a course (tools), but the learner may benefit from understanding each medium, such as a mental model of networked computers as requiring electricity and Internet connection and having capabilities to show motion and provide interactivity. A descriptive model shows the parts of such objects and how they function. A partial descriptive model for a different task is shown in Figure 7.4.

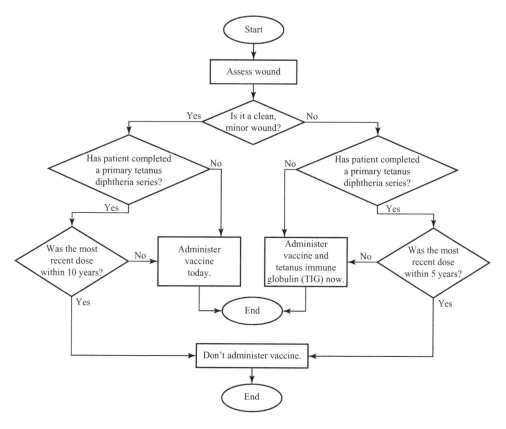

Figure 7.2 Example of a Branching Procedure for Performing Tetanus Prophylaxis.

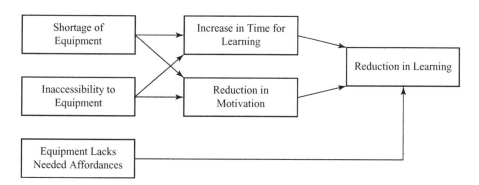

Figure 7.3 Part of an Explanatory Model.

have finished Steps 2 and 3 so that you can evaluate all the content and the entire sequence at the same time.

For a quantitative **rapid prototype** approach, when finished with the one task, proceed to analyze the supporting content. Otherwise, do this for all tasks before proceeding to analyze the supporting content.

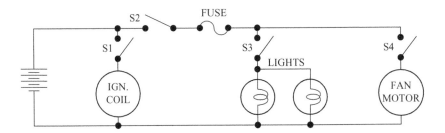

Figure 7.4 Partial Descriptive Model for Troubleshooting an Electronic Circuit.

1B. For Topic Expertise: Select and Sequence the Organizing Content

As you know, this book advocates not only a holistic approach to instructional design and content analysis, but also a **holistic approach to sequencing** instruction. This approach is in direct alignment with schema theory's understanding that meaningful learning is assimilated into a mental model, which provides a meaningful context for what is being learned.

1B.1. Decide on the Kind of Organizing Content – Conceptual or Theoretical – for a Topic

You must analyze the content to make good decisions about both what to teach and how to teach it. Fundamental to this analysis are the two basic kinds of understanding you identified in the mid-level topic analysis – conceptual (addressing "what" – objects, ideas, and events) and theoretical (addressing "why" – causes and effects). Remember that for task expertise, each version of the task has a considerable amount of *different* organizing content – different steps for a branching procedural task and different heuristics for a heuristic task. In contrast, for topic expertise, each application of the topic typically uses mostly the *same* principles or concepts, but in different ways and for different purposes. Consequently, you should analyze the organizing content for a whole topic (whereas for task expertise, you analyze the organizing content for each individual version of a task rather than for the task as a whole), though you may identify some small differences among applications of a topic later.

First, pick a topic from your mid-level ADE document, and note whether you had identified it as primarily conceptual or theoretical (see Table 7.7 for an example of each). Whichever is primary, that is the **organizing content** for that topic and its applications. If both are equally important, you can design a sequence of the organizing content for each (conceptual and theoretical) in the next step (Step 1B.2) and then integrate the two sequences. If it seems that the topic will be too large, break it into two or more subtopics now and decide on the kind of organizing content for each (conceptual or theoretical). Note the topic, its applications, and kind of organizing content in your lower-level ADE document (see Table 7.9 for a sample template).

1B.2. Analyze the Topic and Sequence Its Organizing Content

FIRST, ANALYZE, SELECT, AND GROUP THE ORGANIZING CONTENT

Based on the kind of organizing content (conceptual or theoretical), do *one* of the following two kinds of lower-level topic analysis for each topic: conceptual analysis or theoretical analysis.

Conceptual: analyze, select, and group the conceptual organizing content. When the focus of a topic is on conceptual understanding, its organizing content (concepts) can be identified by asking SMEs (preferably two or more, because they usually have different

Table 7.6 Template for a Lower-Level ADE Document for Task Expertise (Use for Each Version of Each Topic)

Name of Task:
Name of Version # :
Type: |---|---| Procedural   Heuristic
Procedural elements (if any)   Type of procedure: ☐ Linear   ☐ Branching   *[List the steps for a linear procedure. Put a flow chart for a branching procedure.]*   If branching procedure, **sequence** the paths by length/complexity/difficulty:
Heuristic elements (if any):   1. Goals   2. Considerations   3. Descriptive models   4. Causal factors   5. Guidelines   6. Decision rules   7. Explanations
Sequence of organizing content   Learner control: ☐ Yes   ☐ No   (If the version has both procedural and heuristic elements, integrate the two sequences)   (If no learner control, list the elements in sequence.)   (If learner control, put a tree chart showing sequence contingencies.)

Table 7.7 Example of the Two Kinds of Understanding for Organizing Content for the Economics Topic "the Law of Supply and Demand"

Conceptual Understanding	*Theoretical Understanding*
What is "supply"?	What is "the law of supply and demand"? (causal understanding)
What is "demand"?	What are the stages of the economic cycle? (natural process
What are the different kinds of markets?	understanding)

Table 7.8 Examples of a Domain, Subjects, and Topics for Conceptual Organizing Content

Level of Analysis	Description of Content
Domain	Economics
Subjects for Economics	*Microeconomics (see topics below)*
	Macroeconomics
	International economics
	Development economics
Topics for Microeconomics	Supply and demand
	Markets (see concepts below)
	Production, cost, and efficiency
	Specialization
	Firms
Concepts for Markets	Perfect competition
	Monopoly
	Oligopoly

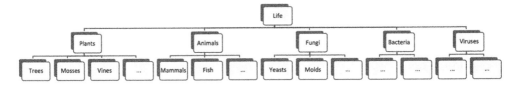

Figure 7.5 Graphic Representation of Organizing Content.

perspectives and biases) what are its *parts* or what are its *kinds* that should be taught (Reigeluth & Darwazeh, 1982). For example, if communication is the topic, the designer might ask what the major different kinds of communication are that should be taught, such as oral, written, and visual. Then think about the sub-kinds of each of those kinds that are important to teach (e.g., oral = conversation and presentation; written = informal and formal). Keep in mind that any given concept can have different ways of thinking about its kinds. For example, written communication could be thought of as informal and formal, or fiction and nonfiction, or books, essays, and letters, and much more. You need to decide which option of kinds is important given your goals, and often more than one option is important. Figure 7.5 shows part of the conceptual organizing content for a course on biology (from Table 6.7 in Chapter 6).

At some point, you might find that **parts** become important, so you could ask what the major parts of a presentation are and so forth. Continue the process of identifying kinds and parts until all the important concepts for this topic have been identified down to the desired level of detail for the target learners (see Table 7.8). It helps to review each of the applications you listed in your mid-level ADE document to make sure you identify all the important organizing content for the topic. You may find that some organizing content is not relevant to some applications. You should note those irrelevancies because they will influence your sequence of applications.

Enter your list of concepts in your lower-level ADE document for topic expertise (see Table 7.9 for a sample template). You should organize your list into groups of concepts that should be taught together, indicating any applications for which any organizing content is irrelevant. Based on this analysis, you may want to make some adjustments to the sequence of applications in your mid-level ADE document. Also, try to estimate whether each application will be of appropriate size (scope, amount of learning time) for the target

Table 7.9 Template for a Lower-Level ADE Document for Topic Expertise (Use for Each Topic)

Topic (or subtopic) Name: **Name of Application #   :**   **Type:** |---|---| Conceptual   Theoretical
Conceptual organizing content (if any): Parts and/or kinds   (List concepts in groups, general-to-detailed)
Theoretical organizing content (if any): Cause-effect relationships and natural processes   (List principles/processes in groups, simple-to-complex)
Sequence of organizing content   Learner control: ☐ Yes   ☐ No   (If hybrid sequence, integrate the two types of organizing content)   (Indicate any applications for which each piece of organizing content is irrelevant)

learners after all supporting content is added (in Step 2). Size should depend on such factors as the age of the learners, the difficulty of the content for the learners, and the level of motivation of the learners for learning the content. The bottom line, as Bruner (1966) explained it for what he called a "learning episode," is that the payoff the learners get from mastering the content of the episode must be greater than the "cost" for the learners to master it. If it looks like an application may be too large or small, try to make adjustments now, but you will have further opportunity to make adjustments when you allocate supporting content to the sequence of organizing content and applications.

Theoretical: analyze, select, and group the theoretical organizing content. When the focus of a topic is on theoretical understanding, its organizing content (causal principles and/or natural processes) can be identified by asking SMEs what are the major *causal*

Table 7.10 Some of the Organizing Content for the Topic "Supply and Demand"

Subtopic (principle): Law of demand
Price and quantity demanded in a given market are inversely related.
Sub-subtopic (principle): Utility maximization
Utility (buyer satisfaction) is maximized when marginal benefit equals marginal cost.
Subtopic (principle): Law of supply
Price and quantity supplied in a given market are directly related.
Sub-subtopic (principle): Profit maximization
Profits are maximized when marginal revenues equal marginal costs.
Subtopic (principle): Market equilibrium
The market will seek an equilibrium price at which quantity supplied equals quantity demanded.

relationships and/or *natural processes* involved in it (Reigeluth, 1987, 2007). For example, Table 7.10 shows the major organizing content for the topic "supply and demand" (domain: economics; subject: microeconomics). Then ask what additional *principles* elaborate on each of these fundamental principles (major causal relationships) and are also important to teach, given the applications you selected for this topic in your mid-level analysis. Such additional principles might address a single concept in the major principle, like the principle of profit maximization for "quantity supplied" in the law of supply (see Table 7.10). And you might look for principles that deal with narrower situations, like those related to a shift in the demand curve (e.g., from an increase in buyers' incomes), a shift in the supply curve (from a change in production costs), or supply and demand under imperfect competition (monopolies and oligopolies). Continue this analysis and selection until you have identified all the principles (often in combinations as causal models) that should be taught, down to the desired level of detail or complexity (based on the applications you selected for this topic).

But not all theoretical understanding is causal; some entails understanding a **natural process**, which is distinct from a process that is consciously performed by humans (called a procedure to avoid confusion). For example, if the subtopic is learning (domain: psychology; topic: cognitive development), *information processing theory* states that selective perception of stimuli is naturally followed by passing them on to sensory memory, where processes of attention and pattern recognition automatically pass them on to short-term memory (or working memory), where rehearsal and encoding processes then pass them on to long-term memory. This process is naturally occurring (not performed consciously) and therefore is not a procedure.

To identify phases in a natural process, ask your SMEs "what happens after this?" or what happens before this?" until you have identified all the phases in the process. Then ask if each phase should be further analyzed into sub-processes, given the applications you identified for this topic. Continue this analysis until you have identified all the natural processes that should be taught and have analyzed the parts of each natural process down to the level of detail appropriate for the applications of this topic.

Enter all the principles and/or processes into your lower-level ADE document for topic expertise (see Table 7.9 for a sample template). You should organize your list into groups that should be taught together, such as causal models (for principles) and process models (for processes). Indicate any applications for which any organizing content is irrelevant. Based on this analysis, you may want to make some adjustments to the sequence of applications in your mid-level ADE document. Also, try to estimate whether each application will be of appropriate size (scope, amount of learning time) for the target learners (as you did for the conceptual organizing content, understanding that supporting content will be added shortly – in Step 2). Size should depend on such factors as the age of the learners, the difficulty of the content for the learners, and the level of motivation of the learners for learning the content. The bottom line, as Bruner (1966) explained it for what he called a "learning episode," is that the payoff the learners get from mastering the content of the episode must be greater than the "cost" for the learners to master it. If it looks like an application may be too large or small, try to make adjustments now, but you will have further opportunity to make adjustments when you allocate supporting content to the sequence of organizing content and applications.

SECOND, SEQUENCE THE ORGANIZING CONTENT

Again, the lower-level analysis and design is a bit different for conceptual, theoretical, and hybrid topics, so choose one of the following three approaches.

Conceptual: sequence the conceptual organizing content. A general-to-detailed sequence provides a meaningful context for assimilating new concepts into a stable schema (Ausubel, 1968; Reigeluth, 1987, 1999, 2007; Reigeluth & Darwazeh, 1982). Typically, the order in which you identified the concepts is a good general-to-detailed sequence for teaching conceptual organizing content. However, concepts usually have branching relationships (parts or kinds) whereby several concepts could be learned immediately after a higher-level (broader, more inclusive) concept has been learned. When feasible (e.g., for online instruction), arrange your groups of concepts in a branching pattern that allows learners to choose the order of those groups (to promote learner control and self-directed learning, which enhances motivation) – for this takes little extra effort for you to do. You can number the groups for a linear sequence or put the numbers in a tree diagram for a branching (learner-controlled) sequence.

Theoretical: sequence the theoretical organizing content. Typically, the principles and processes/phases identified first during your analysis are the simplest ones, and the later ones tend to be more complex. So, the order in which you identified them is typically a good simple-to-complex sequence that provides a meaningful context for learning each subsequent one. Another method for sequencing theoretical organizing content is to use the order in which they were discovered in history. That tends to be a progression from broader, more inclusive principles (which are also simpler and more fundamental) to narrower, more detailed principles. When feasible (e.g., for online instruction), arrange your groups of principles in a branching (rather than linear) sequence that allows learners to choose the order of those groups (within the constraints of broader understandings before narrower ones and prerequisites first) – for this takes little extra effort for you to do. You can number the groups for a linear sequence or put the numbers in a tree diagram for a branching (learner-controlled) sequence.

Hybrid: combine multiple sequences. The third option is to consider the possibility of creating and combining separate general-to-detailed sequences for conceptual-parts, conceptual-kinds, theoretical-causal, and/or theoretical-process organizing content into a single comprehensive sequence, called a multi-strand sequence (Beissner & Reigeluth, 1994). Each sequence needs to be adjusted in order to merge with the others. Consult your SMEs for deciding on those adjustments.

Learner control: branching, learner-controlled sequences. For all three options, if you are designing online instruction, you could design a branching sequence of organizing content so that learners could choose which branch to pursue at any given time, based on their interests.

Record this organizing content and its sequence in your lower-level ADE document (see Table 7.9 for a sample template). Also, you could conduct formative evaluation (described in Step 4) on the results of this step now, but it is usually better to wait until you have finished Steps 2 and 3 so that you can evaluate all the content and the entire sequence at the same time.

If you are using a *quantitative approach* to **rapid prototyping**, then when this step is done for one topic (or even one subtopic, depending on scope), proceed to the next step. Otherwise, perform this step for all your topics, and then continue.

2. Select and Classify the Supporting Content for Each Task or Topic

This guidance is the same for task expertise as for topic expertise.

Now that the "skeleton" of the instruction (sequence of the organizing content) has been designed for each version of the task, the next step is to select and classify the supporting content for each version of the task or for each topic. This is often called a *learning analysis* – an analysis that identifies all the supporting content down to what the learner already knows, and classifies each as to **type of learning** in order to identify the best sequence and instructional methods for each.

Identify All Important Supporting Content Down to Entry Level, and Note the Kind of Learning and Criteria for Mastery for Each

Identify all the supporting content that is directly relevant to each part of the organizing content and has not yet been acquired by the target learners. (Content already acquired by the learners is called *entry knowledge*.) To simultaneously identify the supporting content and the entry knowledge of the target learners, it helps to consult an **experienced instructor** or two – experienced in both the content and teaching it to the target learners. This preliminary assessment of entry knowledge can be confirmed later in a formal target learner analysis.

During this process, **note the kind of learning** for each piece of supporting content identified, for these are important for deciding which instructional strategies to use for each:

- Memorize information (facts)
- Understand relationships (conceptual and theoretical)
- Apply skills (concept-classification, procedure-using, principle-using, and higher-order skills)
- Act on attitudes and values

These kinds of learning are addressed in some detail in Chapter 8. Also, note the **criteria for mastery** for each piece of supporting content, for these are also important for designing the instruction. On this level, it is usually not necessary to note the conditions of performance, for they tend to be the same as for the related organizing content.

Analyze each of those supporting understandings, skills, and affective qualities[1] down to the **level of entry knowledge** (a learning prerequisite analysis), and enter the results in your expanded ADE document (see Table 7.11 for a sample template). For *skills*, the procedural and hierarchical task analysis approaches work well (Gagné, 1968, 1985). For *understandings*, the hierarchical approach can be fairly easily modified to identify prerequisite understandings, which are typically broader, more inclusive understandings that serve as meaningful context for subsequent understandings (consistent with schema theory). For *attitudes*, identify the affective, cognitive, and psychomotor components of each attitude (Kamradt & Kamradt, 1999). During this process, **note the kind of learning** and the **indicators of mastery** for each prerequisite or component part. See Table 7.12 for an example for a topic.

When this is done, you have identified all the content that should be taught for this topic or version of the task – both organizing and supporting content. Now you need to sequence it. You could conduct formative evaluation (described in Step 4) on the results of this step now, but it is usually better to wait until you have finished Step 3, Sequence the Supporting Content for Each Version or Topic, so that you can evaluate all the content and the entire sequence at the same time.

---

1   Facts are not included because they do not have prerequisites.

Table 7.11 Additional Template for the Supporting Content in a Lower-Level ADE Document (Use for Each Version or Topic)

Version or topic name:			
Organizing Content	Supporting Content (in sequence)	Type of Learning	Criteria for Mastery
	[Add rows as needed.]		
[Add rows as needed.]			
Estimated time for target learners to master the version or topic:		*[Adjust as needed.]*	

3. Sequence the Supporting Content for Each Version or Topic

This guidance is partially the same for both task and topic expertise.

3.1. Add the Supporting Content to Your Sequence of Organizing Content

For all the supporting content you have just analyzed (information, understandings, skills, and attitudes), use the following principles to plug that content into your sequence of

Table 7.12 An Example of Supporting Content, Type of Learning, and Indicator of Mastery for a Topic

Organizing Content	Supporting Content	Type of Learning	Criteria of Mastery
Law of Demand	Quantity demanded	Understand Concept	Paraphrase the definition, give examples
	Substitution effect	Understand Principle	Predict, explain
	Purchasing power	Understand Concept	Paraphrase the definition
	Marginal utility	Understand Principle	Predict, explain
	Utility maximization	Understand Principle	Predict, explain
	Perfect competition	Understand Concept	Paraphrase the definition
	Imperfect competition	Understand Concept	Paraphrase the definition, give examples
	Imperfect competition	Understand Principle	Predict, explain
	Shift in demand curve	Understand Concept	Paraphrase the definition, give examples
	Shift in demand curve	Understand Principle	Predict, explain
	Elasticity of demand	Understand Concept	Paraphrase the definition, give examples

organizing content. Keep in mind that these are principles that you should try to implement in combination with each other, as appropriate.

Just-in-time. Sequence the supporting content so it is taught just before it is needed or helpful for learning a piece of the organizing content.

Procedural order. Sequence any procedural supporting content in the order in which it is used (i.e., a procedural sequence) (Merrill, 1976, 1978).

Prerequisites first. Plan to teach prerequisites *just in time* before the content for which they are prerequisite. Prerequisites for a skill are sub-skills that are simpler components of the skill. Gagné (1968, 1985) noted that discriminations are prerequisites for concrete concepts, which are prerequisites for defined concepts, which are prerequisites for rules, which are prerequisites for higher-order rules (see Figure 7.6). But defined concepts can also be prerequisites for other defined concepts, rules (procedures and principles) can be prerequisites for other rules, and higher-order rules can be prerequisites for other higher-order rules. Prerequisites for an understanding (conceptual or theoretical relationships) are other understandings that enable learning it. They are relationships within a schema. Prerequisites for an attitude include the affective component, the cognitive component, and the psycho-motor component of the attitude.

Understanding first. Plan to teach understanding (principles, causal models, or process models) prior to a related procedure (Mayer, 1976).

Coordinate concepts together. Plan to teach coordinate concepts together (M.D. Merrill, Tennyson, & Posey, 1992). Coordinate concepts are those which are subordinate to the same concept. For example, perfect competition and imperfect competition are coordinate concepts because they are both kinds of markets (their superordinate concept). Teaching them together helps learners hone in on the differences between the two, because examples of each are nonexamples of the other.

3.2. Adjust the Size of the Learning Session

When you have designed the sequence, you should adjust the size of each learning session in that sequence. Start by deciding **how long a single learning session** (or what Bruner, 1966, called a learning episode) should be. Too short breaks up the instruction. Too long exhausts the learner. Then, **estimate how long it will take** the target learners to learn each learning session for this topic or version of the task with all its organizing and supporting content. If it exceeds your range for size of learning session, you have three

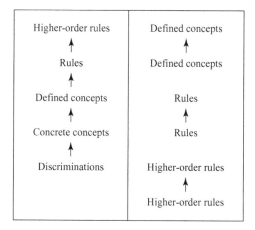

Figure 7.6 Prerequisites for a skill.

choices to adjust its size – choices that are a bit different for a version of a task than for a topic.

3.2A. For a Version of a Task

If the learning session is too large:

1. You may be able to reduce its size by adding another simplifying condition. It is possible to create simplifying conditions that don't exist in the real world, if necessary. While there are obvious disadvantages in doing so, it is often possible to compensate for them (e.g., by warning the learner about what is unrealistic or using extrinsic motivators, if needed).
2. You could reduce the number of variations that this learning session will address and add them to a subsequent learning session.
3. Some supporting content could be moved to a different learning session (whatever such content seems least helpful in learning the organizing content in this learning session), but don't remove any prerequisites for the organizing content.

On the other hand, if the learning session is too short, you might increase its size by removing another simplifying condition or adding supporting content that you were not able to include in an earlier learning session.

3.2B. For a Topic

If the learning session is too large:

1. You could reduce its size by dividing the topic vertically – that is, putting half the sub-topics (with their respective sub-subtopics, etc.) in one learning session and the other half in another.

2. You could reduce its size by dividing the topic horizontally – that is, by putting higher-level subtopics in one learning session and lower-level ones (e.g., sub-sub-subtopics) in the other.
3. You could remove some supporting content from the learning session (and put it in another learning session), but don't remove any prerequisites for the organizing content.

On the other hand, if the learning session is too short (e.g., it breaks up the flow for the learner), you might increase its size by adding another topic or adding supporting content that you had to remove from an earlier learning session.

But different learners may benefit from different sized learning sessions. When your budget allows, you could design personalized, digital instruction to either permit the learner to adjust the size of the learning session, or automatically adjust the size of the learning session to the learner based on the learner's prior performance. This requires that you design a computer system to allow selection of different designs or to design the instruction for each learner in real time, which will not be feasible for most ID projects.

4. Formatively Evaluate and Document the Findings

This guidance is the same for both task and topic expertise.

Your formative evaluation still cannot involve tryouts with learners because the design decisions are still too general. So, among the options described in Chapter 10 (Formative Evaluation), you should still just conduct an **expert review** of the results of Steps 1–3 with both content experts and instructional experts (preferably people who are experts in both the content and teaching it to your target learners) by means of a walk-through exercise. Review and evaluate the selection and sequence of organizing content (from Step 1) and the selection (from Step 2) and sequence (from Step 3) of the supporting content with the SMEs to enhance appropriateness, accuracy, effectiveness, and appeal. You could also review them with learners who have just finished learning this content, as well as with other stakeholders. Refer to your evaluation plan for the project and Chapter 10 for guidance.

5. Identify Resource Requirements, Availability, and Existing Instruction for Each Version or Topic

This guidance is the same for both task and topic expertise. However, the choice of instructional methods (in Step 6) will impact the decisions in this step, and vice versa, so these two steps should be done simultaneously.

Now that there is more information about the instruction, revisit the resource requirements and availability for each version or topic.

5.1. Estimate Resource Requirements for Implementing the Instruction

Estimate the resource requirements for **implementing the instruction** and compare that with the available resources (probably different from the resources for your ID project). If they are insufficient, revise the content and/or methods selected at this point, or contact the client to obtain additional resources to meet the requirements, or in some cases a workaround may be needed to support the instructional needs with available resources.

5.2. Estimate Resource Requirements for the ID Project

Estimate the resource requirements for **designing and developing the instruction** and compare that with the available resources. Also, identify any **existing instruction** that fits the designer objectives (content and methods selected), and assess the extent to which

Table 7.13 Form for Review of Existing Materials

Question	*Yes*	*No*
Does the material meet the requirements of the objective(s)?		
Is the level of learning appropriate (e.g., memorization, application, etc.)?		
Is the material accurate?		
Does the material address motivational factors?		
Can the material be properly sequenced?		
Does the material provide sufficient guidance?		
Are sufficient practice exercises provided?		
Are the learner assessments adequate?		
Is the material proprietary or copyrighted? If so, can you get the rights?		

it could be adopted, adapted, and/or extended to teach the organizing and/or supporting content, given the methods that have been selected so far in the mid- and lower-level designs. Even the use of some portions of existing materials may be economically advantageous. Reusing or revising existing instruction can save time and money and free up personnel resources to complete other tasks. Existing materials could be from textbooks, publications, handbooks, videos, online instruction, and job aids or training materials.

In order **to select the appropriate existing materials**, a deliberate and thorough review of such materials should be conducted. After it has been determined what instructional materials are needed to support the designer objectives and they have been gathered for review, the review process is ready to begin. Questions to keep in mind during the review of existing materials are shown in Table 7.13.

Revise the resource requirements based on your use of existing instruction. If they are insufficient, rethink the content and/or methods selected at this point, or contact the client to obtain additional resources to meet the requirements, or in some cases a workaround may be needed to support the instructional requirement with existing resources.

Copyright, Fair Use, and the Creative Commons

It is important to consider copyright issues when selecting or developing instructional materials, especially online ones, since online materials are often more easily copied, edited, reproduced, and shared. Just because it is online does not mean you can use it without the permission of the author or creator. Copyright law applies to intellectual property that is an original work of authorship, including literacy and musical work. There are some exceptions and limitations to copyright though. For example, works produced by federal employees in the course of their employment (e.g., a food safety guide from the United States Department of Agriculture – USDA) are in the public domain in the United States and not protected by copyright law. Copyright is automatic in that it applies as soon as the original work has been created, as long as it has a copyright notice. In the United States, copyright protection lasts for the life of the author or an additional 70 or 100 years for an institutional author (Creative Commons USA, n.d.). For information on getting permission to use copyrighted material, see Stim (2019).

"Fair use" refers to the right to use portions of copyrighted materials without permission for certain types of uses – such as criticism, comment, news reporting, teaching, scholarship, and research (US Copyright Office, 2019). The educational fair use guidelines (see Stanford University Libraries, n.d.) apply to materials used for educational purposes in educational institutions, such as K-12 schools, universities, libraries, and other nonprofit institutions. "Educational purposes" include:

- Noncommercial instruction or curriculum-based teaching by educators to learners at nonprofit educational institutions
- Planned noncommercial study or investigation directed toward making a contribution to a field of knowledge
- Presentation of research findings at noncommercial peer conferences, workshops, or seminars (Stim, 2019; US Copyright Office, 2019)

Many types of intellectual property, including research, music, books, and software, can be openly licensed. With the Creative Commons, the global standard for sharing content for use and re-use, one can easily get a free copyright license. By providing free, easy-to-use copyright licenses, the Creative Commons aims to develop, support, and steward legal and technical infrastructure that maximizes digital creativity, sharing, and innovation. Using Creative Commons licensing is one way to protect intellectual property. For more information, visit the Creative Commons website at creativecommons.org.

Update the ADE document and ID Project Management Plan, if needed, based on the outcome of this step.

6. Revise and Elaborate the Instruction, Media, and Assessments for Each Version or Topic

Based on the results of the analysis of organizing and supporting content, you should revise and elaborate your instructional methods and media selections and further design instruction and assessments for the lower-level content, if needed. Additionally, you should select the appropriate instructional formats (Step 6.1) and design the instructional scaffolds (Step 6.2) and motivational support (Step 6.3). However, the resources and existing instruction (Step 5) will impact the decisions in this activity, and vice versa, so these two activities should be done simultaneously.

6.1. Select Appropriate Instructional Formats and Tailor Media Selections to Each Format

As you elaborate learning-by-doing approaches and design instruction for each piece of organizing and supporting content, a variety of instructional formats can be selected. The most common formats are shown in Table 7.14. You may select different formats for different pieces of the organizing and supporting content. Different media are likely appropriate for different formats, so adjust your media selections accordingly.

6.2. Design the Scaffolding (Coaching and Instructing), and Tailor Media Selections to Each Scaffold

Scaffolding refers to temporary support provided by teachers, experts, computer-based tutors, or more capable peers to help learners learn so that they can complete a task or solve a problem that they could not accomplish independently (Vygotsky, 1978; Wood et al., 1976). Scaffolds take a variety of forms, including question prompts, feedback, advice, checklists, learner guides, templates, and expert modeling.

Hannafin and colleagues (1999) identified four types of scaffolding: conceptual (guides learners regarding what to consider in the problem-solving process), metacognitive (facilitates metacognitive thinking and processes), procedural (provides guidance on how to

Table 7.14 Instructional Formats

Formats	Definition
Presentation	
Lecture	A formal or semiformal oral presentation of information by a single individual; facts, concepts, problems, relationships, or principles presented orally either directly (as by live instructor) or indirectly (as by video).
Demonstration	Presentation or portrayal of a sequence of events to show a procedure, principle, or natural process; frequently combines an oral explanation with the operation or handling of equipment or material. May be presented directly (as by a live instructor) or indirectly (as by video or simulation).
Exhibit	A material, visual, or print display used to present information; for example, actual equipment, models, mockups, graphic materials, displays, whiteboard, or projected images.
Panel Discourse	Verbal interaction among two or more individuals which is heard by the learner; may be a dramatization, such as role playing, or a dialogue between panel members, or a teaching interview (a question and answer session between instructor and visiting "expert").
Reading	Printed materials, such as books, periodicals, manuals, handouts, or electronic readings. Readings may be course-assigned or self-assigned.
Teaching Interview	Question and answer session between the instructor and visiting "expert" following a highly structured plan.
Learner Interaction	
Questioning	An instructor- and/or courseware-controlled interactive process used to emphasize a point, stimulate thinking, keep learners alert, check understanding, or review material. Questioning may be direct, as by a live instructor, or may be designed into a film or television presentation.
Programmed Questioning	An instructor and/or software-controlled interactive process used to systematically demand a sequence of appropriate learner responses; may be used directly (as by an instructor in a classroom) or indirectly (as by a programmed computer).
Learner Query	The provision by which learners are given the opportunity to search for information, as by questioning a classroom instructor, tutor, coach, or the Internet.
Seminar	A peer-controlled group interactive process in which task- or objective-related information and experience are evoked from the learners. Questions may be used to evoke learner contributions, but the seminar is different from questioning.
Discussion	An interactive process of sharing information and experiences related to achieving a learner objective.
Knowledge Application	
Performance	Learner interactions with things, data, or persons, as is necessary to attain learner objectives; includes all forms of simulation (for example, games and interaction with hardware simulators) and interaction with actual equipment or job materials (for example, forms). Performance may be observed by classroom instructor, tutor, coach, or peer to provide needed feedback. When the performance is done with technology, the technology may be designed to provide the feedback (as in a computer-based simulation). Projects are interrelated sets of performances.
Case Study	A carefully designed description of a problem situation, written specifically to provoke systematic analysis and discussion by learners. This can also be viewed as a form of learner interaction.

utilize resources and tools), and strategic (provides guidance on how to approach learning tasks or problems). These are illustrated in Table 7.15.

Saye and Brush (2002) distinguished between hard scaffolds and soft scaffolds. Hard scaffolds are "anticipated and planned in advance based on typical learner difficulties with a task" (p. 81), while soft scaffolds provide dynamic and spontaneous support based on

Table 7.15 Four Types of Scaffolding with Subtypes and an Example for Each

Type of Scaffold	Subtypes	Illustrations
Conceptual (what the learner should consider)	Project specification Project resources	Project instructions and evaluation criteria Relevant articles and project samples
Metacognitive (how the learner should think)	Templates Question prompts	A template for project planning A template for progress report Question prompts facilitating project planning & monitoring
Procedural (how to utilize resources, tools)	Step-by-step instructions	A video demonstrating how to complete a certain task
Strategic (how to approach problems and learning)	Instructor feedback Tips	Feedback on project plans and progress reports Tips for approaching the project

learner responses. Myers and Reigeluth (2017) propose that scaffolding can be provided by *adjusting* aspects of the task or context in which it is performed, *coaching* the learner, or *instructing* the learner.

There is no question about the importance of scaffolding in instruction, especially in learning-by-doing. Many learners, both adults and children, are accustomed to teacher-centered instruction and overwhelmed by the complexity of applications in learner-centered instruction (LCI), including self-directed learning. Scaffolding can accelerate and broaden learning, while decreasing frustration and increasing learner motivation to learn.

Here we have synthesized the above-mentioned kinds of instructional scaffolding into two major kinds for you to consider adding to the design of the tasks or applications: coaching and instructing.

Coaching Strategies

Coaching is a type of instructional scaffolding that can provide all four of Hannafin et al.'s (1999) kinds of scaffolding – both hard and soft – while the learner is working on a project or application, and it can be provided either by a human or by the learner's virtual mentor (on a digital device). It primarily entails providing information or tips to the learner, though it can include a short demonstration for a skill or topic. More extensive demonstrations and practice with feedback go beyond coaching and are considered instructing. To enhance authenticity, coaching usually requires freezing time in the project or application, as in a "time-out" in sports scrimmages.

When to coach. Coaching should be used when the learner needs only a little help. Larger amounts of help are typically best provided through instructing under authentic conditions. Naturally, there is a blurry line between coaching and instructing.

How to coach. Coaching can take the form of providing *information*, providing a *hint* or tip, or providing an *understanding*. The latter two kinds of coaching can take either an inquisitory or an expository form. The *inquisitory form* occurs as questions to the learner that help the learner to discover an appropriate hint or understanding, as occurs in a Socratic dialogue. The *expository form* occurs as statements or visuals that provide the hint or stimulate the understanding.

Table 7.16 Motivational Strategies in the ARCS Model (Keller, 1987)

Attention Strategies	*Relevance Strategies*	*Confidence Strategies*	*Satisfaction Strategies*
Incongruity, conflict	Experience	Learning requirements	Natural consequences
Concreteness	Present worth	Difficulty	Unexpected rewards
Variability	Future usefulness	Expectations	Positive outcomes
Humor	Need matching	Attributions	Negative influences
Inquiry	Modeling	Self-confidence	Scheduling
Participation	Choice		

Instructional Strategies

The instructional strategies should differ depending on the kind of learning involved: (1) remembering information, (2) understanding conceptual and theoretical relationships, (3) applying skills and higher-order skills, and (4) acting on attitudes and values. Detailed guidance for these instructional strategies is provided in the next chapter. As you select instructional strategies for each of these kinds of learning, tailor your media selections to each.

6.3. Design the Motivational Support

Motivation plays a significant role in learning. Keller (1987, 2010) has developed a general model integrating the various sources of motivation for learning. He calls it the *ARCS model*, an acronym for the four sets of strategies that can be used to motivate a learner (see Table 7.16).

- **Attention** involves grabbing the learner's interest at the beginning of instruction and maintaining that interest throughout the lesson and course
- **Relevance** is the personal significance and value to the learner of mastering the learning objectives
- **Confidence** relates to the learner's expectancy of success
- **Satisfaction** comes from achieving performance goals

Adapt these motivational strategies to your instructional approach. These strategies are done differently depending on whether you are using the learner-centered approach or the teacher-centered approach. Please refer to Chapter 4 for other motivational strategies or frameworks, including self-determination theory and Octalysis. It is usually best to design the motivational strategies while you are designing the instructional scaffolding (i.e., do Steps 6.2 and 6.3 simultaneously).

6.4. Design the Assessments

For each of the types of learning (information, understandings, skills, and attitudes) that is needed for the learner to succeed in the project or application for which you are designing instruction, certification of proficiency should be required before the learner is allowed to resume work on the project. With computer-based instruction, assessment of proficiency should be *fully integrated* with the instruction so that the practice or application also serves as the assessment. Accuracy should be the primary criterion for all kinds of learning, and it is typically measured as x performances correct in a row,

Table 7.17 Example of Dimensions of Divergence (or Equivalence Classes)

Skill: Adding Fractions	
Denominator	Fractions with a common denominator
	Fractions in which the denominators contain a common factor (can be reduced)
	Fractions in which the denominators are not common and have no common factor (cannot be reduced)
Sum	Smaller than 1
	Larger than 1
Type of Fraction	Proper
	Improper
Digits	One-digit numerators and denominators
	(Each of the other possible combinations)

or x out of the last y performances correct, without assistance. The number required should be based on the amount of divergence (what Scandura, 1973, refers to as the number of "equivalence classes" – classes of instances of a generality that vary from each other in consistent ways) for the given kind of learning (see Table 7.17 for an example).

For kinds of learning that should be automatized,[2] the certification also depends on reaching a criterion for speed of performance, such as sufficient speed for x performances in a row or for x of the last y. Alternatively, the learner could be given another task that requires strategic thinking while having to perform the automatized task, but speed of performance is still a factor.

When the practice/assessment cannot be done on a computer or tablet, the instructor will likely have to give an assessment separate from and after the instruction is complete. The assessment should require performances that are as authentic as possible, and it should assess all the major dimensions of divergence (equivalence classes). Criteria for mastery listed in the designer objectives should be used, and when a learner does not meet the criteria, provision should be made for remediation and reassessing.

Having mastery assessments of each individual piece of organizing and supporting content does not guarantee that the learner can put it all together, so it is advisable to assess the learner on the level of performing the whole version of the task or applying the whole topic. Of course, that performance should be as authentic (consistent with real-world situations) as possible.

7. Formatively Evaluate the ADE Document

This guidance is the same for both task and topic expertise.

In a quantitative rapid prototype approach, when you have done the preceding activities for a version of the task or a topic (or large subtopic), you should formatively evaluate as much of this design as is feasible (see Chapter 10) before designing instruction for any other versions or topics. This may require developing parts or all of this design (see Chapter 9 for guidance) so that you will have something approximating real instruction

---

2   Automatization is needed when the real-world performance requires strategic thinking or other cognitive tasks to be performed simultaneously with it.

that you can try out on learners. But it is often advisable to formatively evaluate some designs with simple mock-ups of the instruction before developing that instruction. Finding improvements now should reduce the amount of revision needed for the design of subsequent versions or topics.

Your formative evaluation can finally involve tryouts with learners. So, among the options described in Chapter 10 (Formative Evaluation), if you are designing instruction for group-based learning, you should conduct **individual and small-group tryouts** with representative samples of your target learners for the results of Step 6. If you are designing individualized instruction, you should conduct **alpha tests**. Operational tryouts and beta tests should be done in the later stages of development (Chapter 9). Expert reviews are much less helpful at this stage of the ID process, but they could occasionally be useful. Refer to your evaluation plan for the ID project and Chapter 10 for guidance.

If you are using a qualitative rapid prototype approach, do the preceding activities for each subsequent version or topic, and then proceed to formatively evaluate your designs.

8. Begin Developing the Implementation Plan, and Update the Project Management Plan

Once the instructional system has been designed and before much of the development work begins, it is important to begin developing the implementation plan (see Chapter 11 for guidance), because implementation issues can influence the design. This plan should provide details on how to execute, monitor, and control the instructional system.

Additionally, update the ID project management plan to reflect changes made in the design phase.

For a quantitative rapid prototype approach, when you have finished this step with the one task or topic, go directly to Chapter 10 to develop the instruction for it. Otherwise, repeat this chapter for all remaining tasks and topics before proceeding.

Where Are We?

You had previously completed the mid-level ADE process for both task and topic expertise, resulting in a mid-level ADE document (Chapter 6). In this chapter, you added much more detail to this vision of your new instructional system. This entailed:

1. Selecting and sequencing the organizing content for each version or topic
2. Selecting and classifying the supporting content for each version or topic
3. Sequencing the supporting content for each version or topic
4. Evaluating and documenting the findings
5. Identifying resource requirements, availability, and existing instruction for each version or topic
6. Revising and elaborating the instructional methods for each version or topic
7. Evaluating the ADE document
8. Developing the implementation plan, and updating the project management plan

The next chapter (Chapter 8) provides guidance for designing the instructional strategies in your lower-level ADE for both task and topic expertise, again based on the major considerations described in Chapters 3 and 4 and the designs you have created so far. Finally, Develop and Deploy are addressed in Chapters 9–12. The whole ADE process is again summarized in Table 7.18.

Table 7.18 ADE Process for Task Expertise and Topic Expertise (Differences Are in **Bold**)

	Task Expertise	*Topic Expertise*
Top Level **Ch. 5**	1. Select and sequence top-level content 2. Plan high-level instructional methods 3. Formatively evaluate and document the top-level design	1. Select and sequence top-level content 2. Plan high-level instructional methods 3. Formatively evaluate and document the top-level design
Mid Level **Ch. 6**	1. Identify and sequence **versions of each task** 2. Identify variations within each **version** and create designer objectives 3. Formatively evaluate the findings 4. Develop the learner objectives for each **version** 5. Design learner assessments for each **version** 6. Design the ways that learning by doing will be accomplished for each **version** 7. Select media in general for the **version** 8. Formatively evaluate and document the results	1. Identify and sequence **applications of each topic** 2. Identify variations within each **application** and create designer objectives 3. Formatively evaluate the findings 4. Develop the learner objectives for each **topic** 5. Design learner assessments for each **topic** 6. Design the ways that learning by doing will be accomplished for each **topic** 7. Select media in general for the **application** 8. Formatively evaluate and document the results
Lower Level **Ch. 7**	1. Select and sequence the organizing content for each **version of the task** 2. Select and classify the supporting content for each **version** 3. Sequence the supporting content for each **version** 4. Evaluate and document the findings 5. Identify resource requirements, availability, and existing instruction for each **version** 6. Revise and elaborate the instruction and assessments for each **version** 7. Formatively evaluate the ADE document 8. Begin developing the implementation plan, and update the project management plan	1. Select and sequence the organizing content for each **topic** 2. Select and classify the supporting content for each **topic** 3. Sequence the supporting content for each **topic** 4. Evaluate and document the findings 5. Identify resource requirements, availability, and existing instruction for each **topic** 6. Revise and elaborate the instruction and assessments for each **topic** 7. Formatively evaluate the ADE document 8. Begin developing the implementation plan, and update the project management plan
Ch. 8	Detailed guidance is provided for Lower-Level Step 6: Revise and Elaborate the Instruction and Assessments for Each Version/Topic. It includes instructional strategies for: • Remembering information • Understanding relationships • Applying skills and higher-order skills • Acting on attitudes or values	

Exercises

Here again we offer suggestions for a professor using this book as a textbook in a course, to help the students understand more deeply the contents of this chapter. We suggest that you keep the same teams of about three students each to continue to work on their ID projects throughout the course. However, these exercises can be done individually by any reader who wants to deepen their understanding and skills.

1. Have each team prepare a lower-level ADE document for at least one version of one task or at least one topic in their project. For what you consider to be the best ADE documents, we suggest you get written permission from the students to use them as examples in the next offering of your course.

2. Have each team offer suggestions for improvement for the ADE document of one or two other teams before you review and provide feedback to the students.
3. Have a whole-class, synchronous discussion of the strengths and weaknesses of this lower-level ADE process, including any difficulties or challenges they faced during the process and what changes to the process might have helped. We would love to get your suggestions for improvement.

References

Ausubel, D.P. (1968). *Educational psychology: A cognitive view*. New York: Holt, Rinehart & Winston.

Beissner, K. L., & Reigeluth, C. M. (1994). A case study on course sequencing with multiple strands using the elaboration theory. *Performance Improvement Quarterly, 7*(2), 38–61.

Bruner, J.S. (1966). *Toward a theory of instruction*. Cambridge, MA: Belknap Press.

Creative Commons USA. (n.d.). A brief copyright primer. Retrieved from https://creativecommonsusa.org/wp-content/uploads/2018/01/Copyright-and-Open-Licensing-Primer.pdf.

Gagné, R.M. (1968). Learning hierarchies. *Educational Psychologist, 6*(1), 1–6.

Gagné, R.M. (1985). *The conditions of learning and theory of instruction*. New York, NY: Holt, Rinehart, and Winston.

Hannafin, M.J., Land, S., & Oliver, K. (1999). Open learning environments: Foundations, methods, and models. In C. M. Reigeluth (Ed.), *Instructional-design theories and models: A new paradigm of instructional theory* (Vol. II, pp. 115-140). Mahwah, NJ: Lawrence Erlbaum Assoc.

Kamradt, T.F., & Kamradt, E.J. (1999). Structured design for attitudinal instruction. In C.M. Reigeluth (Ed.), *Instructional-design theories and models: A new paradigm of instructional theory* (Vol. II, pp. 563–590). Mahwah, NJ: Lawrence Erlbaum Associates.

Keller, J.M. (1987). Strategies for stimulating the motivation to learn. *Performance and Instruction*, 26, 1–7.

Keller, J.M. (2010). *Motivational design for learning and performance: The ARCS model approach*. New York, NY: Springer.

Lee, J.Y., & Reigeluth, C.M. (2003). Formative research on the heuristic task analysis process. *Educational Technology Research and Development, 51*(4), 5–24.

Lee, J.Y., & Reigeluth, C.M. (2009). Heuristic task analysis on e-learning course development: A formative research study. *Asia Pacific Educational Review, 10*(1), 169–181.

Mayer, R. E. (1976). Integration of information during problem solving due to a meaningful context of learning. *Memory and Cognition, 4*(5), 603–608.

Merrill, M.D., Tennyson, R.D., & Posey, L.O. (1992). *Teaching concepts: An instructional design guide*. Englewood Cliffs, NJ: Educational Technology Publications.

Merrill, P.F. (1976). Task analysis – An information processing approach. *NSPI Journal, 15*(2), 7–11.

Merrill, P.F. (1978). Hierarchical and information processing task analysis: A comparison. *Journal of Instructional Development, 1*(2), 35–40.

Myers, R.D., & Reigeluth, C.M. (2017). Designing games for learning. In C.M. Reigeluth, B.J. Beatty, & R.D. Myers (Eds.), *Instructional-design theories and models, Vol. IV: The learner-centered paradigm of education* (pp. 205-242). New York, NY: Routledge.

Reigeluth, C.M. (1987). Lesson blueprints based on the elaboration theory of instruction. In C.M. Reigeluth (Ed.), *Instructional theories in action: Lessons illustrating selected theories and models* (pp. 245–288). Hillsdale, NJ: Lawrence Erlbaum Assoc.

Reigeluth, C.M. (1999). The elaboration theory: Guidance for scope and sequence decisions. In C. M. Reigeluth (Ed.), *Instructional-design theories and models: A new paradigm of instructional theory* (Vol. II, pp. 425–453). Mahwah, NJ: Lawrence Erlbaum Associates.

Reigeluth, C.M. (2007). Order, first step to mastery: An introduction to sequencing in instructional design. In F. Ritter, J. Nerb, E. Lehtinen & T. O'Shea (Eds.), *In order to learn, How the sequence of topics influences learning* (pp. 19–40). New York, NY: Oxford University Press.

Reigeluth, C.M., & Darwazeh, A. (1982). The elaboration theory's procedure for designing instruction: A conceptual approach. *Journal of Instructional Development, 5*(3), 22–32.

Saye, J.W., & Brush, T. (2002). Scaffolding critical reasoning about history and social issues in multimedia-supported learning environments. *Educational Technology Research and Development, 50*(3), 77–96.

Scandura, J.M. (1973). Structural learning and the design of educational materials. *Educational Technology, 13*(8), 7–13.

Stanford University Libraries. (n.d.). Educational fair use guidelines. Retrieved from https://fairuse.stanford.edu/overview/academic-and-educational-permissions/non-coursepack/#educational_fair_use_guidelines.

Stim, R. (2019). *Getting permission: Using & licensing copyright-protected materials online & off* (7th ed.). Pleasanton, CA: Nolo.

U.S. Copyright Office. (2019). U.S. Copyright office fair use index. Retrieved from https://www.copyright.gov/fair-use/.

Vygotsky, L.S. (1978). *Mind in society: The development of higher psychological processes* (M. Cole, V. John-Steiner, S. Scribner, & E. Souberman Eds.). Cambridge, MA: Harvard University Press.

Wood, D.J., Bruner, J.S., & Ross, G. (1976). The role of tutoring in problem solving. *Journal of Child Psychiatry and Psychology, 17*(2), 89–100.

8 Lower Level ADE

Instructional Strategies for Just-in-Time Tutorials

Overview

Having now selected all your content (organizing and supporting), this chapter continues the guidance for selecting instructional strategies – lower-level analysis, design, and evaluation (ADE) – from Chapter 7. It provides considerable detail about designing just-in-time tutorials for both organizing content and supporting content, within both task and topic expertise. But keep in mind that such tutorials may well already exist on online platforms like the Khan Academy. This is part of Step 6.2, introduced in Chapter 7. This guidance is overviewed in Table 8.1, where we identify instructional strategies for the four major kinds of learning.

As a part of Step 6 in Chapter 7, you selected the appropriate instructional formats and designed the "coaching" type of instructional scaffolds. In this chapter, we offer detailed guidance for designing just-in-time tutorials for individual pieces of content (which we call *segments* of instruction) on the lower level of the ADE process, when such tutorials are not already available online. It is often beneficial to do some development simultaneously with the design of these individual segments of instruction.

It is helpful to think of two parts of your development activities: scripting[1] and producing. **Scripting** is developing the exact wording and layout, while **producing** is developing the media according to the script. You may find it easier to do much of the scripting as you make the instructional-strategy and motivational design decisions for each individual piece of content.

The instructional strategies should differ depending on the kind of learning involved:

1. **Remembering** information is rote, nonmeaningful learning.
2. **Understanding** conceptual and theoretical relationships is a kind of meaningful learning that is somewhat like a lightbulb – it happens suddenly when the "aha!" moment comes.
3. **Applying skills** and higher-order skills is a kind of learning that happens gradually with practice.
4. **Acting on attitudes and values** can be learned suddenly or gradually and has affective, behavioral, and cognitive components, such that one can cognitively hold a certain attitude but seldom act on it – of course, there are other kinds of learning in the affective domain, which we will briefly describe later.

---

1   We use this term broadly to refer to all the determination of the exact wording and layout of the instruction for all media – print, digital, human, etc.

Table 8.1 Lower-Level Analysis and Design Processes for Task and Topic Expertise (Continued from Table 7.1)

---

6. Revise and elaborate instruction, media, and assessments for each version or topic
  6.2. Design the scaffolding: coaching and instructing

    1. Remember information
- Primary strategies
- Secondary strategies
- Control strategies

    2. Understand conceptual and theoretical relationships
    Understand causal relationships
- Primary strategies
- Secondary strategies
- Performance strategies
- Control strategies

    Understand natural process relationships
- Primary strategies
- Secondary strategies
- Performance strategies
- Control strategies

    Understand conceptual relationships
- Dimensions of understanding
- Primary strategies
- Secondary strategies
- Control strategies

    3. Apply skills and higher-order skills
- Primary strategies
- Secondary strategies
- Control strategies

    4. Act on attitudes and values
- Primary strategies
- Secondary strategies

Table 8.2 provides some general guidance for the timing of the instructional support.

1. Remember Information

Traditionally, remember-level learning has been overemphasized in both training and education. However, when remembering is important for learners to master a task or topic, it can be accelerated by using appropriate primary, secondary, and control strategies.

Table 8.2 Timing for the Instruction

For Learner-Centered Instruction	For Teacher-Centered Instruction
The project or application should typically be introduced before any instruction is provided. The instruction should be provided "just in time" when it is needed during the project or application. It is usually necessary to "freeze time" in the project or application while the instruction is provided. An ideal way to provide the instruction is for each learner to have a tablet that has their own virtual mentor to tutor them in the required supporting and organizing content or to use a website like the Khan Academy. However, it can alternatively be done by an instructor or peer tutor, though certifying mastery is more problematic this way.	The instruction is typically provided to the whole group of learners before any activities are introduced. This can involve many hours and days of instruction that typically occurs out of context, and thus may be less meaningful and motivational than offering the instruction just in time. However, there may be circumstances that require this approach. If learners all progress in their instruction at the same pace, you may find ways to provide some of the instruction just-in-time during student activities.

Primary Strategies

The primary strategies are to *present* what is to be remembered and to *practice* recalling or recognizing it (depending on the post-instructional requirements) with immediate *feedback* (Leshin, Pollock, & Reigeluth, 1992; Merrill, 1983, 2013).

Presentation

Information to be memorized generally has two parts: the stimulus and the response. The *stimulus* is whatever cue that calls for the information to be remembered, while the *response* is the information to be remembered. For example, the stimulus could be the name of a state and the response its capital. The presentation should provide the stimulus followed immediately by the response.

Practice

Decide if recognition or recall is needed for the real-world task. The practice should provide the stimulus and ask the learner for the response (if *recall* is needed), or it should provide both the stimulus and a right or wrong response and ask the learner if the response is correct (if only *recognition* is needed). Sometimes the real-world task can require occasionally reversing the response and the stimulus, in which case the stimulus and response should occasionally be switched. For example, you could give the name of a capital and ask for its state some of the time and give the name of the state and ask for its capital other times.

The practice should be repeated until the learner has met a *criterion for mastery*, making a separate assessment unnecessary and ensuring that mastery has been reached before the learner moves on, rather than having to remediate later. The criterion may be for accuracy (e.g., "the information is successfully recalled or recognized ten consecutive times unaided") or for speed (e.g., "the speed of correct response averages 1.0 second or less ten consecutive times unaided") – using speed of performance as an indicator that the performance has become automatic (called "automatization" in the research literature), important for freeing up the learner's cognitive resources for higher-level strategic thinking during application of the task or topic.

Feedback

The learner should be given feedback immediately after the response, so the learner may learn from the practice. The feedback can merely confirm the learner is *right or wrong*, or it may provide the *correct response* when the learner is wrong, and it may remind the learner of a *mnemonic* (described under Secondary Strategies) to aid the learner's recall or recognition process.

Secondary Strategies

These strategies (see Table 8.3) are not needed if the information is easy to remember (Gropper, 1974, 1983; Merrill, 1983). More secondary strategies should be used when the information is more difficult to remember. However, when in doubt, include fewer secondary strategies (minimalist instruction), and add in more if learners have difficulty in your formative evaluations.

Control Strategies

Control strategies are for controlling the use of the other two kinds of strategies, such as amount and timing of those strategies. The two main control strategies are *instructor* (digital or human) *control* and *learner control*. Memorizing information is a burdensome task and many aspects of the instruction are often best controlled by the instructor, even in learner-centered instruction. Guidelines for the control strategies are shown in Table 8.4, but please keep in mind that the optimal control of instructional strategies can vary a lot from one situation to another and one learner to another.

2. Understand Conceptual and Theoretical Relationships

We have just offered guidance for instructional strategies for remembering information. Here we address understanding relationships. This kind of learning is promoted by different instructional strategies depending on whether the relationships are causal, natural process, or conceptual.

Table 8.3 Secondary Strategies for Remember-Level Instruction

Strategy	Guidance
Repetition	Use for both the presentation and the practice.
Chunking	Divide up large amounts of information into manageable chunks – usually seven plus or minus two items, according to research by Miller (1956) – and use presentation, practice, and feedback until mastery on one chunk before moving to the next chunk. The more complex the information, the smaller the chunks should be.
Spacing	Provide for passage of some time between consecutive practice or assessment items for any given piece of information.
Prompting	Provide hints (e.g., "begins with 'p'") when the learner has difficulty remembering an item.
Mnemonics	Include rhymes, songs, acronyms, images, and so forth, when helpful. You can provide them, or you can request the learners to develop their own. You can also provide prompting to provide hints for remembering the mnemonic.
Review	Periodically assess the learner on an item from an earlier chunk (called the "review pool" by Salisbury, 1990), and if the learner could not remember it, include it in the "active pool."

Table 8.4 Control Strategies for Remember-Level Instruction

Strategies	Control Strategy
Presentation and Practice	Presentation should usually begin under *instructor* control with one round of presentation for a chunk, and then typically revert to *learner* control. Practice should be under *learner* control, but the practice should generally continue until the current chunk is mastered. Ideally, learners should be coached to self-direct the decisions about when to receive presentation or practice.
Repetition of Presentation and Practice	The *learner* should be able to look at the information (stimulus and response together or the entire chunk of information) whenever they want. Also, each item in a chunk should be repeated in each round of practice until it is mastered, based on the criterion for number of consecutive correct responses and/or speed of responses (*instructor* control). When the criterion is met, the item is put into the "review pool" and periodically placed back into the "active pool" for review in subsequent chunks (Salisbury, 1990). Decisions about item selection within a chunk should typically be done randomly unless order of items is a natural part of the remember-level task in the real world (*instructor* control). It is difficult for the learner to manage this process.
Chunking	*Learners* should be helped to self-direct decisions about the size of the chunks, adjusting the size based on the learner's current and past performance with chunks of similar size, complexity, and level of familiarity. However, digital systems are well suited to make such decisions and are usually more effective (*instructor* control).
Spacing (Review)	Decisions about spacing (frequency of review) should be made based on historical data about optimal spacing for review of mastered items for each student (*instructor* control). Typically, the spacing of review gradually increases (farther apart) over time for a given item, unless the learner fails a review, in which case its spacing decreases (its frequency of review increases). These decisions are difficult for learners to make on their own but easy to implement on a digital device.
Prompting	The *learner* could be allowed to request a prompt at any time a response is not forthcoming, but the *instructor* could also provide a prompt if the learner takes a long time to respond. (Of course, prompted practice does not count toward mastery of the item.)
Mnemonics	Mnemonics are typically provided by the *instructor* to all learners, but they could be offered only when a learner has difficulty remembering (*instructor* or *learner* control), or the learner may be prompted and aided to generate a mnemonic of his or her own (*instructor* and *learner* control); or the learner could request a mnemonic or generate a mnemonic of their own unprompted and unaided (*learner* control).

2.1 Understand Causal Relationships

Causal relationships typically exist in sets, wherein there are multiple causes of an effect, multiple effects of a cause, chains of cause-effect relationships, and cycles of cause-effect relationships (see Figure 8.1). These sets are called causal models. This kind of learning can be promoted by using appropriate primary, secondary, performance, and control strategies (Reigeluth, 1983; Reigeluth & Schwartz, 1989; Sloman, 2005; White & Frederiksen, 1990).

Primary Strategies

The primary instructional strategies are related to acquisition and application of the causal relationship(s). **Acquisition** is promoted by telling the learner what the causal relationships are (a *generality*) and providing the learner with examples of them (*demonstrations*). **Application** is promoted by providing opportunities for the learner to use the causal

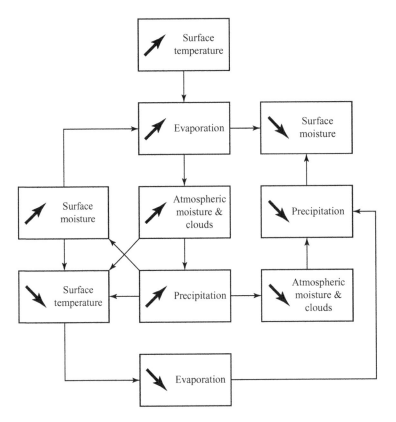

Figure 8.1 Example of a Causal model.

relationships (*practice*), with immediate *feedback* (see Table 8.5). The primary strategy for assessment is unaided practice to a criterion for mastery.

Secondary Strategies

These strategies (see Table 8.6) are not needed if the causal relationships are easy to understand. More strategies should be used as the causal relationships become more difficult to understand. However, when in doubt, include fewer secondary strategies (minimalist instruction), and add in more if learners have difficulty in your formative evaluations.

Kinds of Performance

The basic elements of causal understanding are causes and effects, often in chains and with multiple causes and multiple effects, making for complex causal models. These causal models can be used in three different ways (three kinds of performance) – explanation, prediction, and solution (see the left column in Table 8.7) – meaning that the kind of performance shown in the demonstrations and required in the practice can be any of those three types (Reigeluth & Schwartz, 1989). For complex causal relationships, there are multiple causes, multiple effects, cause-effect chains, and causal loops, and the relationships are probabilistic rather than deterministic. Probabilistic means that the causal

Table 8.5 Examples of the Primary Strategies for Understanding Causal Relationships

Phase of Learning	*Acquisition*		*Application*	
Primary Strategy	*Generality*	*Demonstration*	*Practice*	*Feedback*
Example 1. Principle of Thermal Expansion	Metals expand when heated; the more the heating, the more the expansion.	(Show a video demonstrating that the length of a steel rod changes when it is heated up.)	What would happen to railroad rails on a hot day if they were installed touching end to end on a cold day?	(Ask questions or give hints that help the learner to discover his/her error(s) or misconceptions.)
Example 2. Law of Demand	An increase in demand causes an increase in price, and a decrease in demand causes a decrease in price.	In November 2018, a decrease in demand for Apple Inc. stock caused a 30% drop in price.	What would happen to the price of bananas if they became unpopular?	(Ask questions or give hints that help the learner to discover his/her error(s) or misconceptions.)

Table 8.6 Secondary Strategies for Understanding Causal Relationships

Form of Generality	Can be either expository (wherein a prototypical demonstration of the causal relationship should be provided with the generality) or confirmatory (discovered by the learner from examples).
Form of Demonstration	Can be either passive (observation) or active (involving exploration or manipulation of either the causes to observe their effects, or the effects to observe what caused them).
Form of Feedback	Should almost always be immediate.
	Can be either natural (natural consequences, as in a simulation) or artificial (supplied by the instructor or other medium).
	Can simply confirm (right or wrong), provide a hint, provide the correct answer, and/or provide an explanation.
	Can be informational and/or motivational.
Attention-Focusing Devices	Can be used on the generality, demonstrations, and feedback (e.g., bold, color, loudness, zoom, etc.).
Alternative Representations	Can be used on the generality, demonstrations, and feedback (e.g., verbal, visual, auditory, paraphrase, etc.). If the causal relationships are portrayed with different representations in the real world, then practice should also be portrayed with those various representations.
Easy-to-Difficult Sequence	May or may not be used on the demonstrations and practice, depending on the difficulty of the causal understanding.

factor increases the chances that the effect will happen, whereas deterministic means that the effect is certain to happen. The kind(s) of performance used in the demonstrations and practice (explanation, prediction, and/or solution) should be consistent with those required by application of the task or topic in the real-world.

One other aspect of using causal understanding in the application of a task or topic is that it requires learning a *performance strategy* for doing that kind of performance using the causal understanding. You need to identify the performance strategy, which is typically more heuristic than procedural. This performance strategy should be explicitly taught using a

Table 8.7 Performance Strategies for Causal Understanding

Kinds of Performance, Each of Which Requires a Strategy for Using the Causal Model	Teach a Performance Strategy (for all three kinds of performance)
Explanation: an effect is given, and the learner is asked to explain what caused it *Prediction*: a causal event is given, and the learner is asked to predict what will happen as a result *Solution*: a desired effect (goal) is given, and the learner is asked to implement the necessary events (causes) to bring it about	*Generality*: tell them how to use the causal model to explain, predict, or solve *Demonstrations*: show them how to use it *Practice with feedback*: have them use it, and give them feedback

generality, demonstrations, and practice with feedback (see the right column in Table 8.7). A generality alone may be sufficient if the strategy is an easy one. Automatization (or "overlearning" – meeting a speed criterion after meeting an accuracy criterion) may be important if the real-world performance is done under time pressure or while performing other tasks at the same time.

Control Strategies

As always, the two main control strategies are instructor control (digital or human) and learner control. Guidelines for their use are shown in Table 8.8. Again, it should be apparent that these guidelines for instructor control are easier to implement on a digital medium than by a human. And please keep in mind that the optimal control of instructional strategies can vary a lot from one situation to another and one learner to another.

2.2 Understand Natural Process Relationships

The basic element of process understanding is a natural sequence of events. Sequences performed by humans are not included, for they are a kind of skill. An example is the phases in the life cycle of a flowering plant: a seed sprouts into a seedling, a seedling grows into a mature plant, the mature plant develops a flower, and the flower forms seeds. Strategies for teaching and assessing this kind of learning (Reigeluth & Schwartz, 1989) also include primary, secondary, performance, and control strategies, and they are similar to those for causal understanding. Therefore, the following only focuses on the differences, beginning with primary strategies.

Primary Strategies

The primary strategies are to tell the learner what the events in the natural process are (*generality*), show the learner what they are (*demonstration*), and provide opportunities for the learner to use the natural process (*practice*), with immediate *feedback* (see Table 8.9). The kind of performance shown in the demonstrations and required in the practice is typically *description*, which entails describing the events and their sequence. Such descriptions may include the entire natural process, or they may be as small as describing what immediately precedes or follows a given event (phase) in the process. The kind(s) of performance used in the demonstrations and practice should be consistent with those required by applying the task or topic in the real world. The primary strategy for *assessment* is unaided practice until a criterion for mastery is reached.

Table 8.8 Control Strategies for Causal Understanding

Method	Control Strategy
Type of Performance	The *instructor* (digital or human) typically decides on the type(s) of performance to be taught, based on the real-world applications, but in many cases, this can be done effectively under *learner* control.
Performance Strategy	For difficult causal models, the performance strategy is introduced to the learner (with generality and demonstration) under *instructor* control. Then it is often placed under *learner* control for further access when needed, but wrong-answer feedback typically includes a reminder of the performance strategy under *instructor* control.
Form of Generality	Since deep understanding is particularly important for causal understanding, the decision to use the discovery form of the generality is typically under *instructor* control (universal), but it can be done effectively under *learner* control (making it optional).
Form of Demonstration	Similarly, since deep understanding is particularly important for causal understanding, the decision to use active rather than passive demonstration (as either manipulation or exploration) is typically under *instructor* control (universal).
Timing	The decision as to whether and when to see the generality, demonstrations, and practice are typically under *learner* control (especially with learners coached in making such decisions).
Attention-Focusing	These are often under *instructor* control (universal) at first, then placed under *learner* control.
Alternative Representations	These are also often under *instructor* control (universal) at first, then placed under *learner* control.
Difficulty Level	This is under *instructor* control by default, meaning it is adapted automatically to learner performance – for example, if the learner gets a practice item wrong, an easier one is automatically given – but the *learner* may also request items of a different difficulty.
Automatization	Automatization of a response or skill entails making it automatic – such an ingrained habit that the performer does not need to think about it to do it. It requires overlearning. It is generally under *instructor* control, using a criterion for speed of performance that matches real-world needs. For example, the instruction might be designed to require automatization of the ability to parallel park a car, using a time criterion of five seconds, along with an accuracy criterion of no more than eight inches from the curb and no touching the cars on either end of the parking space.

Table 8.9 Examples of Primary Strategies for Understanding Natural Processes

Strategies	Generality	Demonstration	Practice	Feedback
Examples for the Life Cycle of a Flowering Plant	A seed grows into a seedling, which grows into a mature plant, which develops a flower, which produces seeds	A series of photos (or a time-lapse video) of a particular plant going through these stages	Show a photo of a different plant and ask what will happen next (or what preceded it)	Confirm for a correct answer, or give hints for an incorrect answer until it is correct

Secondary Strategies

These strategies are the same as for causal understanding, except that the need for automatization is rare.

Performance Strategies

A *performance strategy* may be important for using this kind of understanding in the performance of a version of a task or application of a topic and may, therefore, also need to be explicitly taught using a generality, demonstrations, and practice with feedback.

Control Strategies

These strategies are also the same as for causal understanding.

2.3 Understand Conceptual Relationships

Conceptual understanding is primarily a matter of understanding the relationships among concepts (Reigeluth, 1983). Strategies for teaching and assessing this kind of learning also include primary, secondary, and control strategies, but they are heavily influenced by the desired dimensions of understanding (the important kinds of conceptual relationships).

Dimensions of understanding. Different kinds of relationships constitute different dimensions of understanding. The major kinds of relationships include superordinate, coordinate, and subordinate (in which the concepts may be either parts or kinds of each other), analogical, and experiential (for examples, see Table 8.10). Many other types exist but are less common (e.g., order, importance, location). The types of relationships (dimensions of understanding) that you teach should be consistent with those required in the real-world applications.

Primary Strategies

The primary instructional strategies are to portray the relationship (*description*) and to provide opportunities for the learner to use the relationship (*application*), with immediate *feedback*. An example of a description strategy is, "One kind of passenger plane is the Boeing 767." An example of an application strategy is, "What are some kinds of passenger planes?" Demonstrations (examples) are not as relevant here as they are for skills, causal understanding, and process understanding. The primary strategy for assessment is unaided *application* until a criterion for mastery is reached.

Table 8.10 Instructional Strategies for Each Major Kind of Relationship

Kind of Relationship	Instructional Strategy	Example
Superordinate	Context	One dimension of understanding the concept "civil war" is understanding that it is a kind of war (the kinds-superordinate relationship)
Coordinate	Comparison and contrast	One dimension of understanding the concept "civil war" is understanding how it is similar to and different from a revolutionary war (the kinds-coordinate relationship)
Subordinate	Analysis	One dimension of understanding the concept "civil war" is analyzing its major kinds (e.g., religious, geographical, ethnic)
Analogical	Analogy	One dimension of understanding the concept "civil war" is learning about its similarities and differences with a family feud
Experiential	Instantiation	One dimension of understanding the concept "civil war" is studying a case, such as the Irish civil war

Different kinds of relationships require different kinds of descriptions and applications, as shown in Table 8.10. The most common strategies (descriptions and applications) include context, comparison and contrast, analysis, analogy (which entails identifying similarities between the concept and a similar concept outside the area of interest) along with the limitations of the analogy (differences between the two concepts), and instantiation (providing a concrete instance of the concept). Instantiation is perhaps the most fundamental of all dimensions of understanding, for it alone can prevent circularity of definitions by tapping into (or adding to) one's experiential memory store to provide the most basic understanding. All the other relationships are among generalities or definitions of the concepts. In cases where the learner has no preexisting experience with instances of a concept, it is necessary to introduce such experience. Otherwise, it is only necessary to relate the concept to the learner's prior experience. Both are forms of instantiation.

These strategies address the most common dimensions of conceptual understanding, but there are many others. The important point is that each dimension of conceptual understanding (or type of relationship between concepts) requires a different primary instructional strategy, and that strategy entails description and/or application (e.g., describe an analogy to the learner or have the learner describe the analogy).

Secondary Strategies

These strategies (see Table 8.11) are not needed if the concepts are easy to understand. Again, it is more efficient to use a minimalist approach when unsure if secondary strategies are needed, and to add more if your formative evaluation reveals the need.

Control Strategies

Guidelines for the use of the primary and secondary strategies are shown in Table 8.12. Again, instructor control is easier to implement on a digital device than by a human. And please keep in mind that the optimal control of instructional strategies can vary a lot from one situation to another and one learner to another.

3. Apply Skills and Higher-Order Skills

We have offered guidance for instructional strategies for remembering information and understanding relationships. Here we address skills. Strategies for teaching and assessing

Table 8.11 Secondary Strategies for Conceptual Understanding

Method	Secondary Strategies
Form of Description	Can be either expository or confirmatory (discovery through applications)
Form of Application	Can be for a single dimension or for the entire spectrum of dimensions of understanding desired, and can be separate or integrated into a task
Form of Feedback	Should be immediate; it can be simply confirmatory, provide a hint, or provide a paraphrased description; and it can be informational and/or motivational
Attention-Focusing	Highlighting in print, emphasis in audio, and zoom in video, can be used on the descriptions and feedback
Alternative Representations	Paraphrasing, visuals, audio, and video can be used to enhance the descriptions and feedback

Table 8.12 Control Strategies for Conceptual Understanding

Method	Control Strategy
Dimensions of Understanding	The *instructor* (digital or human) typically decides on the dimension(s) of understanding to be taught, based on the real-world applications. (The learner typically doesn't know all the important real-world applications and therefore doesn't know which dimensions of understanding are important.)
Form of the Description	The decision to use the discovery form of the generality is typically under *instructor* control (universal), depending on the difficulty and importance of the understanding. When the discovery form is used, retention rate is typically better, though time-to-mastery tends to be a bit longer.
Timing	In contrast, the decision as to whether and when to see the description and the application is typically under *learner* control.
Attention-Focusing	These are often under *instructor* control (universal) at first, then placed under *learner* control (to choose when useful).
Alternative Representations	These are also often under *instructor* control (universal) at first, then placed under *learner* control.
Number of Applications	This is *instructor* controlled, based on the criterion for proficiency.

this kind of learning (Merrill, 1983, 2013; van Merriënboer, 1997; van Merriënboer & Sluijsmans, 2009) also include primary, secondary, and control strategies.

Primary Strategies

The primary strategies for instruction are to tell the learner how to do it (*generality*), show the learner how to do it (*demonstration*), and provide opportunities for the learner to do it (*practice*), with immediate *feedback*. For assessment, the primary strategy is unaided practice to a criterion for mastery. Each of these instructional strategies (except feedback) differs a bit depending on whether the skills are concept-classification, procedure-using, or principle-using (see Table 8.13).

Table 8.13 Different Primary Instructional Strategies for Different Kinds of Skills

	Concept-Classification	*Procedure-Using*	*Principle-Using*
Generality	Label Superordinate concept Critical characteristics	Goal Steps	Causal change Resulting change (effect) or Phases
Demonstration	Present an instance Say whether or not it is an example of the concept	Present a goal & case Perform the steps	Present a case – cause or effect Show its effect or cause, or Show phases of a case
Practice	Present a new instance Ask whether or not it is an example of the concept	Present a goal & new case Ask student to perform the steps	Present a case – cause or effect or process Ask to predict effect, explain a cause, or achieve a desired effect (goal), or Ask to describe the phases
Feedback	Say right/wrong, or Give correct answer, or Give a hint	Say right/wrong, or Give correct answer, or Give a hint	Say right/wrong, or Give correct answer, or Give a hint

While generality, demonstration, practice, and feedback are all important for higher-order skills, they are different in the following ways:

- Typically, both procedure-using and principle-using strategies are involved.
- Since broader transfer is required, the demonstrations and practice must have considerably greater divergence, but it is best to concentrate on a few variations at a time.
- Since they take longer to master, instruction should be spaced over weeks or years using the simplifying conditions method (see Chapter 6).

Secondary Strategies

These strategies (see Table 8.14) are not needed if the skill is easy to learn. They are increasingly helpful with increasingly difficult skills. Again, it is more efficient to use a minimalist approach when unsure if secondary strategies are needed, and to add more if your product evaluation reveals the need.

Control Strategies

Guidelines for the use of the primary and secondary strategies are shown in Table 8.15. Again, instructor control is easier to implement on a digital device than by a human, and learner control can also be somewhat easier on a digital device.

Table 8.14 Secondary Strategies for Applying Skills

Method	Secondary Strategy
Inductive or Deductive	An inductive approach begins with demonstrations (or practice) and has the learner discover the generality, whereas a deductive approach begins with the generality and follows with demonstrations and practice. Sometimes, the generality is given simultaneously with the demonstration, providing a hybrid approach. The inductive approach can begin with either demonstrations or practice, depending on the learner's tolerance for failure. The inductive approach tends to result in better understanding and retention of the skill, whereas the deductive approach tends to be more efficient. The inductive approach also enhances inductive reasoning and skills.
Attention-Focusing	Highlighting in textual messages, emphasis in audio messages, and zoom in video messages, to name a few, can be used to enhance the generality, demonstrations, and feedback.
Alternative Representations	Paraphrasing, visuals, audio, and video, can be used to enhance the generality, demonstrations, and feedback.
Prototypical Demonstration	Can be provided simultaneously with the generality.
Easy-to-Difficult Sequence	Can be used to enhance the demonstrations and practice.
Item Divergence (variations)	Can be used to enhance the demonstrations and practice (making the items as different as possible from each other, within the full domain of items encountered in the real world, or at least within the types of items encountered at this level of the instruction).
Prompting	Can be used with the practice.
Automatization	Can be used with the practice by including a criterion for speed of performance in addition to a criterion for accuracy.

Table 8.15 Control Strategies for Applying Skills

Method	Control Strategy
Inductive or Deductive Approach	This decision can be universal for all learners based on the requirements of the task (*instructor* control), or it can be tailored to the learning style of each learner based on whether the learner is a concrete or abstract thinker (*instructor* control), or it can be placed under *learner* control based on learner preference. The deductive approach typically begins with simultaneous generality and demonstration (*instructor* control), though the *learner* can be given control over this decision.
Sequence of Primary Strategies	After the initial instruction (inductive or deductive), the *learner* is typically given control over which primary strategy component to use next: another demonstration, another practice, or review of the generality. However, the *instructor* could exercise some control over this decision, based either on the learner's learning style or the desire to expose the learner to multiple ways of learning, or if the learner is not making wise learner-control decisions.
Sequence of Secondary Strategies	The *learner* is typically given control over whether to receive attention-focusing devices or alternative representations, and what difficulty level to receive next for demonstrations and practice. However, the *instructor* could exercise some control over these decisions, based either on the learner's learning style or the desire to expose the learner to multiple ways of learning, or if the learner is not making wise learner-control decisions.
Prompting	Decisions for prompting are generally made by the *learner*, but the *instructor* might intervene with a prompt if the learner takes too long to perform.
Automatization	The decision to automatize the skill is generally under *instructor* control, along with the criterion for speed of performance, based on real-world requirements.

4. Act on Attitudes or Values

As mentioned in Chapter 3, there are many kinds of learning in the affective domain. Krathwohl, Bloom and Masia (1964) categorized this domain into five stages of affective learning: receiving, responding, valuing, organizing, and characterizing. Common categories of affective learning include attitudes, values, morals, ethics, emotions, intrapersonal skills, interpersonal skills, and more. In particular, social and emotional learning (SEL) has received increasing attention since about 2000, but most of the literature is about what to teach, rather than how to teach it (see e.g., Osher et al., 2016). What little there is on how to teach it includes the following instructional strategies (Dusenbury & Weissberg, 2017):

- Attach verbal labels to emotional states to make those states more manageable
- Practice taking the perspective of another to build empathy
- Create a school environment conducive to developing healthy emotional and social behaviors
- Create meaningful real-life opportunities to use SEL skills
- Establish structures to reinforce effective use of SEL skills

These kinds of learning are very complex, resulting in at least 136 frameworks (Berg, Osher, Moroney, & Yoder, 2017) and research is far from conclusive on how best to foster them. Therefore, in this book we only address attitudes and values. Strategies for teaching and assessing this kind of learning (Crano & Prislin, 2008; Kamradt & Kamradt, 1999) also include primary and secondary strategies.

Table 8.16 Examples of Primary Instructional Strategies for Acting on Attitudes

Attitude Component	Cognitive	Affective	Behavioral
Primary Strategy	Persuasion	Operant conditioning	Demonstrations, practice and feedback
Examples for Attitude toward Sexual Harassment in the Workplace	Explore reasons why sexual harassment is bad	Enhance empathy by exploring how their wife/sister/mother would feel about it	Create a roleplay situation and provide intrinsic rewards for good behavior
Examples for Attitude about Courteous Driving	Explore reasons why courteous driving is important	Enhance empathy by exploring (and even experiencing) how the learner would feel in response to courteous and uncourteous driving by others	Create a roleplay situation for the learner to practice courteous behaviors and experience the good feelings that result

Primary Strategies

Attitudes and values have three major components: cognitive, affective, and psychomotor (or behavioral). Each requires a different primary strategy (see Table 8.16). The cognitive component requires *persuasion* through cognitive reasoning during guided discussions. The affective component requires *operant conditioning* (giving or withholding rewards) to develop positive feelings about the attitude or value. This can be done vicariously through social modeling, such as observing a person with whom one can easily empathize in a film. The psychomotor or behavioral component requires *demonstrations* and *practice with feedback* to develop the appropriate behaviors. There is often discrepancy between people's attitudes or values and their actual behaviors. For example, teachers with learner-centered teaching beliefs could be teacher-centered in actual practice. We found that various barriers or factors often prevent teachers from creating learner-centered classrooms even though they have learner-centered beliefs (An & Reigeluth, 2011). Thus, it is important to address all three components to change an existing attitude and consider external factors (e.g., social pressure) to change actual behaviors. Also, the weaker a learner's initial attitude, the easier it will be for the learner to adopt the desired attitude. It is even possible that multiple steps along the continuum will not be necessary.

Secondary Strategies

Since attitudes and values typically exist on a continuum as described in Chapter 3, all three components should be moved to a new position on the continuum as close to simultaneously as possible, where the attitude or value should be consolidated before making another move along the continuum. This process continues until the desired point on the continuum is reached. In the case of attitude toward sexual harassment, the continuum would range from attitude toward very blatant, offensive behaviors all the way to attitude toward behaviors that only a few people might find offensive.

Where Are We?

All of the above guidance (see summary in Table 8.1) is part of Step 6.2, Design the Scaffolding, in Chapter 7. While you are working on the "Instructional Strategies" part of

Step 6.2, you should simultaneously work on Step 6.3, Design the Motivational Support, in Chapter 7. When you have finished with them, you should continue with Step 6.4, Design the Assessments. And when you have finished with Steps 7, Formatively Evaluate the ADE Document, and Step 8, Begin Developing the Implementation Plan, and Update the Project Management Plan, in Chapter 7, you have finished your ADE process for the qualitative approach to **rapid prototyping**. For the quantitative approach, you should repeat all three levels of the ADE process for the next part of your instructional system.

Finally, Develop and Deploy are addressed in Chapters 9–12. The whole ADE process is again summarized in Table 8.17.

Exercises

Here again we offer suggestions for a professor using this book as a textbook in a course, to help the students understand more deeply the contents of this chapter. We suggest that

Table 8.17 ADE Process for Task Expertise and Topic Expertise (Differences Are in **Bold**)

	Task Expertise	*Topic Expertise*
Top Level Ch. 5	1. Select and sequence top-level content 2. Plan high-level instructional methods 3. Formatively evaluate and document the top-level design	1. Select and sequence top-level content 2. Plan high-level instructional methods 3. Formatively evaluate and document the top-level design
Mid Level Ch. 6	1. Identify and sequence **versions of each task** 2. Identify variations within each **version** and create designer objectives 3. Formatively evaluate the findings 4. Develop the learner objectives for each **version** 5. Design learner assessments for each **version** 6. Design the ways that learning by doing will be accomplished for each **version** 7. Select media in general for the **version** 8. Formatively evaluate and document the results	1. Identify and sequence **applications of each topic** 2. Identify variations within each **application** and create designer objectives 3. Formatively evaluate the findings 4. Develop the learner objectives for each **topic** 5. Design learner assessments for each **topic** 6. Design the ways that learning by doing will be accomplished for each **topic** 7. Select media in general for the **application** 8. Formatively evaluate and document the results
Lower Level Ch. 7	1. Select and sequence the organizing content for each **version of the task** 2. Select and classify the supporting content for each **version** 3. Sequence the supporting content for each **version** 4. Evaluate and document the findings 5. Identify resource requirements, availability, and existing instruction for each **version** 6. Revise and elaborate the instruction and assessments for each **version** 7. Formatively evaluate the ADE document 8. Begin developing the implementation plan, and update the project management plan	1. Select and sequence the organizing content for each **topic** 2. Select and classify the supporting content for each **topic** 3. Sequence the supporting content for each **topic** 4. Evaluate and document the findings 5. Identify resource requirements, availability, and existing instruction for each **topic** 6. Revise and elaborate the instruction and assessments for each **topic** 7. Formatively evaluate the ADE document 8. Begin developing the implementation plan, and update the project management plan
Ch. 8	Detailed guidance is provided for Lower-Level Step 6: Revise and Elaborate the Instruction and Assessments for Each Version/Topic. It includes instructional strategies for: • Remembering information • Understanding relationships • Applying skills and higher-order skills • Acting on attitudes or values	

you keep the same teams of about three students each to continue to work on their ID projects throughout the course. However, these exercises can be done individually by any reader who wants to deepen their understanding and skills.

1. Have each team prepare a script for the instruction on at least one difficult piece of content for each of the four kinds of learning for the version or topic in their lower-level ADE document. For what you consider to be the best scripts, we suggest you get written permission from the students to use them as examples in the next offering of your course.
2. Have each team offer suggestions for improvement for the scripts of one or two other teams before you review and provide feedback to the students.
3. Have a whole-class, synchronous discussion of the strengths and weaknesses of this lower-level scripting process, including any difficulties or challenges they faced during the process and what changes to the process might have helped. We would love to get your suggestions for improvement.

References

An, Y., & Reigeluth, C.M. (2011). Creating technology-enhanced, learner-centered classrooms: K-12 teachers' beliefs, perceptions, barriers, and support needs. *Journal of Digital Learning in Teacher Education, 29*(2), 54–62.

Berg, J., Osher, D., Moroney, D., & Yoder, N. (2017). *The intersection of school climate and social and emotional development*. Washington, DC: American Institutes for Research (AIR). Retrieved from https://www.air.org/resource/intersection-school-climate-and-social-and-emotional-development.

Crano, W.D., & Prislin, R. (Eds.). (2008). *Attitudes and attitude change*. New York, NY: Taylor & Francis Group.

Dusenbury, L., & Weissberg, R.P. (2017). Social emotional learning in elementary school: Preparations for success. Retrieved from https://www.rwjf.org/en/library/research/2017/04/social-emotional-learning-in-elementary-school.html.

Gropper, G.L. (1974). *Instructional strategies*. Englewood Cliffs, NJ: Educational Technology Publications.

Gropper, G.L. (1983). A behavioral approach to instructional prescription. In C.M. Reigeluth (Ed.), *Instructional-design theories and models: An overview of their current status* (Vol. I, pp. 101–161). Hillsdale, NJ: Lawrence Erlbaum Assoc.

Kamradt, T.F., & Kamradt, E.J. (1999). Structured design for attitudinal instruction. In C.M. Reigeluth (Ed.), *Instructional-design theories and models: A new paradigm of instructional theory* (Vol. II, pp. 563–590). Mahwah, NJ: Lawrence Erlbaum Associates.

Krathwohl, D.R., Bloom, B.S., & Masia, B.B. (1964). *Taxonomy of educational objectives: The classification of educational goals: Handbook 2, Affective domain*. New York: Longman.

Leshin, C.B., Pollock, J., & Reigeluth, C.M. (1992). *Instructional design strategies and tactics*. Englewood Cliffs, NJ: Educational Technology Publications.

Merrill, M.D. (1983). Component display theory. In C.M. Reigeluth (Ed.), *Instructional-design theories and models: An overview of their current status* (Vol. I). Hillsdale, NJ: Lawrence Erlbaum Associates.

Merrill, M.D. (2013). *First principles of instruction: Identifying and designing effective, efficient, and engaging instruction*. San Francisco, CA: Pfeiffer.

Miller, G.A. (1956). The magical number seven, plus or minus two: Some limits on our capacity for processing information. *Psychological Review, 63*(2), 81–97. doi:10.1037/h0043158

Osher, D., Kidron, Y., Brackett, M., Dymnicki, A., Jones, S., & Weissberg, R.P. (2016). Advancing the science and practice of social and emotional learning: Looking back and moving forward. In *Review of Research in Education, 1*, pp. 644–681).

Reigeluth, C.M. (1983). Meaningfulness and instruction: Relating what is being learned to what a student knows. *Instructional Science, 12*(3), 197–218 doi:10.1007/BF00051745.

Reigeluth, C.M., & Schwartz, E. (1989). An instructional theory for the design of computer-based simulations. *Journal of Computer-Based Instruction, 16*(1), 1–10.

Salisbury, D.F. (1990). Cognitive psychology and Its implications for designing drill and practice programs for computers. *Journal of Computer-Based Instruction, 17*(1), 23–30.

Sloman, S. (2005). *Causal models: How people think about the world and its alternatives.* New York, NY: Oxford University Press.

van Merriënboer, J.J.G. (1997). *Training complex cognitive skills: A four-component instructional design model for technical training.* Englewood Cliffs, NJ: Educational Technology Publications.

van Merriënboer, J.J.G., & Sluijsmans, D.M.A. (2009). Toward a synthesis of cognitive load theory, four-component instructional design, and self-directed learning. *Educational Psychology Review, 21*(1), 55–66.

White, B.Y., & Frederiksen, J.R. (1990). Causal model progressions as a foundation for intelligent learning environments. *Artificial Intelligence, 42*(1), 99–157.

Unit 3

Develop

This unit has two chapters. The first offers guidance for developing the instruction, including such things as producing instructional media, scriptwriting and storyboarding, graphic design, and developing a learner guide and instructor guide. The second, Chapter 10, provides guidance for conducting formative evaluations, an essential part of the development process. Types of formative evaluation include expert reviews, individual tryouts, small-group tryouts, and operational field tests, as well as alpha and beta tests for individual e-learning.

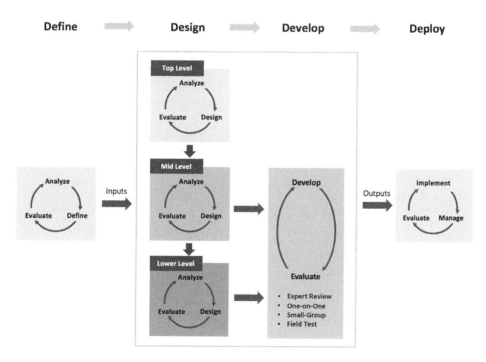

Our Holistic 4D Model of ID.

9 Development

Overview

When a blueprint of the instruction has been created that includes what to teach, how to teach it, and how to assess it, you are ready to realize your design in the development phase. In Chapter 8 we explained that there are two major parts of the development phase: scripting and producing. **Scripting** is developing the exact wording and layout, while **producing** is developing the media according to the script. You may have done much of the scripting as you made the instructional-strategy and other design decisions for each individual piece of content (Chapter 8). However, some additional scripting and script revision will be necessary as you produce your instructional media, be they print, digital, human, or other.

It is important to understand that the development process varies depending on many factors, including the type of instruction as well as development staff and resources available. This chapter begins by discussing how the **type of instruction** influences the work involved in the development phase. Then it offers guidance for developing instructional content for **learner-centered instruction (LCI)**. Further, this chapter provides guidance for producing instructional media, scriptwriting and storyboarding, graphic design, developing technology-enhanced instruction, and developing a learner guide and an instructor guide. Finally, the chapter emphasizes the importance of frequent formative evaluation and revisions (discussed in detail in Chapter 10) throughout the development process.

The Development Process Varies Depending on the Type of Instruction

LCI vs. instructor-centered instruction (ICI). The type of the instruction greatly influences the work involved in the development phase. First, developing learner-centered instruction (LCI) is different from developing ICI. For typical ICI, you might develop PowerPoint presentations or lecture videos, handouts or reading materials, and assessment materials. On the other hand, for LCI you might develop project instructions, project media (e.g., videos, images) for presenting problem scenarios, a learner guide and instructor guide, and just-in-time learning and scaffolding resources.

Online vs. face-to-face. Second, developing online instruction is different from developing face-to-face instruction, and blended learning involves both. For online instruction you need to think about such aspects as navigation, online communication (e.g., synchronous vs. asynchronous), online interactions (e.g., instructor-learner, learner-learner, learner-content), and online accessibility. In contrast, strictly face-to-face instruction involves developing resources to guide instructors and learners in either an LCI or ICI classroom environment.

Learning management system (LMS), development platform, or neither. In Chapter 5 at the end of Step 2 (Plan Big-Picture Instructional Methods), we encouraged you to:

- Determine whether you are required to use, or want to use, a template or pattern for your instruction
- Decide whether the instruction will be delivered on a predetermined platform (course management or learning management system)
- And, if either, to note the limitations of the template and/or platform, so you could take them into account when making instructional design decisions

If you did not have to make a choice then, you should decide now what would work best for your instructional system. A learning or course management system (e.g., Blackboard, Canvas, Desire2Learn, and Moodle) is often a vital part of development for online or blended learning, especially when a large amount of content needs to be taught. **Learning management systems** enable designers and instructors to easily create and deliver online courses by providing various tools. Therefore, we encourage you to explore a variety of LMSs and choose the one that best meets your needs and constraints. In addition, a **development platform** may speed up (and change) the development process, but also may place major constraints on it, especially in e-learning.

Instructor present or not. Fourth, developing instructor-free instruction (instruction in which no instructor is involved) is very different from developing instructor-present instruction (where there is an instructor, however infrequently). Instructor-free instruction, especially instructor-free e-learning, is becoming more popular, because it allows learners to develop knowledge and skills at their own pace at a time and place that is convenient for them. However, without any interactions with instructors and classmates, learners may lack self-direction and time-management skills. Developing effective instructor-free instruction requires developing robust learner guides, embedded scaffolds, immediate informational feedback, and self-reflection and self-evaluation tools, which are otherwise typically provided by effective instructors.

Advanced media. Finally, developing innovative learning environments, such as digital game-based learning, gamified learning, and virtual reality learning environments, often requires collaboration among diverse kinds of development specialists. Typically, a large team is established to carry out a development plan when substantial amounts of advanced or complex media are included.

Developing Instruction for LCI

The following are some of the kinds of instructional content that need to be developed for learner-centered instruction.

a. For projects and applications: the goals, context, resources, etc.
b. For scaffolding: the generalities, examples, practice, and feedback
c. Other pieces: guidance for self-evaluation, reflection, project management, course management, etc.

As mentioned at the beginning of this chapter, some of your instruction is typically developed during the design phase, since design and development activities overlap. For example, many of your design specifications for a project may be largely what needs to be presented to the learners. But some further development will likely be needed to make sure the project instructions are fully developed from the perspective of the learners. You might want to use the following questions as a checklist:

- Are the project goals clearly stated?
- Does the description of the project provide an authentic or meaningful context?
- Are the project instructions clear and easy to understand?
- Are the self-reflection and evaluation processes clearly described?

For those instructors who are inexperienced with the facilitator role in LCI, you could develop an instructor guide on how to provide effective feedback on learners' project processes and products and how to provide scaffolding for learners. Refer to Chapter 8 for more information about feedback and other kinds of scaffolding.

In addition, you may need to develop guidance for self-directed and collaborative learning for learners (and for instructors to scaffold learners in this kind of learning). Keep in mind that many learners are still accustomed to passively acquiring information from the instructor and do not possess knowledge and skills required for successful self-directed and collaborative learning. They may have difficulty completing a real-world project that requires them to step out of their comfort zone. In order to better support the learners in LCI environments, consider developing appropriate guidance for both learners and instructors on self-directed learning, self-evaluation, reflection, group communication and collaboration, and project management. We offer more guidance for this at the end of this chapter.

In some cases, SMEs actively participate in the development process by writing examples, practice, feedback, and/or scripts. In other cases, however, instructional designers are responsible for developing instructional content based on the information provided by SMEs and/or other sources in the design phase. In such cases, it is important to have periodic meetings (e.g., weekly or bi-weekly meetings) with SMEs throughout the development process, to get feedback on the accuracy of the content.

In all cases, it is important to conduct frequent formative evaluations throughout the development process.

Producing Instructional Media

Instructional media refer to objects, print materials, digital resources, or other media intended to carry out instruction and learner assessment. Some of the media that can be used to carry out instruction are:

- Print-based materials
- PowerPoint files
- Infographics
- Videos
- Interactive multimedia, including animations, computer-based training (CBT), computer-based simulations, online instruction, and computer-managed instruction (CMI)
- Objects (procuring actual equipment or materials or developing mock-ups, simulations, or models of such equipment or materials)
- Social media (e.g., collaboration tools)
- Experts (identifying them and making arrangements for their participation)

Media production is a time-consuming and exacting task, regardless of the medium that has been selected. It is essential that quality media be developed, since they are the major vehicle for learning. Adequate development resources (e.g., developers, programmers, production equipment) are required to develop quality instructional media in a timely manner.

Factors to Consider

Production of instructional media may be affected by several factors. The relative importance of each of these factors depends on the type of media selected. These factors include development personnel required, development time required, and development funds required.

When developing instructional media, make sure:

- They are appropriate for the design that was specified in the design phase
- They are developed using appropriate experts in order to create quality instructional media
- They are checked (formatively evaluated) prior to publication/production to ensure quality (e.g., for technical accuracy, completeness, programming errors, blurred visuals)
- They use appropriate vocabulary at the level of the target learners
- They include appropriate safety precautions
- Distance learning segments or courses are developed within the parameters of the learning management or course management system, if this mode of delivery is deemed appropriate for deploying the media

For additional information on development of media, see other resources (Dick, Carey, & Carey, 2005; Dills & Bass, 1984; Dills & Romiszowski, 1997; Gustafson & Branch, 2002; Leshin, Pollock, & Reigeluth, 1992; Morrison, Ross, & Kemp, 2007; Romiszowski, 1986, 1988; Smith & Ragan, 2005).

Activities to Do

Instructional media development requires many activities. The type and number of activities also depend upon the media being developed. Table 9.1 lists some common development activities and kinds of team members (roles) required for production of the different media. Details about formative evaluation are provided in Chapter 10.

Developing instructional media normally requires teamwork and a diversity of skills. You, the instructional designer, are responsible for planning, scheduling, and ensuring the production of the appropriate instructional media.

Development Tools

There are many development tools, including writing tools, graphic design tools (e.g., Adobe Photoshop, Adobe Illustrator), video tools (e.g., Adobe Premiere Pro, iMovie), and e-learning development tools (e.g., Elucidat, Adobe Captivate, Articulate Storyline). In large ID teams, instructional designers often work with professional media developers who use highly advanced and sophisticated development tools. When working with professional media developers, you may focus on writing instructional content and scripts for media development. If your ID teams do not include professional media developers, you may have to develop content and media using less sophisticated tools. In fact, there are

Table 9.1 Media Development Activities and Development Roles

Media	Development Activities	Development Roles
Print	Draft/write material Develop graphics Edit material Formatively evaluate material Publish material	Subject-matter expert Instructional developer Editor Graphic designer Evaluator
PowerPoint Files	Draft/write material Develop graphics Develop animations Edit material Add narration and timing Formatively evaluate material	Subject-matter expert Instructional developer Evaluator
Interactive Multimedia	Draft/write Storyboard/script Shoot and edit video Develop graphics Record audio Program/code computer Formatively evaluate Publish to the Internet	Programmer Script writer Subject-matter expert Instructional designer Video producer and editor Photographer Graphic designer Audio technician Evaluator
Objects	Establish parameters and specifications Identify ones for procurement Make any appropriate modifications Formatively evaluate	Subject-matter expert Instructional developer Third-party manufacturers Evaluator
Social Media	Draft/write material and schedule when to post Identify devices for procurement Formatively evaluate	Subject-matter expert Instructional developer Evaluator
Experts	Establish parameters Develop interview questions Develop demonstration scenarios Formatively evaluate	Subject-matter expert Instructional developer Evaluator

many free development tools that enable designers and educators to easily produce effective instructional media. In this chapter, we do not address specific tools because tools evolve so quickly and we seem to encounter new tools every day.

Scriptwriting and Storyboarding

In many ID project situations, instructional designers work with professional media developers. To develop multimedia, scriptwriting and storyboarding are necessary when working with such developers. You may have already created a first draft of these during the design process. Instructional designers typically write two types of scripts: (1) content scripts including descriptions of media objects and (2) scripts for video scenarios or multimedia presentations.

First, for the **content script**, it is helpful to write in a conversational style and make your sentences concise. Keep in mind that learners should not have to consult an instructor.

Your script should provide all the guidance they need, including concrete directions for interacting with content (e.g., "view the following video to learn about ABC" and "click on the link below to see XYZ"). If you work with developers, your content scripts also need to include detailed descriptions of media objects to be included (e.g., images and videos).

Second, the **scripts** for video scenarios or other multimedia presentations can take a variety of forms. For video scenarios involving actors' dialog, for example, you need to write narrations, realistic conversations between actors, and descriptions of different scenes, including the actors' poses, facial expressions, and gestures, whereas you simply write narrations and descriptions of images for the videos made of still images.

A **storyboard** is a series of sketches or illustrations displayed in sequence. It is used to help developers visualize the animations, videos, or interactive multimedia to be developed. In some cases, you might develop a storyboard first and then write scripts, while in other cases, you write scripts first and then develop a storyboard. It is also possible to do both concurrently.

Again, formative evaluation should be conducted frequently for the scripts and storyboards.

General Guidelines for Graphic Design

Graphic design refers to "a plan for organizing visual objects in space" for the purpose of communication. Good graphic design captures attention, guides the eye's movement across the page or screen, conveys information, and evokes appropriate emotion (Golombisky & Hagen, 2013). On the other hand, ineffective graphic design can result in confusion, misunderstanding, and frustration. Table 9.2 lists five common layout mistakes novice designers make in developing visual materials and ways to avoid the mistakes.

In order to create effective visuals, you need to understand the basics of graphic design, including principles and theories of design (see e.g., Lidwell, Holden & Butler, 2010) and general guidelines for choosing fonts and colors and for working with photos and illustrations. Table 9.3 lists four basic design principles (Williams, 2015).

For additional information on graphic design, we recommend reading such books as *White Space Is Not Your Enemy: A Beginner's Guide to Communicating Visually through Graphic, Web & Multimedia Design, The Non-Designer's Design Book: Design and Typographic Principles for the Visual Novice*, and *Universal Principles of Design*.

Table 9.2 Common Layout Mistakes and Ways to Avoid Them

Common Layout Mistakes	*Best Practice*
Centering everything	Avoid centered alignment. While centered content can create a formal look, it also creates visual flow issues. Left or right aligned layouts give the viewer's eye a nice straight vertical line on the right or the left to follow top to bottom. With centered alignment, the eye bounces around in search of the next eye entry point.
Cluttering the corners	Group items together that belong together rather than spreading out your content to fill every corner.
Too many fonts	Choose one font that is generic and readable for the main text, and choose a second font that contrasts for use in headlines or subheads. Try to stick to two fonts per layout.
Busy backgrounds	Make sure that the background doesn't interfere with your visual communication.
Using all caps	Do not use all caps for body copy.

Table 9.3 Four Basic Design Principles

Design Principle	Design Tips
Proximity	• If items are related to each other, group them into closer proximity. • Separate items that are not directly related to each other. • Avoid too many separate elements on a page. If there are more than three to five elements on a page, see which of them can be grouped together.
Alignment	• Every element should have some visual connection with another element on the page. • Avoid using more than one text alignment on the page. • Choose a centered alignment carefully and rarely.
Repetition	• Think of repetition as being consistent. • Repeat some aspects of the design throughout the entire piece. • Avoid repeating an element so much that it becomes annoying or overwhelming.
Contrast	• If two items are not exactly the same, then make them different. • Add contrast through typeface choices, colors, shapes, sizes, line thickness, etc. • Avoid using two or more typefaces that are similar.

Again, frequent formative evaluations should be conducted during the graphic design process.

Guidelines for Developing Technology-Enhanced Instruction

Clark and Mayer's basic principles of multimedia learning provide research-based guidelines for developing a wide variety of technology-based instruction, including e-learning training and multimedia instruction (Clark & Mayer, 2008; Mayer, 2005). Table 9.4 lists the principles, along with descriptions and guidelines for each, but it is important to keep in mind that exceptions are occasionally appropriate.

Formative evaluation should be conducted throughout the process of developing technology-enhanced instruction.

Developing a Learner Guide

Once the instruction has been designed, a learner guide (e.g., course syllabus) should be prepared to give the learner a big-picture view of the instruction (content and methods), along with guidance about how to navigate the instructional system. For instructor-centered instruction, a *course syllabus* is the standard learner guide. See Merrill (2020) for guidance on syllabi for teacher-centered, problem-centered instruction. For learner-centered instruction, a different format, called a *plan of instruction* or a *learning plan*, is more helpful. Although each kind of learner guide can be in different formats, they are normally organized by modules of instruction and contain the following **information**:

• Course/workshop/project description
• Learner objectives and standards
• How to navigate the online instruction
• Preferred instructional sequence
• Instructional hours and approximate allocations of those hours to units (e.g., modules or projects)
• Instructional methods

Table 9.4 Basic Principles of Multimedia Learning

Principles	Descriptions	Guidelines
Multimedia Principle	• People learn better from words and pictures than from words alone.	• Include both words and graphics.
Spatial Contiguity Principle	• People learn more deeply from a multimedia message when corresponding words and pictures are presented near rather than far from each other on the page or screen.	• Place printed words near corresponding graphics.
Temporal Contiguity Principle	• People learn more deeply from a multimedia message when corresponding animation and narration are presented simultaneously rather than successively.	• Synchronize spoken words with corresponding graphics.
Modality Principle	• Presenting information in a mixed mode (partly visual and partly auditory) is more effective than presenting the same information in a single mode (either visual or auditory alone).	• Present words as speech rather than on-screen text.
Redundancy Principle	• People learn more deeply from graphics and narration than from graphics, narration, and on-screen text. Note: an exception is that information that is redundant for one person may be essential for another. For example, you may need to add on-screen text to narrative graphics if your audience includes learners who have trouble processing spoken words. Also, accessibility requirements may mandate including on-screen text.	• Do not add on-screen text to narrated graphics.
Coherence Principle	• People learn more deeply from a multimedia message when extraneous material is excluded rather than included.	• Avoid instruction with extraneous audio, graphics, and words.
Signaling Principle	• People learn more deeply from a multimedia message when cues are added that highlight the critical aspects of the presented information.	• Use cues (e.g., arrows, circles, bold fonts, different colors) to highlight important information.
Personalization Principle	• People learn more deeply when the words in a multimedia presentation are in conversational style rather than formal style.	• Use conversational rather than formal style.
Voice Principle	• People learn more deeply when the words in a multimedia message are spoken in a standard-accented human voice rather than in a machine voice.	• Put words in human voice rather than machine voice.
Segmenting Principle	• People learn more deeply when a multimedia message is presented in learner-paced segments rather than as a continuous unit.	• Break a continuous lesson into bite-size segments that learners can tackle at their own pace.
Pretraining Principle	• People learn more deeply from a multimedia message when they know the names and characteristics of the main concepts.	• Ensure that learners know the names and characteristics of key concepts before engaging in the activity.

- Procedures
- Where to find learning resources and tools
- Evaluation criteria and/or rubrics for self-evaluation
- Support materials
- Media utilization

The learner guide should be adapted to various instructional situations to meet the needs of the learners. However, there are several basic or general **guidelines** that apply to all learner guides. They should:

- Be easy to understand/use
- Document the plan of instruction
- Provide adequate information
- Be easily maintained
- Vary in format based on the preference of the learners and the organization providing the instruction

Developing an Instructor Guide

An instructor guide, often called a facilitator guide for LCI or lesson plans for ICI, provides detailed information for an instructor to implement the instruction. For LCI, since many instructors are inexperienced with this approach (An & Reigeluth, 2011), they will be inclined to teach in traditional ways even with good problem-based learning (PBL) problems (An, 2013) or authentic projects. Therefore, the facilitator guide must help them overcome that tendency and include guidance for facilitating a learner-centered project or activity, including scaffolding strategies and support for self-directed learning, collaborative learning, and project management.

The lesson plans for ICI, on the other hand, usually include learning objectives, procedures, and directions for a lecture, demonstrations, discussions, media use, assessments, etc. How detailed your lesson plans should be depends on the instructor's experience and familiarity with the content and media used. In some cases, a simple checklist can be sufficient, while other situations may require a very detailed guide including scripts.

The instructor guide should also be formatively evaluated.

Formative Evaluation, Revision, and Finalization

The products developed in this phase should be formatively evaluated as they are developed, rather than evaluating them all at the end of this phase. Due to time and budgetary constraints, it may be helpful to sort the evaluation results by priority (e.g., have to change, should change, and cannot change at this time). Throughout this phase, you should also be continuously evaluating the ID process activities you use. This is a form of "reflection on action" (Donald A. Schön, 1987; Donald A. Schön, 1995). Once formative evaluation has been completed and revisions have been made, the media should be finalized for implementation. During finalization, ensure that all of the last-minute changes have been made to the media and they are ready for use.

It is important to finalize all the media prior to implementing instruction to ensure that they are: current and accurate, complete, and ready to use in the teaching-learning activity. The types and numbers of different media that are developed for a course should determine what needs to be done during finalization of the media. An easy way to ensure that all

Table 9.5 Job Aid for Finalizing Instructional Media

Media	*Finalization Questions*
Printed	Have student workbooks been updated?
	Are student workbooks complete?
	Have student workbooks been published?
	Have the lesson plans been updated?
	Are the lesson plans complete?
	Have the lesson plans been approved and published?
Interactive Multimedia	Have the programs been updated?
	Are the programs complete?
	Have the programs been operationally tested?
	Are the programs ready for use?
Objects	Have the objects been procured?
	Have the objects been modified (if appropriate)?
	Has the use of the objects been operationally tested?

media are finalized is to develop a job aid consisting of questions on specific areas such as plans and control documents. Table 9.5 shows a sample job aid for finalizing instructional media after they have been formatively evaluated and revised.

As the development phase is concluded, it is likely that the **ID project management plan**, which was last updated during the design phase, may again require updating to keep it current and accurate. If the plan is to remain an effective management tool, it should be updated continually so that it provides a roadmap for managing the remainder of the ID project. Some of the information in the plan that may require updating as a result of the development phase is project milestones, resource requirements, and resource constraints.

Where Are We?

This chapter has offered guidance for the third D in the Holistic 4D Model – Develop. It described how the development process varies depending on the type of instruction and the development staff and resources available. Then it offered guidance for developing instruction for LCI and for producing instructional media, scriptwriting and storyboarding, graphic design, developing technology-enhanced instruction, and developing a learner guide and an instructor guide. Finally, the chapter emphasized the importance of frequent formative evaluation and revisions throughout the development process.

The next chapter (Chapter 10) provides guidance for formative evaluation, which is conducted throughout the ID process on all four Ds in the Holistic 4D Model. The fourth D, Deploy, is addressed in Chapters 11–12.

Exercises

Here again we offer suggestions for a professor using this book as a textbook in a course, to help the students understand more deeply the contents of this chapter. We suggest that you keep the same teams of about three students each to continue to work on their ID projects throughout the course. However, these exercises can be done individually by any reader who wants to deepen their understanding and skills.

1. Have each team develop and formatively evaluate the instruction on at least two of the lessons they designed in the Chapter 8 Exercises. If time is a factor, each team could create a formative evaluation plan rather than actually conducting a formative evaluation and preparing an evaluation report. For what you consider to be the best lessons, we suggest you get written permission from the students to use them as examples in the next offering of your course.
2. Have each team offer suggestions for improvement for the lessons and evaluation plans or reports of one or two other teams before you review and provide feedback to the students.
3. Have a whole-class, synchronous discussion of the strengths and weaknesses of this development and formative-evaluation process, including any difficulties or challenges they faced during the process and what changes to the process might have helped. We would love to get your suggestions for improvement.

References

An, Y. (2013). Systematic design of blended PBL: Exploring the design experiences and support needs of PBL novices in an online environment. *Contemporary Issues in Technology and Teacher Education, 13*(1). Retrieved from http://www.citejournal.org/volume-13/issue-1-13/general/systematic-design-of-blended-pbl-exploring-the-design-experiences-and-support-needs-of-pbl-novices-in-an-online-environment/.

An, Y., & Reigeluth, C.M. (2011). Creating technology-enhanced, learner-centered classrooms: K-12 teachers' beliefs, perceptions, barriers, and support needs. *Journal of Digital Learning in Teacher Education, 28*(2), 54–62.

Clark, R.C., & Mayer, R.E. (2008). *e-Learning and the science of instruction: Proven guidelines for consumers and designers of multimedia learning.* San Francisco, CA: Pfeiffer.

Dick, W., Carey, L., & Carey, J.O. (2005). *The systematic design of instruction* (5th ed.). Boston: Pearson/Allyn and Bacon.

Dills, C.R., & Bass, R.K. (Eds.). (1984). *Instructional development: The state of the art.* Dubuque, IA: Kendall/Hunt Pub. Co.

Dills, C.R., & Romiszowski, A.J. (Eds.). (1997). *Instructional development paradigms.* Englewood Cliffs, NJ: Educational Technology Publications.

Golombisky, K., & Hagen, R. (2013). *White space is not your enemy: A beginner's guide to communicating visually through graphic, web & multimedia design.* New York: Taylor & Francis.

Gustafson, K.L., & Branch, R.M. (2002). Survey of instructional development models (4th ed.). Syracuse, NY: ERIC Clearinghouse on Information & Technology.

Leshin, C.B., Pollock, J., & Reigeluth, C.M. (1992). *Instructional design strategies and tactics.* Englewood Cliffs, NJ: Educational Technology Publications.

Lidwell, W., Holden, K., & Butler, J. (2010). *Universal principles of design.* Beverly, MA: Rockport Publishers.

Mayer, R.E. (2005). Cognitive theory of multimedia learning. *The Cambridge handbook of multimedia learning, 41,* 31–48.

Merrill, M.D. (2020). A syllabus review check-list to promote problem-centered instruction. *TechTrends, 64*(1), 105–123.

Morrison, G.R., Ross, S.M., & Kemp, J.E. (2007). *Designing effective instruction* (5th ed.). Hoboken, NJ: J. Wiley.

Romiszowski, A.J. (1986). *Developing auto-instructional materials: From programmed texts to CAL and interactive video.* New York, NY: Nichols Publishing.

Romiszowski, A.J. (1988). *The selection and use of instructional media: For improved classroom teaching and for interactive, individualized instruction* (2nd ed.). New York: Nichols Pub.

Schön, D.A. (1987). *Educating the reflective practitioner: Toward a new design for teaching and learning in the professions.* San Francisco, CA: Jossey-Bass.

Schön, D.A. (1995). *The reflective practitioner: How professionals think in action.* Aldershot, England: Arena.

Smith, P.L., & Ragan, T.J. (2005). *Instructional design* (3rd ed.). Hoboken, NJ: J. Wiley & Sons.

Williams, R. (2015). *The non-designer's design book* (4th ed.). Berkeley, CA: Peachpit Press.

10   Formative Evaluation

Overview

There are two major kinds of evaluation: formative and summative. And there are two basic times that evaluation can be done: while the instruction is being developed (which we call *developmental evaluation* and is always formative) and after implementation of instruction (which we call *operational evaluation* and can be either formative or summative). Formative evaluation has two purposes: one that evaluates and improves the products that result from the instructional design (ID) process (called *product evaluation*, which can be either developmental or operational), and one that evaluates and improves the ID process itself (called *process evaluation*, which is always developmental).

Summative evaluation also has two parts: one that takes place immediately after implementation (*called initial summative evaluation*) and one that takes place periodically throughout the life of the instructional system (called *continuing summative evaluation* or *confirmation evaluation*). The various kinds of evaluation are shown in Table 10.1.

The purpose of formative evaluation is to improve either your instructional product or your ID process. Formative evaluation ensures that:

- The instruction meets training or education requirements
- The instruction is effective and efficient
- Equipment satisfies operational, training, and support requirements
- Facilities meet operational, training, and support requirements
- Instructional design, development, and revision activities are effective and efficient

This chapter offers guidance for all three kinds of formative evaluation. Guidance for summative evaluation is provided in Chapter 12.

Developing a Formative Evaluation Plan

A preliminary plan for formative evaluation should be created during the initial project planning process as part of the ID PM plan (see Chapter 2), and it should be updated throughout the ID process.

Table 10.1 Kinds of Evaluation

	Formative Evaluation		*Summative Evaluation*	
	Product Evaluation	*Process Evaluation*	*Initial*	*Continuing*
Developmental	Developmental Formative Product Evaluation	Formative Process Evaluation		
Operational	Operational Formative Product Evaluation		Initial Operational Summative Evaluation	Continuing Operational Summative Evaluation

Formative Product Evaluation Plan

Developmental and operational formative product evaluations differ primarily in when each is conducted. The methods are largely the same for both. A formative product evaluation plan may contain such information as:

- What kind(s) of formative evaluation to conduct (e.g., expert reviews, individual tryouts, alpha and beta tests, small-group tryouts, and operational tryouts) for each product
- How to conduct each kind of evaluation
- Who will conduct each kind of evaluation
- When to conduct the evaluations
- Evaluation schedule constraints
- Number and availability of experts or learners to be involved in the evaluations
- Criteria for evaluation
- How the results should be documented
- How problems should be resolved

The formative product evaluation plan should be updated periodically to include new or revised information, such as:

- Changes in the evaluation plan for the next phase
- Revisions to the evaluation schedules
- Rationale for changes made to the evaluation plan
- Lessons learned during the latest evaluations

Formative Process Evaluation Plan

Formative process evaluation ensures quality in all phases of the ID process, to ensure process quality, while continually seeking improvements within each activity. Process evaluation enables you to improve your ID process as it proceeds. A process evaluation plan may contain such information as:

- How the ID activities will be evaluated
- Who will conduct the evaluation
- When to conduct the evaluations
- Evaluation schedule constraints

- Other data sources for each activity being evaluated
- How the results should be documented
- How problems should be resolved

Much of this information may need to be added to the preliminary plan just before each activity is evaluated. Nevertheless, everyone conducting an activity in any phase should constantly seek to collect data about what is working well, what is not working well, and how to improve it.

The process evaluation plan should be updated periodically to include new or revised information, such as:

- Changes in the evaluation plan for the next phase
- Revisions to the evaluation schedules
- Rationale for changes made to the evaluation plan
- Lessons learned during the latest evaluations

Conducting a Formative Product Evaluation

Several methods are used for conducting a formative product evaluation: expert reviews, individual tryouts, alpha and beta tests, small-group tryouts, and operational tryouts (see Table 10.2).

Expert Reviews

The expert review is typically the first step of the formative evaluation process. There are two kinds of expert review. The most common is a content review by a subject-matter expert (SME). Often, it is also helpful to conduct an instructional methods review with an expert in the instructional methods you have chosen, especially for large ID projects. This could be an instructor experienced in teaching the methods to your target learners, for they

Table 10.2 Methods for Conducting Formative Product Evaluation

	Participants	*Focus*
Expert Reviews	Chosen SMEs and experts in the instructional method	Content accuracy Instructional quality
Individual Tryouts	Several learners from the target learner population	Clarity, sequencing, and usability of the instruction Problems and difficulties encountered Time required Learners' views about the instruction
Alpha Tests	SMEs	Accuracy of the instruction
Beta Tests	A sample of target learners	Usability of the interface Instructional integrity
Small-Group Tryouts	Small groups of learners	Time required Quality of instruction
Operational Tryouts	Learners and instructors	Operational effectiveness Learning gains Duration of instruction Learners' views of instruction Instructors' views of instruction

are experts in both the content and teaching it to your target learners. Be sure to get input from the experts on what changes they think would likely improve the content and design, and either make revisions during the walk-through exercise, or as soon as possible after it. The earlier in the ID process that a problem is identified and fixed, the less expensive and time-consuming the ID process will be.

If possible, conduct **content reviews** on all content selection decisions. It may be easier to manage with busy SMEs if you give them a sizable chunk of content to review at once. For a **methods review**, we recommend evaluating any given decision before you make a similar decision for other parts of the instruction, so you won't have to make the same revisions for those other parts later. Quantitative rapid prototyping is well-suited to this process. On each of the three levels of the Holistic 4D design process, we have indicated points at which formative evaluation should be conducted (see Table 10.3).

There are many ways to review products for accuracy, completeness, quality, and suitability. The bottom line is to cross-check the products against the experts' opinions, the data sources available (such as technical orders, regulations, directives, and checklists), and learners' reactions. One method of helping conduct the review is to develop useful questions to ask the experts. Sample questions include the following:

- Is the content accurate and current?
- Is the content consistent with the learner's needs?
- What are the "high quality" parts of the product?
- Are there any "low quality" parts in the product?
- How can the product be improved?

When conducting a review, the experts should: take careful notes, make specific comments, identify weaknesses in the products, and recommend ways to improve the products. After the review, the experts and you should discuss their review findings, determine what revisions or changes should be made to the products, decide the best way to make the necessary corrections to the products, and make revisions and changes to the products, as applicable. It is often impossible to address all comments from experts. It is recommended to prioritize feedback from experts and decide what must be changed, should be changed, and cannot be changed.

Individual Tryouts

Conducting individual tryouts is normally the next step in the formative evaluation process as soon as you have instruction in a form that can be shared with target learners. As the instruction is being designed and developed, small segments or units are tried out on individual learners from the target learner population and improved when possible. The instruction should be tried out on several learners, if practical, because learners differ in their instructional needs and preferences. It may not always be possible to conduct individual tryouts due to resource constraints, but they can greatly improve the quality of the instruction, and problems are less expensive to fix at this point in the ID process.

A great deal of care should be used when selecting learners to participate in the individual tryouts. Learners selected for the tryouts should:

- Be evenly distributed between low and high aptitudes
- Have representatively diverse skill levels
- Come from representatively diverse backgrounds

Table 10.3 ADE Process for Task Expertise and Topic Expertise (Differences Are in **Bold**)

	Task Expertise	*Topic Expertise*
Top Level Ch. 5	1. Select and sequence top-level content 2. Plan high-level instructional methods 3. Formatively evaluate and document the top-level design	1. Select and sequence top-level content 2. Plan high-level instructional methods 3. Formatively evaluate and document the top-level design
Mid Level Ch. 6	1. Identify and sequence **versions of each task** 2. Identify variations within each **version** and create designer objectives 3. Formatively evaluate the findings 4. Develop the learner objectives for each **version** 5. Design learner assessments for each **version** 6. Design the ways that learning by doing will be accomplished for each **version** 7. Select media in general for the **version** 8. Formatively evaluate and document the results	1. Identify and sequence **applications of each topic** 2. Identify variations within each **application** and create designer objectives 3. Formatively evaluate the findings 4. Develop the learner objectives for each **topic** 5. Design learner assessments for each **topic** 6. Design the ways that learning by doing will be accomplished for each **topic** 7. Select media in general for the **application** 8. Formatively evaluate and document the results
Lower Level Ch. 7	1. Select and sequence the organizing content for each **version of the task** 2. Select and classify the supporting content for each **version** 3. Sequence the supporting content for each **version** 4. Evaluate and document the findings 5. Identify resource requirements, availability, and existing instruction for each **version** 6. Revise and elaborate the instruction and assessments for each **version** 7. Formatively evaluate the ADE document 8. Begin developing the implementation plan, and update the project management plan	1. Select and sequence the organizing content for each **topic** 2. Select and classify the supporting content for each **topic** 3. Sequence the supporting content for each **topic** 4. Evaluate and document the findings 5. Identify resource requirements, availability, and existing instruction for each **topic** 6. Revise and elaborate the instruction and assessments for each **topic** 7. Formatively evaluate the ADE document 8. Begin developing the implementation plan, and update the project management plan
Ch. 8	Detailed guidance is provided for Lower-Level Step 6: Revise and Elaborate the Instruction and Assessments for Each Version/Topic. It includes instructional strategies for: • Remembering information • Understanding relationships • Applying skills and higher-order skills • Acting on attitudes or values	

If learners do not represent the range of diversity of the target learners, tryout results can be skewed. Thus, revisions may not be helpful for all the target learners and could make the instruction worse for some.

We recommend beginning by designing lean instruction (instruction that assumes the learner does not need much instructional support to master the content), because it is less expensive to add more instructional support to make a lesson easier, than to delete some instruction to make it more appropriately lean. (Any unnecessary instructional support you end up removing is expensive because of the extra time it took to create it in the first place, plus the extra time to remove it. In contrast, starting lean and adding it later does not really take much more time than if you had included it from the beginning.) Often, this entails evaluating some instruction in a preliminary form, or "mock-up," because the earlier you catch problems, the less expensive it is to correct them, and it helps you to avoid creating similar problems in your future design work.

The nature of the tryout should depend, to some degree, on the media selected for use in the course. (Remember that "medium" refers to all means by which instruction is delivered, including instructors, digital media, print materials, and real-world objects.) Certain types of media may be too expensive for use during the individual tryouts, or they may not be available. However, there are ways to evaluate the instruction without using the intended media. Table 10.4 shows some examples.

Before conducting the individual tryouts, you should prepare the learners for the tryouts. Learners need to know:

- The purpose of the tryout
- They are not being evaluated – the instruction is
- Their role in the tryout
- Their active participation is essential if the individual tryout is to be successful
- Their feedback is necessary in determining ways to improve the instruction

During the individual tryouts, you should:

- Closely observe learners as they go through the instruction
- Make careful note of where learners seem to have problems or uncertainties
- Give assistance to learners only when it is essential to learner progress
- Administer the relevant test items at the appropriate time
- Get the learners' views about the difficulties encountered during the tryout and how best to address them

Sources of individual-tryout information are provided in Table 10.5.

Often, the following problems are identified during the first tryouts:

- Improper sequencing of the instruction
- Instruction not clear and concise
- Lack of supporting instructional media
- Confusing test items
- Test items that do not measure objectives
- Insufficient practice time

Table 10.4 Media Use during Tryouts

If Media Selected Are …	*Conduct Individual Tryout by …*
Available, such as job aids, simulators, trainers, or Capable of being quickly and economically developed, such as paper-based materials, slides, graphics	Using the actual media that will be used in the course.
Not available, or Dangerous to use, or Expensive to develop	Devising storyboard versions of the instruction. For example, paper script with drawings can be used in place of multimedia, and mockups can be used to replace the actual media.

Table 10.5 Sources of Data for Individual Tryouts

Source	Activity
Diagnostic tests	• Administer a pretest to identify entry knowledge and behavior. • Administer a posttest to assess learning as a result of the tryout.
Learner performance during instruction	• Observe and record learners' performance. • Determine which exercises or tasks result in errors, types of errors made, and how many learners are making the same error(s).
Learner comments	• Get learner reaction to the instruction and materials, especially their difficulties. • Ask learners for suggestions on how the instruction and materials can be improved.

After a tryout, you need to analyze the resulting data to determine if error patterns or problems have occurred on successive tryouts. If so, changes or revisions to the instruction or test are appropriate. For example, if each learner participating in the individual tryouts fails to meet the performance standard for a particular objective, you should review the objective, instruction, and test, and revise as necessary. In most cases, several tryouts should be conducted before making any significant revisions or changes to the instruction or test. When significant revisions are required in the instruction or test, we recommend that additional individual tryouts again be conducted in order to determine if the problem was solved.

Small-Group Tryouts for Group-Based Instruction

If the instruction is going to be conducted in groups when implemented, after the individual tryouts have been completed and all necessary revisions have been made, it is advisable to conduct the next stage of formative evaluation, which is small-group tryouts. Small-group tryouts are not needed if the instruction does not include any group work. The instruction and tests are tried out on small groups of learners. Up to this point, the evaluation of the instruction has been based on a small sample of learners. Small-group tryouts are focused on the full range of target learners under conditions approximating the actual teaching-learning situation. It may not always be possible to conduct small-group tryouts due to resource constraints, but they can greatly improve the quality of the instruction, and problems are less expensive to fix at this point in the ID process.

Learner selection for a small-group tryout is very important. See the criteria for selecting learners for individual tryouts. Representativeness of learners helps determine if the instruction and tests will be effective under implementation conditions. The number of learners included in the small groups should be determined based on factors such as:

- Need for teams of learners within the target instructional context (for example, some tasks may require learners to work in teams of three; if so, the small-group size should be based on multiples of three)
- Planned normal group size, if any, for the target instructional context (e.g., classroom size)
- Availability of equipment for the tryout
- Availability of facilities for the tryout

Up to this point in the formative evaluation process, time required for learners to master a task or topic has not been of major concern, because the instruction has been frequently interrupted by formative evaluation activities. However, time becomes a critical factor in the small-group tryouts. Learning the material or performing a task successfully is not sufficient; learners should be able to master what is required within a reasonable time period. Therefore, effort should be made to ensure that learning can be accomplished within any time constraints based on training requirements and the capability of the slowest learners. For individualized instruction, this should be done during the beta test.

Before a small-group tryout, you should:

- Determine the number of learners to include in each small group
- Determine the number of small groups to use in the tryouts
- Select a broad range of representative learners from the target learners
- Ensure that the instruction and tests have been revised based on the applicable information resulting from individual tryouts
- Ensure that learner materials are available in adequate quantities
- Ensure that instructional resources such as equipment, personnel, and facilities to be used during the tryout approximate the operational conditions
- Ensure that the course management system is operating and can collect, analyze, and report data, if possible

During a small-group tryout, you should:

- Ensure that the time required for each learner to complete the instruction and/or test is accurately recorded. This information is used to determine the size (amount of content) of projects, modules, and courses.
- Record the levels of learner performance. This information should help determine deficiencies in the instruction or assessments.
- Establish the number of trials a slow learner needs to meet performance requirements.
- Let the instruction stand on its own. Supplementing the instruction or assisting on tests may skew the results of the tryout.

You should conduct a sufficient number of small-group tryouts to improve the quality of your instruction and assessments. One rule of thumb is to continue tryouts until you no longer get useful information, but resource constraints may preclude this.

After each tryout, the data collected should be analyzed to determine:

- The maximum time required to complete each project, module, or other unit of instruction. (This information is used to set the approximate times for each unit, or to adjust the size of each to fit the time slots available.)
- The need to revise equipment requirements, make changes to facilities, and adjust personnel requirements.
- Revisions warranted in instruction and assessments.
- Priority for accomplishing revisions and plan of accomplishment.

As with the individual tryout, if the instruction or assessments require significant revisions or changes, we recommend that additional small-group tryouts be conducted on the revisions.

Operational Formative Product Evaluation

The operational formative product evaluation, often called a "pilot test," is conducted under normal instructional conditions by an instructor and developer. It normally takes place for an entire course (or other autonomous unit of instruction). It evaluates the instructional system's operational effectiveness, maintainability, supportability, and suitability. It identifies any operational and logistic support deficiencies and any needed modifications. In addition, the operational tryout provides information on organizational structure, personnel requirements, support equipment, policies, training, and tactics. It should also provide data to verify operating instructions, maintenance procedures, training programs, publications, and handbooks. Its purposes are to:

- Ensure that all four functions of the instructional system (delivery, management, support, and administration – see Chapter 11) work well under implementation conditions
- Make further revisions or refinements to all four functions of the instructional system based on feedback from managers, instructors, and a large sample of the target learners
- Work out any implementation or operational problems, such as equipment and facilities

For operational tryouts, learners are selected from the target population to participate, using the normal learner scheduling process. Operational tryout data are collected before, during, and after the instruction is provided.

- Before conducting instruction, the instructional designer or instructor should:
  o Determine if learners have met course prerequisites and identify their entry skill and knowledge levels
  o Collect data using such methods as pretest, oral examination, or directly asking learners if they have specific skills and knowledge
- While conducting instruction, the instructional developer or instructor should identify breakdowns in instruction, check learner progress, and record duration of instruction
- After conducting instruction, the instructional developer or instructor should administer the posttest, interview learners, and critique the instruction

The data collection is summarized in Table 10.6.

Before an operational tryout, ensure that:

- Resources are available, such as equipment, facilities, and instructors
- Instruction and tests have been revised based on the results of previous formative evaluation activities
- Materials are available in adequate quantities
- Learners have been scheduled to participate
- Size of the tryout group is compatible with actual implementation conditions

Table 10.6 Stages of Data Collection

Stage	Data to Be Collected	Data Collection Methods
Before	Learner entry skill/knowledge level	Pretest Oral examination Learner interviews
During	Number of errors learners make Questions raised by learners Learner work samples Duration of instruction	Observation Recording learner questions Collecting work samples
After	Learner learning gains Learner views of instruction, materials Instructor's or supervisor's views of instruction, materials	Posttest Learner interviews, critiques Instructor interviews, critiques

During an operational tryout, you should:

- Ensure that instruction is conducted in the normal implementation environment
- Collect data such as time requirements, test results, instructor and learner comments, and problem areas, using adequate data samples to ensure valid and reliable data

After an operational tryout. When an adequate number of operational tryouts has been conducted, you should:

- Analyze data gathered during the tryouts
- Revise all four functions of the instructional system as necessary
- Continue cycles of tryout and revision as long as the quality of the instructional system is in need of improvement and resources allow

Alpha and Beta Tests for e-Learning

In the e-learning field, you often hear the terms alpha test and beta test. Both alpha and beta tests are conducted to formatively evaluate e-learning before you actually implement it. However, they have different purposes and are conducted in different phases. The **alpha test** takes place during the development phase when the first working draft of the instruction (often referred to as an alpha version) is complete (though often before full media development) in order to ensure accuracy and quality of the instruction. SMEs are the primary participants for the alpha test, but target learners may also be brought in at this point to see how they react to the instruction and better understand their perspectives.

On the other hand, the **beta test** takes place once the instruction has been polished into something closely resembling the final version and is done with a representative sample of target learners. It is a kind of operational tryout. Because the beta test is the last step before the release of the e-learning product, it is critical to get input from a representative sample of actual users of the instruction. The beta test has multiple purposes: to gather feedback on the usability of the interface, to ensure instructional integrity, and to find errors (Lesniak, 2002). However, it is recommended to have editorial and technical reviews completed by editors before beta tests so that learners can focus on learning, not on finding typos, broken links, and other errors. The beta test usually takes about twice as long as the actual instruction because you often stop during the beta test to receive feedback from representative learners (Piskurich, 2015). So, you need to schedule enough time and let your participants know that the beta test will take longer than the expected learning time. When e-learning will take place individually rather than in small groups, no small-group tryouts will be conducted, so you should finish your beta testing by determining how long the instruction typically takes with a sample of the target audience, and make sure the modules are of appropriate length.

Using the Kirkpatrick Model for Formative Evaluation

The Kirkpatrick model, developed by Donald Kirkpatrick, has been widely used to evaluate training and educational programs. The model consists of four levels:

- Level 1: Reaction
- Level 2: Learning
- Level 3: Behavior
- Level 4: Results

Level 1, Reaction, measures the degree to which learners find the training favorable, engaging, and relevant to their jobs or lives. Level 2, Learning, measures the degree to which learners acquire the intended knowledge, skills, attitudes, confidence, and commitment based on their participation in the training. Level 3, Behavior, measures the degree to which participants apply what they learned during instruction when they are back in the real world. Finally, Level 4, Results, measures the degree to which targeted outcomes occur as a result of the instruction and any related interventions (e.g., support and incentives) (Kirkpatrick Partners, 2018). Levels 1 (reaction) and 2 (learning) are used most often for formative evaluation, but Levels 3 (behavior) and 4 (results) could also be used in some situations.

Level 1: Evaluating Participant Reaction

This looks at what learners and instructors (and for training contexts, managers) thought and felt about the quality of instruction for the purpose of improving its quality. Table 10.7 shows an example of a questionnaire designed to obtain learner feedback.

After the data are collected and analyzed, the next stage is to correct deficiencies in the instruction. Due to resource constraints, it is often necessary to prioritize the improvements and work your way down the list until resources run out. Revisions should be made as soon as possible to receive the greatest benefit from the changes.

Level 2: Evaluating Learning

This level of evaluation determines the specific learning that occurred (information, understandings, skills, and attitudes) through learner assessments and compares it to the learning requirements (goals and objectives). It is important to collect sufficient assessment data for the analysis, since insufficient data may skew the analysis results, possibly leading to poor decisions. Several methods of collecting the data are listed in Table 10.8.

Before beginning analysis of the data, ensure that data have been collected from each unit of the instruction and that an adequate number of data samples has been collected in order to validate the reliability of the findings. During data analysis, review assessment data to ensure that learners are meeting course objectives and to determine if assessment methods are valid and reliable. After data analysis, identify specific parts of the course that are not working well, use participant reactions to identify ways those parts can be improved, rank-order those improvements, and then make as many of those improvements as resources allow – as soon as possible.

Levels 3 and 4: Evaluating Behavior and Results

Level 3 looks at the learners' behavior when they are back in the real world. Learners don't always use what they have learned, and if this is the case, the instruction has failed. Level 3 evaluation could be done after a full operational evaluation (pilot study), if it is important enough and resources allow. Such an evaluation requires observing learner behaviors (related to the instruction) in the real world. When those behaviors do not meet expectations, look for ways the instruction and/or other performance interventions could be revised to overcome those shortcomings.

Level 4 looks at organizational or societal results related to the instruction. Even if learners are behaving as hoped or expected, the impact of those behaviors may not meet expectations for organizational or societal change. This level of evaluation requires looking for the kinds of changes hoped for in an organization or society (Kaufman,

Table 10.7 Learner Reaction Questionnaire

LEARNER REACTION TO INSTRUCTION

COURSE:	DATE:
INSTRUCTOR:	LEARNER:

One way that instruction is improved is by sampling learner reaction to the instruction. Please answer the following questions.

1. Prior to this instruction, my experience in this area was:
   ___ extensive   ___ moderate   ___ little or none

2. Did your knowledge of the subject increase as a result of the instruction?
   ___ yes   ___ no

3. If your knowledge increased as a result of the instruction, to what extent did it increase?
   ___ not applicable (my knowledge didn't increase)
   ___ slightly   ___ moderately   ___ extremely

4. Based on my experience, the level of instruction was:
   ___ too advanced   ___ about right   ___ too elementary

5. The organization of the instruction was:
   ___ very helpful   ___ helpful   ___ not very helpful

6. The lecture outline (main points of instruction) was:
   ___ very helpful   ___ helpful   ___ not very helpful

7. Audiovisual aids were:
   ___ of great value   ___ valuable   ___ of little or no value
   ___ not used, but could have helped   ___ not used and not needed

8. Answers to learner questions were:
   ___ meaningful   ___ somewhat helpful   ___ not helpful
   ___ not applicable (no questions asked)

9. Should the subject matter covered be changed?
   ___ yes (please explain below)   ___ no

10. Should the methods of instruction be changed?
    ___ yes (please explain below)   ___ no

11. Overall, the instruction was:
    ___ outstanding   ___ good   ___ fair   ___ poor

12. Instruments (including tests) to evaluate learner performance were:
    ___ outstanding   ___ good   ___ fair   ___ poor

COMMENTS, EXPLANATIONS, OR RECOMMENDATIONS:

Table 10.8 Data Collection Methods

Data Collection Method	Purpose
Monitor Your Measurement Program	To check the assessment program for compromise. If an assessment has been compromised, it cannot provide useful feedback. To monitor the assessment program to ensure quality.
Compile Measurement Data	To evaluate instruction in terms of learner performance. Use performance measures to determine learners' achievement of objectives.

2000), which may not occur immediately. When the changes fall short, look for ways the instruction and/or other performance interventions could be revised to overcome those shortcomings.

Conducting a Formative Process Evaluation

You should continually evaluate your ID process while you are conducting it, so you can make it more effective and efficient. The major questions are who should do it and how should it be done.

Who. Generally, those who are conducting the process should be the ones to evaluate it.

How. Two methods for conducting a formative process evaluation are reflection-in-action and reflection-on-action (Schon, 1995).

Formative process evaluation focuses on enabling instructional developers to improve their ID process. A preliminary evaluation plan should be created during the ID project planning phase (see Chapter 2), and it should be updated throughout all phases of the ID process. A formative process evaluation plan may contain such information as:

- Description of ID activities to be evaluated in each phase
- Who will conduct the evaluation
- Data sources for each activity being evaluated
- Evaluation procedures
- Evaluation schedules
- Evaluation schedule constraints
- How the results should be documented
- How problems should be resolved

Everyone conducting an activity in any phase should constantly seek to collect data about what is working well, what is not working well, and how to improve it. The process evaluation plan should be updated periodically to include new or revised information, such as:

- Changes in the evaluation strategy for the next phase. For example:
  - o Types of activities to be evaluated
  - o Procedures to be used in evaluating the activities
  - o Standards or metrics to be used in the evaluations.
- Revisions to the evaluation schedules, such as:
  - o Number or quantity of activities to be evaluated
  - o When the activities should be evaluated
- Documentation of the results of the evaluations
- Rationale for changes made to the evaluation strategy
- Lessons learned about the evaluation process during evaluation of each phase

Where Are We?

This chapter has offered guidance for all three kinds of formative evaluation: developmental formative product evaluation, operational formative product evaluation, and formative process evaluation. It described how the formative evaluation process should be conducted throughout the ID process, including expert review, individual tryouts, small-group tryouts, and operational tryouts, as well as alpha and beta tests. Finally, it reviewed how Kirkpatrick's four levels of evaluation can inform your formative evaluation activities.

The fourth D, Deploy, is addressed in Chapters 11 and 12. It includes implementation and summative evaluation. The Holistic 4D Model is summarized at the beginning of the next unit.

Exercises

Here again we offer suggestions for a professor using this book as a textbook in a course, to help the students understand more deeply the contents of this chapter. We suggest that you keep the same teams of about three students each to continue to work on their ID projects throughout the course. However, these exercises can be done individually by any reader who wants to deepen their understanding and skills.

Expert reviews were conducted for the exercises in Chapters 5–7, and expert reviews, individual tryouts, and small-group tryouts (if appropriate) were conducted as parts of the exercises in Chapter 9. This leaves the following activities if target learners and context are available.

1. Have each team conduct an operational tryout (pilot test) for at least two of the lessons they developed in the Chapter 9 Exercises. Each team should prepare an evaluation report that describes what they did during the evaluation, what strengths and weaknesses they found, and what revisions they recommend be made. For what you consider to be the best reports, we suggest you get written permission from the students to use them as examples in the next offering of your course.
2. Have each team offer suggestions for improvement for the reports of one or two other teams before you review and provide feedback to the students.
3. Have a whole-class, synchronous discussion of the strengths and weaknesses of this formative evaluation process, including any difficulties or challenges they faced during the process and what changes to the process might have helped. We would love to get your suggestions for improvement.

References

Kaufman, R.A. (2000). *Mega planning: Practical tools for organizational success.* Thousand Oaks, CA: Sage Publications, Inc.

Kirkpatrick Partners. (2018). The Kirkpatrick model. Retrieved from https://www.kirkpatrickpartners.com/Our-Philosophy/The-Kirkpatrick-Model.

Lesniak, B. (2002). Putting it to the test: Quality control for e-learning courses. *The Elearning Developers' Journal.* Retrieved from https://www.elearningguild.com/pdf/2/073002dev-h.pdf.

Piskurich, G.M. (2015). *Rapid instructional design: Learning ID fast and right* (3rd ed.). Hoboken, NJ: John Wiley & Sons, Inc.

Schön, D.A. (1995). *The reflective practitioner: How professionals think in action.* Aldershot, England: Arena.

Unit 4

Deploy

This unit has two chapters. The first offers guidance for implementing the instructional system, which includes ensuring that systems are in place for four major functions: delivery, management, support, and evaluation. The second, Chapter 12, provides guidance for conducting summative evaluations, which are often important for determining whether to continue, replace, or terminate the instructional system.

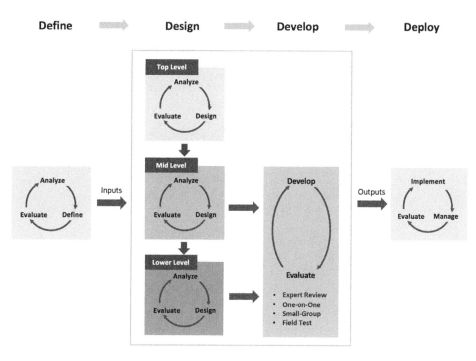

Our Holistic 4D Model of ID.

11 Implementation

Overview

After the instruction has been formatively evaluated and revised, you are ready to implement the instruction. Once the instructional system becomes operational, it will require continuous support, maintenance, and evaluation to ensure that it operates effectively and cost-efficiently and meets the needs of the target audience and organization.

The instructional system functions of delivery, management, support, and evaluation (see Figure 11.1) should be in place and working if the instruction is to operate effectively and efficiently. System functions provide the structure that supports, operates, and maintains the system. We describe these four functions, followed by additional guidance for instructor-present instruction and instructor-free instruction.

The Four Functions for Implementation

Delivery Function

The instructional system delivery function is the means by which instruction is provided to the learners. In the design and development phases of instructional design (ID), appropriate delivery methods were selected and developed to deliver instruction to the learners. Prior to implementing the instructional system, you should ensure that the delivery function is ready to support the operation of the system. You need answers to questions about the delivery function, such as:

- Are there adequate numbers of **instructors** qualified to support the instructional requirements? If not, hire and, if necessary, train them.
- Are there adequate **facilities** for any face-to-face instruction (numbers, sizes, configurations)? If not, procure and, if necessary, reconfigure them.
- Is the necessary **equipment** available and operational, such as computers, Internet connections, simulators, tablets, and projectors? If not, procure and prepare them.
- Do online learners have access to appropriate **technology**? If not, take any necessary steps to ensure such access.
- Are there adequate amounts of **learning materials** to support the instruction? If not, take any necessary steps to ensure adequate amounts.

Support Function

Support is the function of maintaining all parts of the system. It should be preplanned but also done in response to emerging needs, requests, or complaints. The importance of the

Figure 11.1 Four System Functions.

instructional system support function cannot be overstressed. Without adequate support, it may be impossible to implement the instructional system, or at best, its implementation may suffer reduced effectiveness and efficiency.

Again, in most implementation situations, support structures already exist to carry out most of these activities. Your responsibility as a designer of the system is to make sure that such structures exist and are well structured, and if they are not, to then promote the design or improvement of those structures. Support is required in the form of a wide variety of basic support activities, including:

- **Supplying** equipment, parts, and materials
- **Maintaining** equipment and facilities
- **Reproducing** instructional materials
- **Constructing** new instructional aids and facilities
- **Providing** academic and technology support to learners and staff
- **Providing** funding

Evaluation Function

Formative evaluation should be conducted continuously throughout the implementation of the instructional system. See Chapter 10 for guidance. Summative evaluation should be conducted whenever the "owner" of the instructional system is concerned about whether or not to continue it or proof of effectiveness is needed to justify its continuation or to increase support for the system. However, we caution that initial summative evaluation could lead to the termination of a program that hasn't had enough time to work out the inevitable kinks that come with a new instructional system. See Chapter 12 for guidance.

Management Function

Management is the function of directing or controlling instructional operations, such as assigning individuals to roles and responsibilities associated with the instructional program, or acquiring, installing, and maintaining equipment and materials, or hiring and managing staff. Management has the overall responsibility for ensuring that the three other functions and all other components of the system are fully integrated, compatible, and running smoothly. The management function should be in place and working throughout the life of the instructional system from the initial planning stage on. Effective management is crucial for an effective and efficient instructional system.

In most implementation situations, organizational structures already exist to carry out most of these activities. Your responsibility as a designer of the system is to make sure that such organizational structures exist and are well structured, and if they are not, to then promote the design or improvement of those structures. The basic activities to be carried out by the management function are:

- **Planning** for the other three functions
- **Managing** the other three functions
- **Hiring** and **managing** personnel
- **Maintaining** learner records, typically in a database system that includes data on enrollment (registrations), engagement (interactions), performance (on course requirements), and activities (what learners are doing)
- **Informing** instructors and learners about course management issues, including technical problems, updates, and other problems or changes
- **Organizing** the resources, which involves identifying, arranging, and bringing together resources required for the instructional system
- **Scheduling and monitoring** the resources, such as classrooms, lab equipment, real-world objects and equipment (e.g., electronic equipment in an electronics repair course), and real-world or simulated project environments
- Continuously **evaluating** the appropriateness, effectiveness, and efficiency of each element in the instructional system (see Chapters 10 and 12 for guidance)
- **Reporting** status and progress of the revision of instruction or operation of the instructional system
- **Developing and implementing** marketing plans for the instruction
- **Reviewing** if the projected costs of the instructional system are within the budget, and if not, then seeking remedies with the stakeholders
- **Ensuring** that any conflicts of interest relevant to the instruction are resolved

Additional Guidance

Implementing Instructor-Present Instruction

Before implementing instructor-present instruction, careful planning is required to recruit qualified instructors and schedule their time. Also, keep in mind that many people who serve as instructors may be subject-matter experts (SMEs) who have no or little formal training in teaching and learning. Even many teachers and professors have little experience with certain instructional approaches and technologies. In many contexts, therefore, you may need to train the instructors to improve their knowledge and skills required for successfully delivering the instruction. To effectively implement learner-centered instruction, for example, you should provide training on how to facilitate learner-centered instruction to those instructors who are inexperienced with the facilitator roles. For online instruction, the instructors may also need training on various aspects of online teaching and learning (e.g., how to interact with learners online).

Further, if the designed instruction involves new technologies, technology training should be provided.

Implementing Instructor-Free e-Learning

Before implementing instructor-free e-learning, last-minute checks need to be made to ensure that all feedback from beta testing has been addressed and that the course is ready to implement (see Chapter 10 for more information on beta tests). Once the instruction is ready, all target learners should be informed why they should complete the instruction, how to access it, how to successfully complete it, when to complete it by, whom to contact if they encounter any problem or need help, and any other critical information needed to complete the instruction. You should also ensure that all the target learners have the necessary technology and know how to use it in all the ways that are required.

Where Are We?

This chapter has described the first part of the fourth D (Deploy) in our Holistic 4D Model – implementing the four instructional system functions of delivery, management, support, and evaluation. It also offered additional guidance for implementing instructor-present instruction and instructor-free e-learning. The next chapter addresses the second part of Deploy – summative evaluation.

Exercises

Here again we offer suggestions for a professor using this book as a textbook in a course, to help the students understand more deeply the contents of this chapter. We suggest that you keep the same teams of about three students each to continue to work on their ID projects throughout the course. However, these exercises can be done individually by any reader who wants to deepen their understanding and skills.

1. Have each team develop a plan for implementing the instruction they have designed and developed – or, preferably, for the entire instructional system of which their instruction would be a part. The implementation plan should address all four system functions. For what you consider to be the best reports, we suggest you get written permission from the students to use them as examples in the next offering of your course.
2. Have each team offer suggestions for improvement for the implementation plans of one or two other teams before you review and provide feedback to the students.
3. Have a whole-class, synchronous discussion of the implementation process, including any difficulties or challenges they may face during the process. We would love to get your suggestions for improvement.

12 Summative Evaluation

Overview

Summative evaluation is conducted to verify the effectiveness of instruction. It helps educators make informed decisions about whether to maintain currently used instructional systems, abandon them, or seek a new one that has the potential to meet their needs better. However, we caution that conducting a summative evaluation too soon after its implementation could lead to the termination of a program that hasn't had enough time to work out the inevitable problems that come with a new instructional system. We recommend waiting until after sufficient operational formative evaluation and revision (see Chapter 10) before conducting a summative evaluation.

As mentioned in Chapter 10, summative evaluation has two parts: the first one that takes place after implementation (called *initial summative evaluation*) and those that take place periodically throughout the remaining life of the instructional system (called *continuing summative evaluation or confirmative evaluation*). The ultimate goal of continuing summative evaluation is to ensure that the instruction continues to effectively and cost-efficiently develop learners who meet established educational needs or training requirements. The methods are the same for both initial and continuing summative evaluation – only the timing differs.

The CIPP model (Context, Input, Process, Product) is a useful framework for conducting summative (and formative) evaluations of an instructional system. It was developed by Daniel Stufflebeam and colleagues in the 1960s (see e.g., Stufflebeam, 2000, 2003). It entails evaluating the context, input, process, and product when evaluating an instructional system.

- The **context** evaluation concerns what the instructional needs, problems, and opportunities are in order to define goals and judge the significance of outcomes – what should be done?
- The **input** evaluation concerns the quality of the design of the instructional system – how should it be done?
- The **process** evaluation concerns how well the design has been implemented or executed – is it being done as planned?
- The **product** evaluation concerns the intended and unintended outcomes to determine the extent to which the instructional system succeeds in meeting the needs – did it work?

For more detailed guidance on conducting summative evaluations, we recommend the Kirkpatrick model.

Figure 12.1 An Example of a Reactionnaire Recreated.

Using the Kirkpatrick Model for Summative Evaluation

In Chapter 10 we introduced the Kirkpatrick model and discussed how its four levels are used for formative evaluation. In this chapter, we offer guidance for using the Kirkpatrick model for summative evaluation. The four levels of the model (Kirkpatrick Partners, 2018) are:

- Level 1: Reaction
- Level 2: Learning
- Level 3: Behavior
- Level 4: Results

Level 1: Evaluating Participant Reaction

Summative evaluation at this level measures how learners react to the instructional program by focusing on their opinions and perceptions. Reactionnaires, also called "happy sheets" or "smile sheets," and interviews are the most frequently used data collection methods (see Figure 12.1 for an example). Level 1 evaluation is conducted in most instructional systems because it is easy and inexpensive to administer compared to other types of evaluation. However, you need to be skillful in designing the questions in order to get

Table 12.1 The Kirkpatrick Model.

Level	Function
1 Reaction	Measures the degree to which learners find the training favorable, engaging, and relevant to their work or life.
2 Learning	Measures the degree to which learners acquire the intended knowledge, skills, attitudes, confidence, and commitment based on their participation in the instruction.
3 Behavior	Measures the degree to which graduates apply in their work or lives what they learned during the instruction.
4 Results	Measures the degree to which targeted organizational or societal outcomes occur as a result of the instruction and related interventions (e.g., support and incentives).

useful information. Beyond simply asking if graduates are satisfied with an instructional program, try to ask specific questions about various aspects of the program, including:

- Learner objectives
- Instructional resources
- Content organization
- Instructor
- Instructional environment
- Timeline
- Ease of navigation (for e-learning)

Participant reaction is conducted during or immediately after the instruction and is most often used for formative evaluation. However, it can also provide useful summative information from learners after sufficient formative evaluation has improved the quality of the instructional system.

Level 2: Evaluating Learning

This level of evaluation measures learners' knowledge gains, skill development, and attitude changes. These data are normally gathered through assessments, observations of performance (often with a checklist), and/or artifacts created by graduates. It is critical to collect sufficient assessment data, since insufficient data may skew the evaluation results, possibly leading to incorrect decisions being made. Before data analysis, ensure that data have been collected from each unit or part of the instruction and that an adequate number of data samples has been collected in order to validate the reliability of the findings. As with participant reaction, evaluation of learning is conducted during or immediately after the instruction and is most often used for formative evaluation. However, it can also provide useful summative information from learners after sufficient formative evaluation has improved the quality of the instructional system.

Level 3: Evaluating Behaviors

This level of evaluation measures graduates' real-world behavior changes and the extent to which the newly acquired knowledge, skills, and/or attitudes are being used at work or in life (learning transfer). Typically, it is conducted by evaluators from the organization that provides the instruction. Most of these evaluation data come from the graduates and their supervisors in the field. We caution that, when the initial summative evaluation takes place some months or years after the implementation, some graduates likely went through the instructional system before operational formative evaluation and revision led to improvements. Therefore, the Level 3 evaluation results should be compared with any changes that have been made since those graduates were in the instructional system, and conclusions should be qualified accordingly.

Unfortunately, learning transfer does not always happen. In many cases, what is learned in the instruction does not get applied in the real world. Often, it is not because the instruction is ineffective, but because of various organizational, social, or other contextual barriers that prevent graduates from applying what they learned, especially in job situations.

Some possible problems that may be identified during a Level 3 evaluation are:

- The criterion test did not measure graduates' ability to meet real-world performance requirements

- Objectives did not reflect real-world performance requirements
  - o   Performance requirements were incorrectly identified during task analysis
  - o   Performance requirements changed after task analysis
- Instruction did not address the influence of contextual factors

The Level 3 evaluation data are typically collected through (1) questionnaires, (2) field visits, and (3) performance evaluations. Detailed guidance on the common data collection methods is provided below.

Questionnaires

Questionnaires or surveys are effective, cost-efficient evaluation tools. In Level 3 evaluation, questionnaires are used to:

- Determine the perceived ability of graduates to perform the specific tasks in the real world or apply specific topics on which they received instruction
- Identify the specific nature of any deficiency
- Determine how competent performances are actually being done by graduates

Types of questionnaires. Two types of questionnaires can be used to collect Level 3 evaluation data:

- One is for the graduates. This questionnaire is designed to find out how they believe they are performing in the real world after completing the instructional program.
- In job situations, the other is for the graduate's immediate supervisor, to find out how she or he believes the graduate is performing.

Table 12.2 summarizes the advantages and disadvantages of questionnaires.

Preparing questionnaires. Well-constructed questionnaires that are properly administered are extremely important to the Level 3 evaluation process. Table 12.3 identifies the five basic stages of questionnaire development.

Guidelines for developing questions. Guidelines for developing effective questions are:

- Use closed-end questions when you want the respondent to choose answers from a small number of possibilities. However, this may not allow for the range of answers

Table 12.2 Advantages and Disadvantages of Questionnaires

Advantages	*Disadvantages*
• They are comparatively inexpensive to administer • They can be used to collect large samples of graduate and supervisor data • They yield data that can be easily tabulated and reported • Respondents typically give their opinions freely	• They may not be the most reliable form of evaluation; data validity depends on preparation and distribution • Communication is one-way; respondents may not understand some of the questions and evaluators may not understand some of the responses • They may not ask the most relevant questions • They collect only opinions, which may not be as reliable as other methods of collecting data • Low completion rates and inappropriate responses could occur, affecting accuracy

Table 12.3 Stages of Questionnaire Development

Stage	Activity
1	Define the purpose of the questionnaire. Focus only on relevant information.
2	Determine specific information to be collected. Specify exactly what is needed in a list of objectives.
3	Develop questions that ask for specific information such as: • Conditions/equipment required to perform well • Exact action to accomplish the performance • Standards of performance • Results of the performance
4	Consider motivational factors when developing questionnaires. You want the respondents to answer fully and conscientiously. Questionnaires should motivate respondents if they: • Explain the purpose of the questionnaire • Tell the respondents how they can benefit from answering the questionnaire • Write clear and concise instructions • Make the questionnaire format uncluttered and easy to answer. For example, using boxes for check marks should make the questionnaire easier to answer • Arrange the questions in logical order • Ask specific questions
5	Test the questionnaire on sample respondents. Ask them to: • Evaluate the cover letter or email introduction • Check instructions and questions for clarity and brevity • Explain how they feel about answering the questions • Revise the questionnaire, if necessary, before distribution

desired. Consider adding "Other" so that the respondents can provide information that was not included in the provided options.

• Use open-end questions when you don't know all the possible answers.
• Word questions at the respondent's level of understanding. Use vocabulary and concepts that are easy for the respondent to understand.
• Limit each question to one aspect of a topic or one relatively stand-alone part of a task.
• Decide on the logical order of the questions (typically the order of performance for a task, or general to detailed for a topic). Thereby, each question provides a frame of reference for upcoming questions.
• Avoid questions that make it easier to answer one way over another.
• Avoid questions that convey biases or exceptions.
• Word questions so they will not threaten the respondents.
• Supplemental "information-seeking" questions may be used. Such questions may ask how much time the graduates spend on individual tasks or what equipment or materials they use.

Guidelines for constructing questionnaires. When constructing a questionnaire, several guidelines should be considered.

• Provide short, concise, and specific directions for completing the questionnaire
• Include demographic questions (e.g., name, title, organization, age, gender)

- Provide clear verbal descriptions when using rating scales (e.g., 1 – Strongly Disagree, 2 – Disagree, 3 – Neutral, 4 – Agree, 5 – Strongly Agree)
- Make sure that all responses are mutually exclusive and there is no overlap (as in Figure 12.2)
- Make the questionnaire easy to read and understand
- For paper-based questionnaires:
  o Number the questionnaires to allow for administrative control
  o Number each page of the questionnaire
  o You may want to print on both sides of the pages to conserve materials
  o Send self-addressed, stamped return envelope with the questionnaire
  o Fold the questionnaire in such a manner that the respondent can refold it the same way to place it in the return envelope after completion
  o You may want to include an incentive of some kind with each questionnaire to get a higher response rate

Guidelines for preparing an introduction. Each questionnaire should have a cover letter (for paper format) or introduction (for online format). When developing the cover letter/introduction, ensure that it:

- Explains the purpose of the questionnaire and its importance for improving instruction
- Includes a statement that assures the respondent that the information will be treated confidentially
- Provides information on how to return or submit the questionnaire
- Indicates the approximate time required to complete the questionnaire
- Shows the recommended return date
- If paper-based questionnaire, uses appropriate letterhead stationery signed by a responsible authority

Before you distribute the questionnaire, it should be administered to a small number of representative individuals for pilot testing, to:

- Provide valuable feedback on the quality of the questionnaire
- Allow correction of problems in the questionnaire before distribution

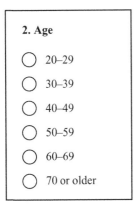

Figure 12.2 A Survey Question with Mutually Exclusive Responses.

- Preclude acquiring misinformation resulting from administration of a faulty questionnaire

Distribution of questionnaires is a critical aspect of evaluation; don't just pick a few graduates' names and send a questionnaire to them. Plan the distribution to ensure that the data collected are valid and reliable. When distributing the questionnaire, you should:

- Decide to whom you are sending the questionnaire: a graduate, his or her supervisor, or both. You may collect important information from both.
- Select a representative sample to ensure valid results. Graduates may have different life needs, job requirements depending on such factors as their major responsibilities, geographic location, or organization level, requiring differences in their performances. Therefore, your sample should be selected as representatively as possible.
- For paper versions, determine how many questionnaires you need to send out. That decision is based on:
  - o Expected response rate.
  - o Level of confidence (a statistical consideration which means the size of the sample required for you to be, say, 95 percent sure the sample truly represents the larger population). The graduate sampling chart in Table 12.4 shows how to determine the number of questionnaires you need based on this consideration.

Decide when to distribute the questionnaires. Timing is critical. Usually, question-naires should be sent to the graduates within three to six months after completion of the instruction. Beyond six months, it may be impossible to tell whether the graduate learned the skill or knowledge in the instruction, or after it. If the questionnaire is sent too early, the graduate may not have had time to perform many of the tasks that were taught. To ensure that sufficient numbers of the questionnaires are completed for analysis, contact non-respondents and encourage their response.

Field Visits (Interviews and Observations)

Field visits are a very effective method of conducting evaluations but are more expensive. They are normally conducted by an evaluator, often assisted by an instructional designer or instructor. The purposes of a field visit are to get first-hand information on graduates' real-world performance (how well they are applying what was learned), and to validate information gained from other evaluation activities. Interviews and observations are pri-mary data-collection methods for field visits. Evaluators should interview graduates and those with whom the graduates interact (e.g., their supervisors) and observe the graduates' on-the-job performance when possible. However, observations are almost useless unless the observer is familiar with the tasks being performed. Ideally, field visits should include experts in the graduates' performances. However, in most cases this is not possible due to limited funds, scheduling constraints, and number and variety of graduates to be inter-viewed. Table 12.5 summarizes the advantages and disadvantages of field visits. Checklists are often used during observation.

Preparing for the field visit. Visits to the field to collect evaluation data require ade-quate planning to ensure that useful data are gathered. To prepare for the visit, you should:

- Develop a list of questions (interview protocol) to get honest, pertinent answers and to keep the discussion focused

Table 12.4 Graduate Sampling Chart

Graduate Sampling Chart

Course Graduates (during sampling period)	Sample Size for 95% Confidence*	Sample Size for 90% Confidence	Sample Size for 80% Confidence
10	10	10	9
20	19	19	18
40	36	35	32
60	52	49	44
80	67	62	54
100	80	73	62
120	92	83	69
160	114	101	81
200	133	115	90
250	154	130	99
300	171	142	106
350	187	153	112
400	200	161	116
450	212	169	120
500	222	176	123
600	240	186	129
700	255	195	133
800	267	202	136
900	277	208	139
1,000	286	213	141
1,500	316	229	148
2,000	333	238	151
2,500	345	244	154
3,000	353	248	155
3,500	358	251	157
4,000	**364**	253	157
4,500	367	255	158
5,000	370	257	159
10,000	383	263	161
25,000	394	268	163
100,000	398	270	164

How to use this table. The table can be used as shown in the following example: Annual course production is 4,000, and a 95% confidence level is desired. * From the table, 364 usable questionnaires are required. The estimated return rate of usable questionnaires is 85% (0.85). Therefore, the number of questionnaires to mail (M) is computed as follows: 0.85M = 364   M = 364/0.85   M = 428
* It is recommended that the 95% confidence level be chosen. This is the level commonly used in business and education decisions.

- Determine the places to be visited
- Establish the schedule for the visit
- Select the individuals to be interviewed and observed

Conducting the field visit. The following are some of the tasks to be performed during the field visit.

- Inform graduates and supervisors of the purpose of the visit. Tell them that their answers will furnish valuable information for improving the instruction.
- Interview the graduates and their supervisors.

Table 12.5 Advantages and Disadvantages of Field Visits

Advantages	Disadvantages
• Information is gathered first-hand by the evaluator from graduates and their supervisors. Any questions or assumptions can be clarified. • Field visits help validate and elaborate on questionnaire data. • Field visits build rapport between the instructional personnel and the graduates. • Additional information can be gained by observing nonverbal messages and asking leading or probing questions.	• They are time-consuming. Travel to several different locations requires considerable time. Interviews and observations also require a lot of time if they are done correctly. • The sample is limited. Since the evaluator typically only goes to a few locations, the number of interviews and observations conducted is limited. • The cost is high. Field visits require evaluators to spend limited funds to travel to the various locations. • Information gathered by the evaluator can be subjective and biased. • Graduates may feel they are being scrutinized. • Evaluators are not always skilled at interviewing and observing.

- Determine the graduates' proficiency.
- Determine how the knowledge and skills learned during instruction are being used.
- Guide the interviews with your list of questions. (As the interview progresses, you may need to add, delete, or revise questions.)
- Have the supervisor (or others impacted by the graduate's performance) rate the performance confidentially.
- Observe graduates performing the tasks. (This may not be beneficial if the evaluator does not have expertise in the performance or the task is not observable.) Take careful notes on the graduate's performance. After the task has been completed, ask questions to clarify actions taken by the graduates during the performance.
- Take accurate and complete notes during interviews and observations.

Analyzing the data. Data collected from interviews and observations is analyzed in the same manner as questionnaires: that is, compiled, collated, and analyzed by the evaluator.

Validating the findings. The analysis results of the field visits and questionnaires should be combined and compared in order to validate the findings.

Performance Evaluations

The purpose of performance evaluations is to determine how well graduates perform what they were supposed to learn. In work settings, performance evaluations are conducted on-the-job by the supervisor. Data are collected periodically through observations and quality of results and are reported by the supervisor to an evaluator for analysis. For education contexts, they are typically conducted at-a-distance by the educators or an evaluator through questionnaires (see the Questionnaires section) or interviews (see the Field Visits section). Table 12.6 summarizes the advantages and disadvantages of performance evaluations.

Preparing for the evaluation. As with any evaluation method, you should make adequate plans before starting. Planning includes:

- Selecting graduates and those impacted by their performance (e.g., their supervisors or customers) to participate in the performance evaluation
- Meeting with, or otherwise contacting, the graduates to explain performance evaluations

Table 12.6 Advantages and Disadvantages of Performance Evaluations

Advantages	*Disadvantages*
• In work contexts, evaluations are conducted on the job by the supervisor, reducing the cost to the evaluator • Such evaluations are typically thorough and accurate assessments of the graduates' performance • Data can be used to validate other forms of field evaluations	• If performance evaluations are not conducted in a work context, it will take a lot of the supervisor's time and effort to conduct the evaluation • The sample is limited

- Getting the commitment of those impacted to support the evaluation (especially the supervisor in work contexts)
- Determining performances to be evaluated based on the goals of the instruction
- Determining the criteria for the performances to be evaluated
- Establishing milestones for the evaluation process

Conducting performance evaluations. Once the participants have been selected and briefed on the process and its importance, it is time to begin the evaluation. For work contexts, the evaluation consists of the following activities:

- The supervisor evaluates the graduates' performance on each task performed
- The supervisor reports on the quality of the performances. Sometimes it is helpful to include:
  o The frequency of performance
  o The time required to perform
  o Equipment used
  o The standard of performance exhibited
  o Any special circumstances for the performance

For non-work contexts, the performance evaluation consists of the following:

- The evaluator asks the graduates for names of those affected by their performance and either interviews or gives questionnaires to those people. Alternatively, the evaluator could ask the graduates to gather feedback from those affected by their performance and forward that information to the evaluator. Anonymous questionnaires are important for accurate information.
- While not an evaluation of performance, the evaluator should also ask the graduates to comment on the quality of preparation provided by the instruction (strengths, weaknesses, and suggestions for improvement) because it is useful for deciding whether to continue, discontinue, or replace a program.

Data analysis and reporting. When the evaluator receives the performance reports from the supervisor or graduate, they are analyzed to determine how well the graduates are performing the tasks they were taught during the instruction, as an indicator of whether the instructional program should be continued, discontinued, or replaced. Evaluators should watch for reports that indicate the graduate:

- Cannot perform a task that he or she learned in the instruction
- Requires excessive help to perform the task

- Any special circumstances that may have impacted the quality of performance (circumstances that the instruction may not have adequately addressed)

In these situations, data analysis should focus on determining why the graduate is not able to meet job performance requirements, to accurately decide whether the instructional program should be continued, discontinued, or replaced.

Level 4: Evaluating Results

This level of evaluation measures the organizational or societal impact of the instructional program – that is, the impact of the instruction on the organization's performance. For work contexts, some of the organizational performance indicators include:

- Increased sales
- Decreased costs
- Improved quality of products and service
- More efficient processes
- Improved customer satisfaction
- Improved employee satisfaction
- Reduced frequency of accidents

For education contexts, some of the organizational or societal performance indicators include:

- Improvement in meeting the organization's goals (e.g., for a family as the organization, improved relationships among the family members or improved financial situation)
- Improvement in the functioning of society (e.g., more informed voter participation, lower crime rate, lower teen pregnancy rate, or higher literacy rate)

The Level 4 evaluation is rarely done because gathering the organizational or societal data is difficult and typically requires support from management or government and involvement by finance and budgeting people. However, the results of Level 4 can communicate the success of the instructional program in terms that leaders understand and can provide the most important indicator as to whether the program should continue or be either discontinued or replaced with a better one. Nevertheless, we caution that, when the initial summative evaluation takes place months or years after the implementation, some graduates likely went through the instructional system before operational formative evaluation and revision led to improvements. Therefore, the Level 4 evaluation results should be compared with any changes that have been made since those graduates were in the instructional system, and conclusions should be qualified accordingly.

Where Are We?

This chapter has offered guidance for summative evaluation. It reviewed Kirkpatrick's four levels of evaluation and described how summative evaluation could be conducted at the four levels. Along with Implementation (Chapter 11), Summative Evaluation completes the last D (Deploy) in the Holistic 4D Model. In our epilogue, we offer some concluding remarks.

Exercises

Here again we offer suggestions for a professor using this book as a textbook in a course, to help the students understand more deeply the contents of this chapter. We suggest that you keep the same teams of about three students each to continue to work on their ID projects throughout the course. However, these exercises can be done individually by any reader who wants to deepen their understanding and skills.

Given that only a small amount of instruction has been developed during your course, full implementation and summative evaluation are seldom possible. However, you could identify a small instructional system that is currently operating, such as a two-hour workshop, and have your students conduct a summative evaluation of it, as follows:

1. Have each team conduct a summative evaluation of the selected instruction. Each team should prepare an evaluation report that describes what they did during the evaluation, what strengths and weaknesses they found, and what conclusions they draw regarding whether to continue, terminate, or replace the instruction. For what you consider to be the best reports, we suggest you get written permission from the students to use them as examples in the next offering of your course.

   Alternatively, you could just have each team prepare a summative evaluation plan for the larger instructional system of which the team's previous exercises addressed one small part.

2. Have each team offer suggestions for improvement for the reports (or plans) of one or two other teams before you review and provide feedback to the students.

3. Have a whole-class, synchronous discussion of the strengths and weaknesses of this summative evaluation process, including any difficulties or challenges they faced during the process and what changes to the process might have helped. We would love to get your suggestions for improvement.

References

Kirkpatrick Partners. (2018). The Kirkpatrick model. Retrieved from https://www.kirkpatrickpartners.com/Our-Philosophy/The-Kirkpatrick-Model.

Stufflebeam, D.L. (2000). The CIPP model for evaluation. In D. L. Stufflebeam, G. F. Madaus & T. Kellaghan (Eds.), *Evaluation models* (2nd ed.). Boston, MA: Kluwer Academic Publishers.

Stufflebeam, D.L. (2003). The CIPP model for evaluation. In T. Kellaghan & D.L. Stufflebeam (Eds.), *International handbook of educational evaluation. Kluwer international handbooks of education* (Vol. 9). Dordrecht: Springer.

Afterword

Over the past few decades, dramatic advances have been made in learning theory, instructional theory, and technological tools for both instruction and instructional design (ID). The Holistic 4D Model has been developed to incorporate these advances into the ID process. But additional significant advances will surely continue over the next few decades, and the Holistic 4D Model needs to continue to evolve. We do not view this model as proprietary – as ours. We encourage contributions to its evolution from other ID experts. Our vision is that the next edition of this book will have sections authored by other experts. We recognize that many instructional design decisions are situational – that the designs (instructional methods) need to change from one situation to another. This model does not yet include all kinds of instruction for all kinds of situations. So, if you see ways this model can be improved, please write up your ideas and contact one of us to discuss them. Our field will advance more if we collaborate and build on each other's ideas and experiences.

Second, for those of you who teach ID, we encourage you to share your ideas and resources for using this book in your courses. We have created a website to facilitate such sharing: www.reigeluth.net/holistic-4d. Send us your ideas and resources – syllabi, student projects, course schedules, examples, suggestions, and so forth – and we will post them with full credit to you (and your students, if appropriate). We will also likely start a blog as a vehicle for you to communicate directly with each other. If you have any suggestions at all, we would love to hear from you. You can contact us at reigeluth@indiana.edu or yunjo.an@unt.edu.

Appendix

This appendix contains all the templates or forms offered in this book, as a convenience for you to photocopy. You can also find electronic versions of these forms at www.reigeluth.net/holistic-4d.

Template for a Top-Level Analysis, Design, and Evaluation (ADE) Document for Task Expertise

Top-Level ADE Document for Task Expertise	
Name of Job:	
Name and Sequence of Duties	**Name and Sequence of Tasks**
1.	1.1 1.2 1.3 …
2.	2.1 2.2 2.3 …
…	…
Big-Picture Instructional Methods	

Mastery approach? ☐ Yes ☐ No
Learner-centered? ☐ Yes ☐ No
Pacing strategy? ☐ Self-paced ☐ Group pacing ☐ Group lockstep

Initial thoughts about learning by doing:

Initial thoughts about delivery methods:

Initial thoughts about templates and course management systems:

Template for a Top-Level ADE Document for Topic Expertise

Top-Level ADE Document for Topic Expertise	
Name of Domain:	
Name and Sequence of Subjects	**Name and Sequence of Topics**
1.	1.1 1.2 1.3 …
2.	2.1 2.2 2.3 …
…	…

Big-Picture Instructional Methods
Mastery approach?　☐ Yes　　☐ No **Learner-centered?**　☐ Yes　☐ No **Pacing strategy?**　☐ Self-paced　　☐ Group pacing　　☐ Group lockstep
Initial thoughts about learning by doing:
Initial thoughts about delivery methods:
Initial thoughts about templates and course management systems:

Template for a Mid-Level ADE Document for Task Expertise (Use One Form for Each Version of the Task)

Mid-Level ADE Document for Topic Expertise		
Name of Task: **Simplifying Conditions:** **Number and List of Versions:** **Sequence of Versions:**		
Name of Version # :		Duplicate from here on for each application
Variations in …	**Factors**	**Difficulty (1-5)**
Behaviors		
Conditions — Contextual factors		
Environmental factors		
Tools and other resources		
Standards		
Learner Objective (if any at mid level) Kind: ☐ Demonstration ☐ Abstract Description:		
Learner Assessment (if any at mid level) ☐ Criterion-referenced ☐ Norm-referenced Description: ☐ Performance ☐ Predictive		
Learning-By-Doing Teams? ☐ Yes ☐ No Names of projects:		
Media: ☐ Text ☐ Pic's/text ☐ Video ☐ Interactive media ☐ Physical objects ☐ Experts General description:		
Info about formative evaluation:		
Name of Project # : Duplicate from here on for each application		
Project environment: ☐ Real ☐ Staged ☐ Simulated ☐ Narrated Description:		
Scenario for this project:		
Details for this scenario:		

Template for a Mid-Level ADE Document for Topic Expertise (Use One Form for Each Application of the Topic)

Mid-Level ADE Document for Topic Expertise

Name of Topic:
Kind of Topic: ☐ Conceptual   ☐ Theoretical   ☐ Hybrid
Number of Applications:
List of Applications:

Sequence of Applications:

Name of Application # :	Duplicate from here on for each application

Variations in …	**Difficulty (1-5)**
Behaviors	
Conditions	
Standards	

Learner Objective (if any at mid level)   Kind: ☐ Demonstration   ☐ Abstract
Description:

Learner Assessment (if any at mid level)   ☐ Criterion-referenced   ☐ Norm-referenced
Description: ☐ Performance   ☐ Predictive

Learning-By-Doing   Teams?   ☐ Yes   ☐ No
Contexts for applying the topic: ☐ Authentic   ☐ Fantasy
Description:

Media: ☐ Text   ☐ Pic's/text ☐ Video   ☐ Interactive media   ☐ Physical objects   ☐ Experts
General description:

Info about formative evaluation:

Name of Variation # :	Duplicate from here on for each application

Scenario for this variation:

Details for this scenario:

Template for a Lower-Level ADE Document for Task Expertise (Use for Each Version of Each Topic)

Name of Task:	
Name of Version # :	
Type: |---|---| Procedural Heuristic	

Procedural elements (if any)   Type of procedure: ☐ Linear   ☐ Branching
[List the steps for a linear procedure. Put a flow chart for a branching procedure.]

If branching procedure, **sequence** the paths by length/complexity/difficulty:

Heuristic elements (if any):
1. Goals

2. Considerations

3. Descriptive models

4. Causal factors

5. Guidelines

6. Decision rules

7. Explanations

Sequence of organizing content   Learner control: ☐ Yes   ☐ No
(If the version has both procedural and heuristic elements, integrate the two sequences)
(If no learner control, list the elements in sequence.)
(If learner control, put a tree chart showing sequence contingencies.)

Template for a Lower-Level ADE Document for Topic Expertise (Use for Each Topic)

Topic (or subtopic) Name:
Name of Application #   :
Type: |---|---| Conceptual   Theoretical
Conceptual organizing content (if any): Parts and/or kinds   (List concepts in groups, general-to-detailed)
Theoretical organizing content (if any): Cause-effect relationships and natural processes   (List principles/processes in groups, simple-to-complex)
Sequence of organizing content   Learner control: ☐ Yes   ☐ No (If hybrid sequence, integrate the two types of organizing content) (Indicate any applications for which each piece of organizing content is irrelevant)

Additional Template for the Supporting Content in a Lower-Level ADE Document (Use for Each Version or Topic)

Version or topic name:			
Organizing Content	**Supporting Content (in sequence)**	**Type of Learning**	**Criteria for Mastery**
	[Add rows as needed.]		
[Add rows as needed.]			
Estimated time for target learners to master the version or topic:		*[Adjust as needed.]*	

Form for Review of Existing Materials

Question	Yes	No
Does the material meet the requirements of the objective(s)?		
Is the level of learning appropriate (e.g., memorization, application, etc.)?		
Is the material accurate?		
Does the material address motivational factors?		
Can the material be properly sequenced?		
Does the material provide sufficient guidance?		
Are sufficient practice exercises provided?		
Are the learner assessments adequate?		
Is the material proprietary or copyrighted? If so, can you get the rights?		

Learner Reaction Questionnaire

LEARNER REACTION TO INSTRUCTION

COURSE: DATE:

INSTRUCTOR: LEARNER:

One way that instruction is improved is by sampling learner reaction to the instruction. Please answer the following questions.

1. Prior to this instruction, my experience in this area was:
   ___ extensive   ___ moderate   ___ little or none

2. Did your knowledge of the subject increase as a result of the instruction?
   ___ yes   ___ no

3. If your knowledge increased as a result of the instruction, to what extent did it increase?
   ___ not applicable (my knowledge didn't increase)
   ___ slightly   ___ moderately   ___ extremely

4. Based on my experience, the level of instruction was:
   ___ too advanced   ___ about right   ___ too elementary

5. The organization of the instruction was:
   ___ very helpful   ___ helpful   ___ not very helpful

6. The lecture outline (main points of instruction) was:
   ___ very helpful   ___ helpful   ___ not very helpful

7. Audiovisual aids were:
   ___ of great value   ___ valuable   ___ of little or no value
   ___ not used, but could have helped   ___ not used and not needed

8. Answers to learner questions were:
   ___ meaningful   ___ somewhat helpful   ___ not helpful
   ___ not applicable (no questions asked)

9. Should the subject matter covered be changed?
   ___ yes (please explain below)   ___ no

10. Should the methods of instruction be changed?
    ___ yes (please explain below)   ___ no

11. Overall, the instruction was:
    ___ outstanding   ___ good   ___ fair   ___ poor

12. Instruments (including tests) to evaluate learner performance were:
    ___ outstanding   ___ good   ___ fair   ___ poor

COMMENTS, EXPLANATIONS, OR RECOMMENDATIONS:

Index

Note: Page numbers in *italics* indicate figures and page numbers in **bold** indicate tables.